# Building Workforce Strength

# Building Workforce Strength

*Creating Value through Workforce and Career Development*

RON ELSDON, EDITOR

 PRAEGER

AN IMPRINT OF ABC-CLIO, LLC
Santa Barbara, California • Denver, Colorado • Oxford, England

**Library of Congress Cataloging-in-Publication Data**

Building workforce strength : creating value through workforce and career development / Ron Elsdon, editor.
    p. cm.
  Includes bibliographical references and index.
  ISBN 978-0-313-37926-0 (alk. paper) —ISBN 978-0-313-37927-7 (ebook)
1. Career development.   2. Personnel management.   I. Elsdon, Ron, 1950–
  HF5549.5.C35B85   2010
  658.3'124—dc22        2010007379

ISBN: 978-0-313-37926-0
EISBN: 978-0-313-37927-7

14  13  12  11  10  1  2  3  4  5

This book is also available on the World Wide Web as an eBook.
Visit www.abc-clio.com for details.

Praeger
An Imprint of ABC-CLIO, LLC

ABC-CLIO, LLC
130 Cremona Drive, P.O. Box 1911
Santa Barbara, California 93116-1911

This book is printed on acid-free paper (∞)

Manufactured in the United States of America

This book is dedicated to the authors' and editor's families

> We cannot eliminate hunger,
> but we can feed each other.
> We cannot eliminate loneliness,
> but we can hold each other.
> We cannot eliminate pain,
> But we can live a life
> of compassion.

Mark Nepo, from *Accepting This*

# Contents

# Illustrations

# Preface

In the early 2000s, when I was writing *Affiliation in the Workplace,* it seemed that the dot-com meltdown was as close to financial Armageddon in today's world as we would come. This challenge in the early 2000s was largely sector dependent. However, events of 2008 and 2009 unearthed a much more serious and broader crisis, driven this time not by unbridled optimism for emerging technologies. Instead, hubris had brought us again to a precipice our forebears had faced in the 1920s and 1930s. In the absence of effective corporate governance in some U.S. companies, senior-level compensation became divorced from company performance and economic reality, reaching extremes in the financial sector. This was abetted by a political climate where policies were aimed largely at securing more for those who already had much while eviscerating strong government. Not surprisingly, just as in the 1920s and 1930s, these policies brought us to the brink of economic collapse. These words from Adrienne Rich's poem "In Those Years" say it well: "In those years, people will say, we lost track / of the meaning of *we*, of *you*" (Intrator and Scribner 2007).

So now we grapple to find a path forward, glad that this takes place at a time and place in the U.S. when we hope policies will attempt to honor all people. It is in this new, brave world that we come face-to-face with one of the cornerstones of a healthy society: organizations that inspire, and that are inspired by, the people in them. It is with a sense of optimism, of enthusiasm, knowing the value of affiliation in organizations, that we explore building workforce strength in this book, for workforce strength is central to economic prosperity.

In some respects this book was born out of the journey that led *to Affili-ation in the Workplace*. While it builds on those principles and perspectives, this book at its core honors and brings forth new voices. These are voices of practitioners whose learning has been forged from the experience of individual and workforce development. Each is a heroic voice that "does . . . strive to do the deeds; who knows great enthusiasms, the great devotions" in the words of Theodore Roosevelt (1910). These are voices of practitioners writing for practitioners. These voices care about development, that beautiful, gradual unfolding. It is this gradual unfolding, whether of individuals or organizations, that we explore in this book. However, any errors in this book are solely my responsibility.

I well remember attending an early Kaiser Permanente workforce planning meeting several years ago at Bob Redlo's invitation. Kaiser Permanente, founded on a core value of broad access to healthcare, is a leader in the healthcare field. At that time, Bob had recently been appointed to manage Kaiser Permanente's workforce development function. There were about 50 people present. As I think back to that occasion, I am stuck today, as I was then, not so much by what was said but by the makeup of the group: about an equal number of management and labor participants, each enthusiastically engaged in exploring workforce issues of major importance to the organization and its labor unions. This was not the top telling the middle what to do to the bottom, as so often happens. This was broad participation, engagement, and contribution. This was building affiliation in a tangible way at the heart of the organization. So when the opportunity arose some years later to propose delivery of career development services within the organization, I knew this would take place in the context of real partnership between Kaiser Permanente's management, its unions, and its employees. It was clear that this was, and is, a special relationship. This book contains much learning from that process, and from work with other organizations.

As my wise friend and colleague Rita Erickson observed, from the beginning, delivery of career services flowed naturally. It was as if, in the words of Franz Kafka, it is necessary to "become quiet, and still and solitary. The world will freely offer itself to you to be unmasked. It has no choice; it will roll in ecstasy at your feet" (Kafka, www.themodernword. com). In this spirit of beautiful unfolding we offer this book and our learning for you.

*Ron Elsdon*
*Danville, California*

# Acknowledgments

For me one of the great pleasures in creating a book is being close to the kindness and commitment of many people. I am deeply grateful to our thoughtful and insightful chapter authors, Zeth Ajemian, Nancy Atwood, Michele DeRosa, Anna Domek, Cynthia Brinkman Doyle, Martha Edwards, Rita Erickson, Lisa Franklin, Shannon Jordan, Amy Lichty, Mark Malcolm, Darlene Martin, Michele McCarthy, Bob Redlo, and Richard Vicenzi. Each gave much of their time and wisdom and stayed the course. It was a pleasure taking this journey together. This book is a celebration of their voices.

There are many others whose presence is reflected here. We are fortunate to be blessed with a marvelous team at Elsdon, Inc. While many team members have contributed directly as chapter authors, others have contributed much with their knowledge, encouragement, and ideas. They include Seth Bernstein, Alia Lawlor, Beth Levin, Lynda Jones, and Maggi Payment. For this I am most grateful. How fortunate we also include others in our broader team circle: Marilyn Hertzberg, Carol Peterman, Maureen Shiells, and Robin Wortley Hammond, whose thoughtfulness is always enriching. And it is good to recall past team members Deb Carr, Simona Cherlin, Mary Holdcroft, Carol Kem, Joan McMahon, Kathryn Remick, and Rebecca Smith. Each brought a special part of herself that is in some respect reflected here.

All those mentioned with gratitude and affection in *Affiliation in the Workplace* helped prepare the foundation for this book, and it with much pleasure that I recall their kindness. At Elsdon, Inc., we have been fortunate to work with many organizations that invited our contributions and partnership. Kaiser Permanente, one such organization, is a beacon of light in the healthcare field, and in its labor-management collaboration. Many people at Kaiser Permanente have contributed to this book both directly as chapter authors and through their examples. In addition to our chapter authors from Kaiser Permanente, others who have enriched our partnership include Tim Alberts, John August, Bertha Aviles, Anjali Bedi, Julissa Barajas, Mary Ellen Farrell, Allyne Beach, Bonnie Bender, Susie Bulf, Jessica Butz, Brandon Byars, Ann Cahill, Edine Davis, Mary Deming-Boone, Pat Finnegan, Gary Flaxman, Linda Focht, Toong Gee, Barbara Grimm, Barbara Ishikawa, Tamara Johnson, John Kolodny, Enpei Lam, Karin Lim, Laura Long, Mike Lynd, Nicole Marshall, Paul Martin, Jim Miranda, Frances Monteiro, Pati Nicholson, Jim Ogden, Janet O'Halloren, Carol Pomerantz, Karen Price, Patrick Raymond, Paul Records, Jessica Rivera, Des Santos, Ellen Scully-Russ, Connie Savoy, Kathy Shen, Greg Smith, Mary Ellen Smith, Chris Talbot, Tracy Truong, Lori Wambold, and Iris Woodard.

It has been a pleasure to work with APS in Arizona, and our thinking has been deepened by many there, including Susie Bechtle-Mason, Jeff Brodin, Tamara Carro, Judy Norris, Linda Ricciardi, Lori Sundberg, Shelly Shaffer, and Linda Thompson. We also have valued our relationship with colleagues at Qualcomm, including Dhalia Balmir, Mike Foster, Megan Graham, Ben Hamson, Ed Hidalgo, Julianna Sanchez, Adam Ward, and Linda Watorski. Our work has been enriched by our contacts with many in the public sector: in the town of Danville, Joe Calabrigo, Denise Phoenix, Tai Williams, and many others; in the city of San Ramon, Lisa Bobadilla and Lisa's team; and in the Tennessee Department of Human Services, Dave Avans, Kimberlee Becton, Linda Daniel, Pam Davenport, Doris Doherty, Susan Kirk, Ed Lake, Gina Lodge, Eva Mosby, Kerry Mullins, Jeff Owens, Jeff Roberts, Glenda Shearon, Lionel Senseney, Lori Shinton, Leslie Sperrazza, Pat Stubblefield, Melvin Taylor, Linda Williams, and others, including all those heroic frontline eligibility counselors and field supervisors.

It has been a pleasure to stay connected with colleagues at several universities: Pat DeMasters, John Morel, and many others at the Haas School of Business of the University of California–Berkeley; Gail Lynam Dutcher and others at John F. Kennedy University in Pleasant Hill, California; Kathy Ullrich at the Anderson School of Management at UCLA; and many people at Vanderbilt University, including Mark Cannon, Teresa Suarez, Tom Ward, Cissy Mynatt, and Steve Thompson. My association with Vanderbilt University and with the Tennessee Department of Human Services came about through Pearl Sims, who has been a wise and trusted friend and colleague for many years. I am most grateful for Pearl's presence and support, and for our association with Carter Andrews, whose kindness and compassion are inspirations.

Other friends and colleagues continue to be a source of motivation. Their presence demonstrates, on a personal level, many of the principles in this book. They include Barbara Langham of DBM; Dottie Moser of Easter Seals, Inc.; Audrey Southard, Angela Williams, and Suzanne Markus of the Follett Higher Education Group; many volunteers and staff at the Taproot organization whose lives have enriched mine through volunteer projects; colleagues at the American Institute of Chemical Engineers and the American Chemical Society who have opened doors to help bring career development into the worlds of science and engineering; and friends at Shell Ridge Community Church and the Health Care for All movement in California, whose principles of social justice are a light in our community.

I continue to be so grateful to individual career counseling clients who allow me into their lives and show by their example the resilience and beauty of the human spirit. Our work together informs this book. Two people have been central to this project. My friend and colleague Rita Erickson has brought a deep insight to the work of our organization, compassion in the guidance and leadership of our team, and wisdom in the exploration of new frontiers. Rita is an inspiring presence in this book.

Seeing is something most of us take for granted. I took it for granted until several years ago when a detaching retina suddenly caused the field of vision in one of my eyes to begin to disappear. Because of Bob Redlo and Kaiser Permanente, I experienced one of the miracles of modern healthcare as my sight was restored. I am so grateful for the healing that came from Bob's kindness and Kaiser Permanente's skills. Bob has also been instrumental in sponsoring the career development work at Kaiser Permanente that informs much of our discussion in this book, in addition to being a chapter author. I am deeply grateful to Bob.

It has been a pleasure to work with editors at Praeger. Hilary Claggett was a continuous source of encouragement during the writing of *Affiliation in the Workplace*. Hilary was able to connect me to Jeff Olson, who has been a pleasure to work with in preparing this book, as has Jeff's successor, Brian Romer. Brian's and Jeff's encouragement and support are so much appreciated.

It is with much love and caring that I dedicate this book to my family. To my parents, Barbara and Frank, and the foundation they gave me. To our children, Mark and Anna, and their spouses, Erica and Andy, who are all a beautiful presence in our lives, and to Andy for kindly bringing his communication talents in helping to edit chapter 3. To our special grandchildren, Emma and Sophie, who bring so much life and exuberance to us all. I hope that in some small way this book will help create a world that honors, embraces, and loves Emma and Sophie as we do, and comes closer to being a good and caring place for all children. Finally, I am so grateful to my wife, Linda, for our shared love, and for Linda's ever-present support and encouragement. For this is surely a small miracle in a large world.

# List of Abbreviations

| | |
|---|---|
| ACT | American College Test |
| AFSME | Association of Federal, State, and Municipal Employees |
| BHMT | Ben Hudnall Memorial Trust |
| CEO | Chief Executive Officer |
| Coalition | Coalition of Kaiser Permanente Unions |
| EAP | Employee Assistance Program |
| E.S.A. | Employment Security Agreement |
| GDP | Gross Domestic Product |
| GED | General Educational Development Test |
| GPA | Grade Point Average |
| HR | Human Resources |
| IT | Information Technology |
| KP | Kaiser Permanente |
| LMP | Labor Management Partnership |
| MBTI | Myers-Briggs Type Indicator |
| N | Sample size |
| NACE | National Association of Colleges and Employers |
| OPEIU | Office and Professional Employees International Union |
| PDC | Professional Development Center |

| | |
|---|---|
| PLA | Prior Learning Assessment |
| ROI | Return on Investment |
| SEIU UHW | Service Employees International Union United Healthcare Workers—West |
| S.M.A.R.T. | Specific, Measurable, Achievable, Results-oriented, Time-bound |
| S.W.O.T. | Strengths, Weaknesses, Opportunities, Threats |
| WFD | Workforce Development |
| UFCW | United Food and Commercial Workers International Union |
| U.S. | United States of America |

# Introduction

## Ron Elsdon

Fragments of past memories sometimes come together with new meaning when seen through a present-day lens. This is particularly so when the lens is seasoned by recent economic and societal distress. It has been more than 30 years, but I still remember going through job interviews with a number of companies during those final months of struggle and relief as I completed an engineering degree at Cambridge. Each interview with these established companies had a distinct flavor—not unpleasant, but a bit disconcerting. One was conducted in a small room at the top of a long, circular staircase in a house off a quiet London square. Another, a group interview, was conducted at a large chemical manufacturing complex in the northeast of England; a third was in a rural setting at a small manufacturing site in the south of England; and a fourth was at an imposing headquarters building in London. In retrospect it is not the content of those interviews that is most interesting today; rather, it is the path those organizations have taken since that time in the mid-1970s.

Two of the companies were in the film business, the kind of film we used to put in cameras. Both companies are shadows of their 1976 selves. Ilford had the small manufacturing site in the south of England. Today, the remaining vestiges of Ilford are part of the Japanese company OJI. Eastman Kodak, the company with the imposing headquarters building in London, employed 124,000 people worldwide in 1976. These numbers had decreased to about 20,000 people by the end of 2009. ICI, the large chemical manufacturing complex, dominated the chemical industry in the U.K. in the 1970s and employed about 148,000 people by the end of that decade. What is left of ICI today is part of the Dutch company AkzoNobel.

Amoco, the company for which the interview was conducted in a room located at the top of the staircase and was the one I joined, employed 47,000 people in 1976 and was twelfth on the U.S. Fortune 500 list. It does not exist today, having been acquired by BP in 1998. These four companies employed more than 300,000 people in the 1970s. Three of them have vanished, and one is struggling to survive. Each enjoyed success at one time but ultimately was unable to capitalize on the ingenuity and creativity of its workforce. This book is about how to avoid a similar demise. It is about creating and sustaining a vibrant and strongly affiliated workforce. It is about building foundations for thriving organizations that are central to prosperous and caring communities.

Workforce strength benefits individuals by providing meaningful and rewarding work; it benefits organizations by building a solid foundation for creating value; and it benefits communities through fulfilling, shared experience and financial prosperity. The individual, the organization, and the community each become giver and receiver. For example, the community provides educational resources and receives financial support. While workforce strength is observed at the system or institutional level, it is created at the individual level. So it is necessary to look through both organizational and individual lenses to understand how to build and sustain workforce strength. We will explore in this book how relationships of people with each other and with organizations are at the core of workforce strength. We will find that ongoing development, whether at the organizational level or the individual level, is a connecting theme, and we will explore what this means in practice. We will examine the interaction of workforce capability and flexibility and explore how the combination of these attributes speaks to workforce strength.

Our focus is on the interconnection between organizations and individuals, including the linkage to specific community resources such as educational institutions. So this book will be of most interest to practitioners working in, or with, organizations. Organizational interactions take place in the context of public policy that can have far reaching influence. For example, the influence of funding for particular public-sector initiatives or community support services for individuals, and the influence of the overall legal and ethical framework within which we live and work, can have significant implications. While this book is not about public policy, to the extent that policy is informed by working lives and institutions, we hope that material here may also be of interest to those in the public policy arena.

Workforce strength is about people, and that will be our focus. In a world of almost seven billion people in 2010, more than three billion are economically active (Laborsta 2008), which means they are participating in the global economy. It is tragic that many are left out and need support. Of those who are economically active today, more than 80 percent are in less-developed regions of the world, a substantial increase from

73 percent in 1980 and projected to increase further to 83 percent by 2020. North America currently accounts for only about 6 percent of the world's economically active population. However, this is an important group given the opportunities to learn and apply approaches in North America, as well as in other developed economies, which can be rapidly transferred to other parts of the world for the benefit of all.

The recent global economic upheaval provides pause for thought about unbridled pursuit of self-interest. In the U.S., income and wealth inequality recently exceeded the disparities of the late 1920s that preceded the Great Depression (Pizzigati 2008). By 2006 the average income of the top 0.01 percent of U.S. families rose to almost 1,000 times the average income of the bottom 90 percent, and this inequality continued to increase in 2007 and 2008 (Saez 2009; U.S. Census Bureau 2009). It is not surprising that economic policies from the 1980s through 2008, which led to such income inequality, also led to an economic crisis similar to that of the Great Depression. Laboring under the euphemism of trickle-down economics, wealth was systematically transferred from the poorest to the richest. This transfer violates fundamental premises of most major ethical systems, namely equitable distribution of resources, and support for disadvantaged members of society. Such ethical principles are central to the growth and vitality of a healthy society. A new spirit is emerging again in the U.S. that recognizes these principles. It is in keeping with this spirit of communal responsibility that we approach the topic of workforce strength. For workforce strength is one place where the individual, the organization, and the community meet for the benefit of all, and for the creation of economic growth and vitality. It is in this spirit that we begin our path of exploration.

Evolving shifts in global workforce demographics extend well beyond the cost-driven geographic migration of manufacturing operations. These shifts are driven by changes in the fundamental attributes needed to practice in work world's of today and of the future. Levy and Murnane (2005) demonstrate that dramatic shifts to more complex tasks are inherent in the current evolution of work. An example from healthcare, a sector examined in this book, is the emergence of electronic medical records systems that fundamentally change the nature and structure of certain jobs. This shift in the nature of work to greater complexity elevates the importance of ongoing development to stay abreast of such changes. Meanwhile, the emergence of readily accessible, low-cost communication and information processing tools is changing the context within which work takes place. Access to such technology is no longer the prerogative only of large organizations. Indeed, there are diseconomies of scale associated with the costs of staying current with technology change. It is easier and less costly for a small organization to upgrade its technology platforms than it is for a large organization. Consequently, it is not surprising to see entrepreneurial activity increasing in the U.S. (Fairlie 2009).

These changes affect the risk/return landscape for people in terms of their work options. Figure I.1 provides one perspective about personal risk/reward profiles recognizing that this perspective is subjective, and that others may express it differently. The significance of the figure is not in the absolute placement of different options; rather, it is that these options exist.

Figure I.1 examines the benefits and challenges of five alternative forms of work engagement for an individual:

- Conventional position in an organization
  - Having a full-time employment relationship
- Part-time position in an organization
  - Having an ongoing relationship that allows parallel work activities
- Contract or consulting position
  - Bringing expertise to assignments on a project basis
- Ownership: starting or buying a business or starting a nonprofit entity
  - Creating ownership through purchase or development of a for-profit business or nonprofit entity
- Portfolio career
  - Combining various work elements, for example contract work, teaching, or building a consulting practice

A conventional position in an organization, shown in the lower right in the figure, offers the benefits of short-term income, in the U.S. access to group benefits such as healthcare at preferred rates, and the opportunity to be part of a team. In the emerging work world of the future,

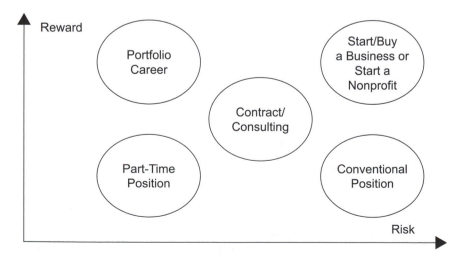

Figure I.1.   Risk/reward characteristics of different forms of work engagement

disadvantages of the conventional position include instability resulting from frequent workforce restructuring and being subject to others defining options, including employment continuity and location. It has the unenviable combination of high risk (others make determinations about the future) and low return (rewards in most large organizations accrue disproportionately to those at the top).

A part-time position, at the lower left, can provide flexibility to accommodate parallel work activities. It suffers from the disadvantages of likely higher cost of benefits in the U.S. as these benefits need to be secured independently, and a more tenuous link to the organization, with possibly a lower sense of inclusion. Securing benefits independently does provide some assurance of continued availability, which is compromised by participating in, and then leaving, a group plan in a large organization in the U.S. The part-time position carries both lower reward and lower risk. Rewards are capped by the organization, and risk is mitigated by the ability to engage in more than one opportunity at a time.

Contract or consulting work, in the center of the figure, is based on bringing specialized expertise that others value and are willing to purchase. There is much freedom to set direction. Disadvantages include the need for a broad skill set that encompasses both selling and delivering services, although some of these elements may be available through partnership. In the U.S. it also means securing benefits independently. There is less opportunity to mitigate risk than with a portfolio career; however, contract or consulting work offers greater rewards than a part-time position.

Starting or buying a business or starting a nonprofit, shown at the upper right, offers great freedom in terms of setting direction and, in the case of a for-profit entity, the possibility of significant wealth creation. Success here means meeting the challenge of bringing organizational savvy to the various stages of growth, and it likely means extensive time demands. This choice offers the potential for high reward, either material or emotional, but at a high risk, particularly if significant initial investment is required.

The portfolio career, shown in the upper left, may contain elements of the part-time position, contract or consulting work, and buying or building a business or nonprofit interwoven to match personal interests. As a result, the direction chosen can match personal aspirations most closely. Potential disadvantages include possibly heavy time demands and uncertainty about success, although these are mitigated by the breadth of activities included. For this option, benefits also need to be secured independently in the U.S. The portfolio career can be characterized by high reward and low risk. Here, risk is mitigated by breadth of activities. Reward, whether tangible or intangible, is substantial and personal, being built on knowledge, commitment, and execution.

One astute observer commented that the conventional position and the portfolio career have exchanged their respective risk/reward profiles over the past 10–20 years. For those charged with workforce responsibility in an organization, competition for people may increasingly come not from other organizations, but from these alternative forms of work relationships, which allow people an opportunity to exercise individual choice and initiative. Addressing this form of competition will mean reexamining the organization's employment proposition relative to these other options. It will also mean that those charged with organizational responsibility must carefully examine operating practices such as equitable compensation throughout the organization. It will mean building depth and continuity of workforce relationships, so that affiliation with an organization is an attractive option for individuals, built on integrating personal aspirations with organizational needs. It is here that the concepts of workforce and career development become especially important.

Workforce and career development are built on a strong relationship between an individual and an organization. This is a two-way relationship of affiliation (Elsdon 2003, 7), reflecting mutual respect and benefit, not a one-way relationship of retention, something done by the organization to the individual. Strong affiliation is built on understanding individual needs, providing options and choices for people, fostering learning, supporting breadth in development, and engaging individuals as free agents. It is with this in mind, and with the knowledge that internal and external factors are interwoven in career decisions (Duffy and Dik 2009), that we explore workforce strength.

The book begins in part I by establishing a foundation for examining workforce strength. Part II looks at effective implementation of workforce and career development processes at the organizational level, while part III explores working with individuals in organizations. Part III also includes example cases illustrating the implementation of workforce and career development in organizations. The book concludes with a review of the themes that emerge out of the reflections on building workforce strength.

As expressed in part I, the benefits of a strong workforce in an organization are felt by the people in it, by owners, by shareholders and those charged with governance responsibility, by those who work with the organization, and by the communities within which it operates. In chapter 1 Ron Elsdon and Rita Erickson review what is meant by workforce strength, how it is characterized, and why workforce strength is important for different constituencies. This chapter also examines the link between workforce development and career development, and the allocation of development and learning resources; further, it explores, and provides examples of, establishing a need and sense of urgency for committing resources.

In chapter 2, Rita Erickson and Michele McCarthy address the importance of understanding the needs of different individuals in organizations. While many opportunities and challenges associated with workforce and career development are common regardless of the context, there are also significant differences according to individual perspectives. The chapter establishes and then builds on a framework for understanding individual differences, illustrating the framework with examples of effective practice. Part I concludes with chapter 3, in which Nancy Atwood, Anna Domek, and Richard Vicenzi examine the links to educational systems and community developments, and mentoring processes in organizations. One important aspect of workforce and career development is the opportunity for educational institutions to support growing organizational needs for particular capabilities and skills. This includes equipping those new to the workforce, and those with experience, with needed competencies that evolve over time. This chapter explores how to build effective bridges between organizations and educational institutions to meet such needs, and it examines building effective internal bridges for development through mentoring.

Part II, which focuses on implementation in the organization, begins with chapter 4, in which Bob Redlo and Ron Elsdon look at workforce planning and development from an organizational perspective. Workforce planning provides a compass to gauge the needs of the organization in the future. It focuses on projecting required capabilities and identifying where there are potential gaps. As such, it guides workforce development efforts designed to close those gaps. Workforce development provides a systematic approach to enhance organizational capabilities, connecting individual aspirations to organizational needs. This chapter examines approaches to workforce planning and development and their contribution to organizational strength, with healthcare as a primary example.

Chapters 5 and 6 then examine the application of career development processes, which are key components of workforce development in an organization. In chapter 5, Rita Erickson and Ron Elsdon focus on designing, developing, and measuring career development processes and systems. Career development provides both a developmental path that enables people to move toward meeting their aspirations, and the opportunity for organizations to build and develop strength in depth. This chapter addresses understanding and assessing career development needs in an organization, recognizing differences in organizational culture, and building the needed infrastructure and capabilities to foster shared learning. The chapter also addresses measuring progress and establishing a launch timeline for career development services. In chapter 6, Amy Lichty and Darlene Martin describe approaches to implementing and carrying the message about the value of career development in an organization. Engaging people in career development conversations means reaching out and establishing a reason why it is important. Sustaining individual and organizational interest means creating ongoing value. This chapter examines how to reach out effectively to people within an organization to communicate career development's benefits and value, and it explores the opportunities and challenges that accompany implementation of career development processes. It also addresses the needs of managers who carry both personal career development aspirations and the responsibility for supporting others in their development.

Part III addresses working with individuals in organizations. In chapter 7, Michele DeRosa and Cynthia Brinkman Doyle examine components of career fitness for individuals. Career and workforce development take shape with individuals. It is here that personal transformation can occur, which then cascades into the organization. This chapter provides a foundation for working with individuals in organizations, identifying the elements that constitute individual career fitness and the skills associated with becoming effective in each of these areas. The chapter also examines the different stages of personal experience when engaging with an organization: entry, integration, development, and transition, and shows how to provide mutually beneficial support at each stage. Effectively implementing career development in an organization means addressing the specific needs of different populations. In chapter 8, Shannon Jordan, Lisa Franklin, and Martha Edwards address this topic by examining three groups as examples. These groups are those with specialized technical expertise, a labor union–represented population, and those who are over 50 years of age. The chapter explores the attributes of these populations and how to tailor career development approaches to address their needs.

The section concludes with chapter 9 and example cases at the organizational level. Zeth Ajemian and Mark Malcolm's case study of a major healthcare provider, Kaiser Permanente, illustrates the implementation of a broad-based workforce and career development initiative within an organization. In the second case study, from the high-technology sector, Ron Elsdon illustrates the implementation of a career development pilot project sponsored from within a particular group as a beginning foundation. These examples identify the driving forces that led to the workforce and career development initiatives, the approaches adopted, and observations about successes and challenges. Chapter 10 then weaves the threads of the book together. This final chapter links the foundation principles of workforce and career development with learning from the examples, and summarizes themes emerging in the book. It addresses the challenge of organizational change and underlines the contribution that workforce and career development efforts make to personal fulfillment, organizational success, and community prosperity.

The approaches adopted by chapter authors vary from descriptions of general principles that are then illustrated with specific examples, to the use of specific examples from which general principles are derived. In some cases authors interweave both of these approaches. Chapter authors show the benefits and positive outcomes of their work, and on occasion they also describe challenges and how they were addressed. We hope that the combination of practice and purpose, of accomplishment and challenge, will support you in your path forward, and we are grateful for fellow travelers on this journey of discovery.

# PART I

## Laying the Foundation

The hope that we can learn together, teach together, be curiously impatient together, produce something together, and resist together the obstacles that prevent the flowering of our joy.

—Paulo Freire, *Pedagogy of Freedom*

# CHAPTER 1

# What Does Workforce Strength Look Like and Why Does It Matter?

*Ron Elsdon and Rita Erickson*

American Airlines and Southwest Airlines together account for more than a quarter of all passenger airline miles in the U.S. They held their annual meetings on the same day in 2008 in the Dallas–Fort Worth area. And there the similarity ends. An hour before the American meeting began, members of the Association of Professional Flight Attendants and the Allied Pilots Association began picketing, handing out anti-management packets (Nocera 2008). In the meeting Gerald Arpey, the chief executive of AMR, American's parent company, bemoaned the state of the industry and described a combination of upcoming route cuts and passenger surcharges that American would implement. Nocera goes on to describe the Southwest annual meeting. Herb Kelleher, the company's co-founder, was stepping down as chairman after 37 years. "When Mr. Kelleher, 77, entered the main meeting room, shareholders gave him the kind of standing ovation usually reserved for rock stars...not only did the Southwest pilots not set up a picket line, they took out a full page ad in USA Today thanking Mr. Kelleher for all he had done. 'The pilots of Southwest Airlines want to express our sentiment to Herb that it has been an honor and a privilege to be part of his aviation legacy,' said the union president, Carl Kowitzky, in a statement....when he (Mr. Kelleher) brought up the pilots ad—and when he talked about how much the company's employees meant to him—he wept....More than a few people in the audience wept right along with him" (Nocera 2008).

What does this have to do with workforce strength? Southwest Airlines has been consistently profitable for 70 quarters. Southwest's after-tax profit margin in 2007 was almost three times that of American Airlines, and its growth rate was about three times as fast over the previous two years. In the October 16, 2008, third-quarter financial news release, Gary Kelly, now Southwest's chairman of the board speaks about the Southwest workforce (Southwest 2008): "I am very proud of the substantial progress our People have made...." Gerald Arpey of American, in the October 15, 2008, third-quarter financial news release, speaks of the need to "retire inefficient aircraft" and of "bolstering our liquidity" (American 2008). It is not surprising that Southwest's mission statement prominently includes the following: "Above all, Employees will be provided the same concern, respect, and caring attitude within the organization that they are expected to share externally with every Southwest Customer." And it is not surprising to see workforce strength at the core of Southwest's success. What is surprising is how many other organizations miss this crucial foundation for success.

## WHAT IS WORKFORCE STRENGTH?

Let's examine workforce strength from the perspectives of capability and flexibility. Capability means having the skills needed to deliver services or make products better than others. It means embedding these skills in systems that focus on providing exceptional outcomes for customers, whether internal or external. It means creating an environment that values contributions from all in the organization and builds a consensus about the right path forward. For example, Southwest Airlines' mission is stated as "dedication to the highest quality of Customer Service delivered with a sense of warmth, friendliness, individual pride and Company Spirit." Notice there is nothing about flying planes.

At Kaiser Permanente, a leader in healthcare delivery, workforce planning and career development take place in partnership with management and labor. Here's how people benefit. These are recent words from one Kaiser Permanente employee, responding to the question, how has this (career development support) changed your life? "Oh gosh. I'm a single mother...and...a lot. It's helped me so much...when I didn't think I could get help. I got help....Once you put your feet forward then you start running." Here's Bob Redlo, director of National Workforce Planning and Development for Kaiser Permanente: "Workforce planning and development is really a strategy by which we have internal mobility." In healthcare, Kaiser Permanente possesses broad strength in depth in delivering healthcare services and has the many disciplines required, whether through physicians; nurses; or pharmacy, laboratory, or radiology staff. And it is equipped to adjust for changes in the environment. This brings us to flexibility.

Workforce flexibility is the capacity of an organization to adjust capabilities and systems to changing needs. Here are some examples:

- In the airline industry, adjusting to changing reservation patterns as more reservations are made online

- In healthcare, adjusting to using electronic medical records for rapidly sharing patient information anywhere in the system by equipping doctors, nurses, and other primary healthcare providers with the ability to enter medical data directly, rather than having handwritten medical records transcribed

- In the world of high technology, adjusting to the business opportunities presented by increased processing speed or emerging information delivery capabilities

Providing needed flexibility includes blending permanent and contingent staff to handle shifts in demand, as in nursing or in high-technology recruiting. It may also mean service or product providers working hand in hand with educational institutions to create a steady flow of people with requisite skills. It may mean organizations working together to match skill and learning needs to changing industry standards. We will see examples of related situations as we examine workforce strength in practice throughout this book.

We can create a workforce capability and flexibility profile as shown in Figure 1.1.

The bottom left quadrant houses organizations with low workforce capability and limited flexibility to adjust to external changes. These are organizations in decline or stagnant; examples from recent experience are those banks that made excessively risky loans because of a lack of understanding of evolving market dynamics. In the lower right quadrant are

# Workforce Capability and Flexibility

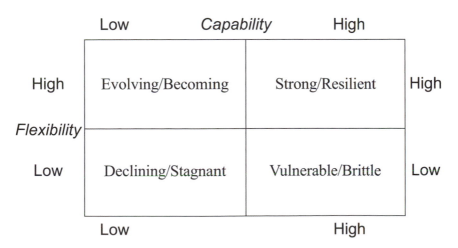

Figure 1.1.   Workforce strength expressed in terms of capability and flexibility

organizations that are vulnerable to changing conditions, having become strong in an area that is no longer needed. Their brittleness speaks to the challenge of changing with the needs of the market or environment. The big three U.S. automotive companies, prior to 2009, may fit here. In the upper left are evolving organizations with great flexibility but with the need to develop core capabilities. They are in a stage of becoming something greater. Many start-ups fit here, for example, Google in its early days when it was evolving its core search capability. In the upper right are strong, resilient organizations with both established capability and the ability to flex. DuPont, in the chemical industry, is one such example, able both to build workforce strength in depth in its core business areas and to evolve business focus on a regular basis over its more than 200-year history. Organizations in the upper left and lower right quadrants can shift to the top right quadrant. Doing so means building workforce strength in either or both capability and flexibility.

Workforce strength, then, is the combination of knowledge, skills, practices, and shared values, embedded in the workforce, which enable an organization to deliver exceptional performance while adapting to constantly changing needs. This builds on the concept of organizational value as "the sum total of the organization's knowledge, capabilities, operating practices, connections inside and outside, how they fit together, and the ability to marshal these to meet customers' needs" (Elsdon 2003, 51). Workforce strength, just as with organizational value, is created one person at a time. Understanding workforce strength means looking from the perspectives of the individual and the organization. It means looking at the context for assessing workforce strength and the nature and extent of resources needed to sustain it. Let's first examine the context and why workforce strength matters.

## WHY WORKFORCE STRENGTH MATTERS

Consider the viewpoint of the stewards of an organization while acknowledging that stewardship of an effective organization is distributed throughout the organization. In most developed economies, formal stewardship is vested in the boards of publicly held for-profit or nonprofit organizations. Formal stewardship for public-sector organizations is vested in elected or appointed officials charged with oversight responsibility. However, practical stewardship is present throughout the organization, for all connected with the organization are stewards of their time, resources, and relationships with others. All have a vested interest in the success of the organization. In organizations with a strong workforce, all share in the rewards of this success. For a nonprofit or public-sector organization, success is likely defined by program outcomes. For example, in a public-sector human services organization, the percentage of people eligible for food stamps who receive the benefit may be a key indicator. In a for-profit enterprise, financial performance will be one important measure of success.

Let's look from the viewpoint of outcomes. Rucci, Kirn, and Quinn (1998) conducted an extensive study at Sears, examining links between employee attitudes, customer impression of the organization, and revenue growth. They were able to demonstrate and quantify a direct relationship between positive employee attitude about the company and work that led to improved customer impressions about service and value, which in turn correlated with increased revenue growth. On a values level, we see that creating a supportive relationship with employees leads to tangible, positive business outcomes.

This is also borne out by Holmes and Zellner (2004), who observed Costco significantly outperforming competitor Sam's Club of Wal-Mart. Employee attrition at Costco was less than a third of that at Sam's Club, and labor and overhead costs as a percentage of revenue were less than two-thirds of those at Sam's Club, resulting in sales per square foot 54 percent higher, profits per employee 24 percent higher, and more rapid income growth. This was achieved with Costco having hourly wages 39 percent higher than Sam's Club, 64 percent higher per-person healthcare costs, 78 percent higher per-person retirement costs, and a CEO who chose to have his compensation be in the lowest 10 percent of his peers. Here's Jim Sinegal, CEO of Costco: "Having an individual who is making 100 or 200 or 300 times more than the average person working on the floor is wrong" (qtd. in Greenhouse 2005). Creating a strong and supportive workforce environment leads directly to business success at Costco.

From the perspective of the many stewards associated with an organization, workforce strength benefits the shareholders or owners through improved financial performance, it benefits sponsors of non-profit entities in the ability to more effectively achieve mission and program objectives, it benefits employees in terms of the nature of the work environment and the potential for sharing in the organization's success, and it benefits union partners in providing better working conditions for members. This is further supported by studies of high-performance workforce systems by Becker, Huselid, and Ulrich (2001, 210) who observed that a 33 percent increase in their measures of high-performance work systems led to an increase in market value of 24 percent, an increase in gross return on assets of 25 percent, an increase in sales per employee of 4.8 percent, and a reduction in employee attrition of 7.6 percent. High-performance work systems include such elements as a strong backup ratio for key positions, significant commitment of resources to developing people's competencies, and effective employee feedback systems (64). Again there is a direct link between the strength of the workforce and organizational performance.

The importance of workforce strength and its contribution to organizational performance is further underlined by feedback from individual clients, gathered in the course of providing career counseling services for an organization by Elsdon, Inc. Figure 1.2 shows the relationship between clients' self-assessed strength of affiliation with their work group in the organization, the extent to which they are working at their full potential (top chart), and the length of time they intend to stay with the organization (lower chart). Strong affiliation, a characteristic of workforce strength,

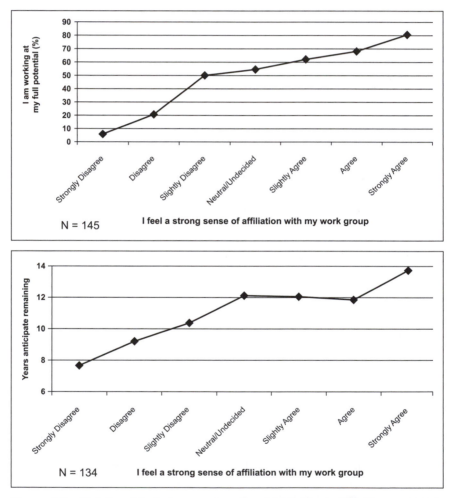

Figure 1.2.   Relationship between strength of individual affiliation, extent to which people are working at full potential, and time they intend to stay with the organization. Time responses in the lower chart coded as follows: less than one year = 0.5, 1 to less than 2 years = 1.5, 2 to less than 3 years = 2.5, 3 to less than 4 years = 3.5, 4 to less than 5 years = 4.5, 5 to less than 10 years = 7.5, 10 years of more = 16 (the average tenure of clients with 10 or more years of service).

is accompanied by lower attrition and by people more closely approaching their full potential. Indeed, since people must contribute value that exceeds their compensation for an organization to survive and prosper, the upper chart in Figure 1.2 provides an example of quantifying potential productivity gains from strengthened affiliation. In this case, increasing the measure of affiliation from that of disagreement to agreement, with the statement that a person feels a strong sense of affiliation with their work group, resulted in a 47 percent increase in the perceived approach to working at full potential. Capturing only one-tenth of such an increase as a productivity gain for a workforce of 10,000 people with an average compensation of $50,000 and a benefit loading of 40 percent would contribute $33 million annually to financial performance.

In assessing important workforce issues and how to proceed, the stewards of an organization can operate within various ethical frameworks. Saner (2004) identifies two primary options, one based on commonly shared values and one based on compliance with a set of agreed-upon standards. In the values-based approach, the emphasis is on important goals, means to achieve these goals, and motivations driving the organization, for example, growth or maintaining service excellence. Such an approach provides broad guidance for decision making, is flexible, and can be used in situations that were not anticipated when the foundation principles were created. The U.S. Bill of Rights is an example of such an approach.

A compliance-based approach, on the other hand, emphasizes rules and limits that need to be respected by all. Features are clarity, specificity, and the ability to readily incorporate performance measurement and audit processes. Unfortunately, a compliance-based approach can rapidly become encyclopedic in size and still not be sufficiently comprehensive. It also tends to stifle individual initiative. It tends to be implemented top down by edict, whereas a values-based code is built more by consensus. An example of a compliance-based approach is the U.S. tax code.

The preferred approach, whether values-based, compliance-based, or a blend of the two, depends upon context. For example, Southwest Airlines strictly enforces a compliance code when it instructs pilots precisely how to fly planes to ensure safety standards are met. However, in meeting customer needs, Southwest encourages great flexibility by pilots and flight attendants in making the flying experience as cheery as possible. Considering stewardship as holding something in trust for another (as framed by Block 1993, xx), a blend of the values- and compliance-based approaches can inform our understanding of why workforce strength is important to an organization's multiple stewards. Given the benefits of workforce strength, the role of stewardship is supported well by building workforce strength. Indeed, this extends externally, where workforce strength can also lead to an organization enhancing the quality of life for those in its constituent communities—its social contribution—the essence of the long-term contribution of an organization (Elsdon 2003, 228).

## CHARACTERIZING AND BUILDING WORKFORCE STRENGTH

### Characterizing Workforce Strength

Having defined what workforce strength means, explained why it is important, and discussed the ethical framework within which it is created, it is appropriate to ask what measures are available to characterize workforce strength. While many frameworks are possible, it is important to craft an approach that recognizes the specific needs of a given organization. One framework that can be a helpful starting point is to look through two lenses. The first lens is that of stage of engagement for people with the organization, as follows:

- Selection and hiring
- Integration
- Development and growth
- Transition

The second lens looks at workforce attributes, both at the individual level and at the organization level, as follows:

- Individual perspectives
  - Views people hold about the nature of their working relationship with the organization
- Individual behaviors; competencies
  - Observable actions that occur as part of work related activities; clusters of related knowledge, skills, abilities, and other personal characteristics that lead to specific performance outcomes
- Workforce capabilities
  - System-level strengths that are central to the organization meeting its goals, driven by workforce development activities

These two lenses combine to create the grid shown in Figure 1.3.

This grid becomes an organizing framework for understanding workforce strength that can be tailored to each organization. I recall giving a talk to a group of both HR and finance practitioners. Those in HR were surprised at how hard it was to get resources. The finance group said, "Just give us a good basis for your proposals, and we'll be happy to support them." An organizing framework provides a means for groups to communicate effectively with each other about building workforce strength.

Examples of items that might fit into this grid include the following:

- In the Selection and Hiring/Individual Perspectives box, surveys to gather feedback from those new to the organization about the hiring process

| | Individual Perspectives | Individual Behaviors and Competencies | Workforce Capabilities |
|---|---|---|---|
| Selection and Hiring | | | |
| Integration | | | |
| Development and Growth | | | |
| Transition | | | |

Figure 1.3.   Grid used to characterize workforce strength

- In the Development and Growth/Workforce Capabilities box, measures of key competencies such as communication effectiveness or conflict management, aggregated across the organization.
- In the Individual Perspectives/Transition box, exit interviews to understand why people leave the organization and how to address concerns that surface

Diagnostic tools that identify individual perspectives within the organization are one foundation for understanding and then building workforce strength. These tools, when coupled with systems for supporting internal development, tracking the external environment, and accessing external talent pools, provide a powerful basis for action. One example of using exit interviews as a diagnostic tool comes from more than 2,500 exit interviews conducted for many organizations between 2000 and 2009 (Elsdon, Inc. information). The following top 10 reasons, in order of priority, were why people looked outside the organization for another job:

1. Negative work environment
2. Lack of development opportunities in existing role
3. Lack of promotional opportunities
4. Better opportunity/more challenge
5. Lack of recognition/appreciation
6. Poor communication with manager
7. Financial—base pay

8. Lack of meaningful work/opportunity to add value

9. Lack of resources

10. Increased stress

Building workforce strength means understanding such issues and creating an environment that eliminates or minimizes concerns. This is primarily a management and leadership issue, and it is controllable. Leadership sets the tone within the organization, for example Southwest Airlines. In healthcare, Kaiser Permanente's leadership is strongly committed to working in partnership with the many unions representing various groups of employees. This partnership leads to support systems that make it easier for people to develop, for their benefit and for the organization's.

### An Organizational Context for Building Workforce Strength

In looking at building workforce strength, in this book we will examine the organizational context within which such development occurs. This includes looking at the internal systems that support workforce planning and development and the career development of individuals, and the external linkages that contribute to the potential flow of talent into an organization. It also includes exploring the needs of particular groups in the organization. In examining the context for building workforce strength, there are several aspects to bear in mind:

- Potential barriers
- Evolving forms of career relationship
- Optimized development and learning resources
- Role of career development

### *Potential Barriers*

Examples of barriers that can stand in the way of building workforce strength are as follows:

- Parochialism—a focus on only a subgroup in the organization to the detriment of the greater organizational good
- Lack of recognition that individual development is necessary for the long-term viability of the organization
- Lack of leader and manager skills in fostering an environment that builds workforce strength
- Lack of communication within the organization about the need to value and develop the workforce
- Lack of support for an equitable balance among individual, manager, and organization in sponsoring individual development

The approaches examined in the book are offered to help mitigate such barriers.

### Evolving Forms of Career Relationship

An important component of the context for building workforce strength is the interdependent nature of individual development, for such interdependence is a now a core factor in the evolving world of work. Here is a paraphrase of words from a recent client: "It is so good to see these opportunities come to life." Enthusiasm and energy cascaded from the phone. He was describing a journey from the corporate world through the world of consulting to a new opportunity, building a business in a field he cares deeply about. Each step along this path required courage, personal initiative, and support from others. These steps epitomize the career world of today and the future. How different this is from career worlds of the past.

From the 1950s through the 1980s, large organizations were prominent employers in the career landscape, whether in the public or private sectors. People in many such organizations enjoyed a measure of employment stability in exchange for their continued presence and fealty. This relationship fractured in the 1990s as the concept of career tenure disintegrated in the private sector. Survival skills became those of career self-reliance: survival of the fittest. Indeed, in the mayhem of the technology meltdown in the early 2000s, such an approach is an understandable response to an unknown and radically reshaped career landscape. However, it is becoming increasingly apparent that an approach based on satisfying only parochial needs, whether on an individual or organizational level, won't suffice in the future. The parochial perspective leads to tenuous or intractable relationships that suppress full expression of talents in individuals, and that limit organizational value creation.

Which brings us to career interdependence. Career interdependence recognizes the strengths and benefits that come from integrating personal aspirations with communal resources. It is based on a concept of abundance, where collaboration benefits all, rather than a zero-sum concept, where one person can only gain at the expense of others. Gladwell (2008) illustrates the power of interdependence for individuals in the book *Outliers*. On an organizational level, interdependence translates into the concept of affiliation, that of mutual partnership between individuals and organizations (Elsdon 2003, 7). Let's examine where interdependence fits into evolving forms of career relationship, and what this means for workforce strength. To do this, it is helpful to map forms of career relationship based on the extent to which we define our career paths ourselves and the extent to which our paths are supported by others. This framing leads to four primary directions summarized in Figure 1.4.

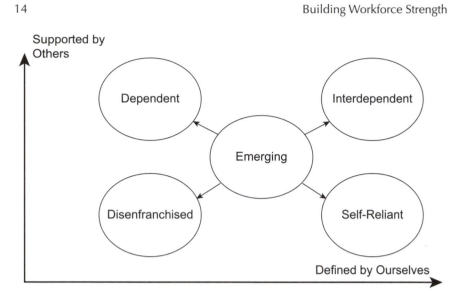

Figure 1.4.   Evolving forms of career relationship

Entry to the work world is shown by the "Emerging" oval in the center of the figure. This may come many times during our lives as we explore different phases. From this entry there are four primary directions:

- Disenfranchised (neither supported by others nor defined by ourselves)
- Dependent (supported by others and not defined by ourselves)
- Self-Reliant (defined by ourselves and not supported by others)
- Interdependent (both defined by ourselves and supported by others)

Those who are Disenfranchised neither own their own career direction nor feel supported by others. Some rural and urban communities in the U.S. have poverty rates exceeding 25 percent, college participation rates below 5 percent, and lack of access to effective medical care. Not surprisingly, in the absence of developed skills and effective community support, and while characterized by the reality of poverty and ill health, this Disenfranchised domain can become a black hole in the career relationship realm with a clear entry point but few exit opportunities. It is not a strong foundation for building workforce strength. Conversely, those who have much support from others but limited personal definition of their career path enter the Dependent relationship. This describes the organizational world of the 1950s–1980s. And there are vestiges of this relationship in the public sector in the U.S. today, where the overall separation rate is only 36 percent of that in the private sector (U.S. Department of Labor 2010b). This can lead to brittle workforce structures with limited ability to flex as needed. The third relationship, that of Self-Reliance, is driven by self-definition and independence, not by the support by others. It can be characterized by lack of engagement and constrained organizational value creation since it limits shared learning.

The fourth relationship, that of Interdependence, both personally defined and supported by others, includes these characteristics:

- Individual success and aspirations are interwoven with the success and aspirations of others so that individual and organizational benefits ensue.
- Progress and development for one person contributes to the progress and development of many. An early example of this is given in a paper by Barnett and Miner (1992) that examines the influence of hiring temporary employees on the progress of permanent staff.
- Mutuality occurs in connecting with others, with people both giving to and receiving from others according to the situation. This may mean, for example, giving and receiving mentoring, knowledge, resources, and contacts.
- The contribution of partnerships as a means to create value exists so that specialized expertise and capability are developed individually and pooled collectively.

It is this relationship of Interdependence, both among individuals and within organizations, that is the primary focus for building workforce strength.

### *Optimizing Development and Learning Resources*

Implicit in such interdependent relationships is alignment of individual development with organizational needs as a central component. Individual development enhances the two core aspects of workforce strength: capability and flexibility. At a system level, decisions about how much, and where, to commit an organization's development resources can generate substantial long-term value by strengthening capability and flexibility. Such decisions are an important issue for leadership, and a major reason for linking workforce development to career development. Making smart choices about how much and where to commit resources for individual development is not easy. At one extreme, no investment in individual development, the benefit that would come from new knowledge is lost. At the other extreme, overinvesting in individual development, these time-consuming efforts reduce productivity. Consequently, there is an optimum level of investment in development resources between these extremes. The tools of modeling (quantitatively describing a situation) and simulation (identifying the best solution) can provide some insights into what this optimum level looks like and how much to invest in development. An example is how to best allocate development resources across groups of employees performing at different levels. For example, should all of the organization's development resources be targeted to a small group of high-performing individuals, or should the resources be more evenly distributed throughout the organization? Elsdon (2004) applied the modeling and simulation approach to examine where resources could best be allocated among groups performing at different levels, as well as the substantial benefit that comes from such an allocation approach. The optimum distribution of resources for the example studied demonstrated the major value contribution of the middle performing group, as well as the benefit of increasing development resources for higher performing individuals.

## The Role of Career Development

As critical as the level of resource commitment is, so is the nature of the development activities and where they should be focused. Historically, resources committed by organizations to individual development have often been viewed as a perk for individuals rather than an issue of strategic importance both to the organization and the individual. So it is not surprising that one of the main reasons people in exit interviews say they leave organizations is lack of support for development, even though more than $56 billion was spent in the U.S. in 2008 on training activities (*Training* 2008). Training has also often been viewed largely from the sole perspective of enhancing skills for immediate performance. While this is a key component, equally important is development that supports longer-term career aspirations for the individual and benefits the organization in building workforce strength. Doing this well means building an effective process to guide individual development, linked to organizational needs. Career development practices provide an important way to establish this link and help guide those development activities that will be most valuable. For example, recent studies (IBM 2008; Mallon 2009) illustrate the prominent value of on-the-job training. It is in addressing the most effective approaches to individual development that career development practices provide a link between the needs of the organization and the needs of the individual to create and sustain workforce strength.

Our organizational context for exploring workforce strength recognizes barriers that need to be overcome, the evolution of interdependence as a core form of career relationship, the value of optimizing development resources at a system level, and the important contribution of workforce and career development practices.

## BUILDING A CASE FOR INVESTING IN WORKFORCE STRENGTH

### Overview

With these aspects in mind, establishing a sound case for investing in workforce strength is a critical step in implementation. This means building a business case. The following factors are central to building this case:

- Establishing strategic and business relevance
- Matching the approach to organizational culture
- Creating a sense of urgency
- Communicating potential value contribution

### Establishing Strategic and Business Relevance

For many practitioners in the field, it is self-evident that building workforce strength through workforce and career development is central to securing organizational prosperity. In some organizations such views are shared by senior leaders. For other senior leaders, however, such endeavors may appear benign, perhaps even marginally useful, but peripheral to the real work of the organization. This latter group may include those in senior management with limited exposure to organizational and individual development, particularly in highly analytical cultures. In these cases regularly communicating the linkage of workforce strength to the organization's critical drivers is essential. For example, workforce strength in high-technology organizations, where intellectual capital is continuously and rapidly evolving, links directly to competitive advantage and to securing growth opportunities such as those presented by geographic expansion. In customer-facing groups within organizations, workforce strength, built through development, secures the organization's revenue stream. In organizations focused on continuously improving operating efficiency, workforce strength is central to securing ongoing productivity improvements. Where innovation and creativity are the organization's lifeblood, workforce strength can catalyze the introduction of new ideas and address emerging skill needs. For organizations such as those in healthcare, facing a scarcity of people with needed skills, workforce strength is central to an organization's ability to service current needs and capture future growth potential. In each type of organization, a separate and distinct business case is needed to demonstrate the link between resources invested and critical organization drivers.

### Matching the Approach to Organizational Culture

While establishing business relevance addresses the driving forces for building workforce strength, it does not address how to introduce the conversation into the organization. This conversation needs to respect organizational culture. For example, securing resources in a strongly hierarchical, more traditionally oriented organization usually requires sponsorship at senior management levels. Identifying and securing one or more senior champions is central to moving forward. In decentralized, fast-moving entities, ideas from a central source may be rejected as antithetical to local needs. Here, forward movement will require local sponsorship for adoption.

### Creating a Sense of Urgency

Once the rationale and the form of approach are defined, movement requires creating a sense of urgency, for invariably there will be competing needs for resources. Creating a sense of urgency means understanding the demographics of the workforce, as well as future issues and their timing. This includes defining the potential contribution of workforce strength to the organization either through securing opportunities or addressing challenges, many of which are time dependent. For example, the impending retirement of a significant fraction of an organization's workforce presents time-dependent challenges in the conduct of ongoing business and in the retaining of intellectual capital, while at the same time presenting development opportunities for the current workforce.

### Communicating Potential Value Contribution

Having defined the rationale and the approach, and having established urgency, it is then necessary to communicate a path forward in such a way that recommendations can be heard. Analytical, frequently quantitative, information expressed in the language of business, economics, and finance will appeal to the intellectual and thinking domains of decision makers. Anecdotal perspectives that speak the language of relationship and community will provide a strong emotional connection. A combination of both, the analytical and the emotional, is a powerful form of communication to influence forward movement and help secure resources.

### Examples of Building Business and Organizational Relevance

Understanding the experiences of others in establishing the business and organizational relevance of building workforce strength can provide valuable insights. Let's examine some examples related to career development services. In order to assess the need, level, and composition of demand for career development services, Erickson (2004) conducted in-depth structured interviews with more than 80 career counselors, coaches, human resource consultants, and organization development leaders in various organizations:

- Ten niche market leaders
- Three firms that had recently completed initial public offerings (IPOs)

- Forty Fortune 500 firms
- Two firms that were moving to offshore production

The sampling composition was primarily business and professional services (50%), followed by manufacturing (25%), financial services (15%), and healthcare (10%). The results of the interviews were analyzed via content analysis and then applied to Moore's Technology Adoption Lifecycle (Moore 1995). These techniques were used to better highlight the connection between the organizational stage and the nature of demand for career development services. All respondents indicated their firms aligned leadership development offerings with organizational strategy. Although 60 percent of these firms employed a balanced-scorecard type process (Kaplan and Norton 1996) for this, under 20 percent of these respondents indicated that strategy and employee development efforts were aligned at the individual contributor level.

### Ten Niche Market Leaders

Only the 10 niche leaders were successful in aligning strategy and development throughout the organization. All these firms were in the professional services industry, and most were in custom software development or computer consulting niches. These firms ranged in size from 10 employees to over 2,000, with 6 of the 10 respondent firms employing between 50 and 100 employees. The smaller the firm, the more likely it was to have invested in value creation mapping, with clear linkages between skills, competencies, and sales. All these firms leveraged both in-house and external talent to educate employees about the market space. This included informal lunch and learn sessions aimed at understanding the needs of the customer, with presentations led by senior executives, senior sales staff, or technical thought leaders within the firm; presentations by industry analysts; or custom offerings from professional associations. Developmental and leadership coaching was offered on topics ranging from transferable skills to business acumen and emotional intelligence. Workforce planning forecasts and the development of talent pipelines ensured that employees in these firms were well ahead of changes in business conditions.

Niche market leaders developed expertise not only in their product or service offerings but also within their customers' business dynamics. Moore refers to this period of niche development and differentiation as "the bowling alley" (1995, 99, 130). Employees needed high levels of functional expertise, business acumen, and interpersonal skills. Because the technology, tools, and processes were evolving at an extremely rapid rate, few of these firms had traditional job descriptions. For development, deployment, and resource planning purposes, employees were assessed against a variety of technical and functional competencies. Employees opted into sharing their competencies via internal talent bank databases. From the perspective of the employee, both robust and evolving skills were visible to resource managers. This increased project-to-project mobility for employees and allowed for continual challenge. From an organizational perspective, the value added from corporate-sponsored career development stemmed from the ability to continuously develop its workforce and thus capitalize on existing talent to fill rapidly changing roles. Harnessing evolving talent ensured continued ability to meet the firm's high product or service quality standards, and thus further growth in profitable client relationships. Both the organizations and the individual clients sought sustainable competitive advantage. While several of the firms invested in custom econometrics for multiple human capital initiatives, an effective proxy for the value created by a single human capital development initiative was average revenue per employee.

### Three IPO Firms

Three of the respondent firms had completed the IPO process within the preceding 12 months. All three were undergoing the rapid phase of growth Moore refers to as "the tornado" (1995, 99, 130). The switch from privately held to publicly held status is often followed by standardization in processes, more defined role descriptions, and increased financial scrutiny. Development professionals in these firms acknowledged that employees who thrived in a talent-driven, customer-centric environment were challenged by the faster pace and longer hours during the ensuing rapid growth of these firms. Career services were delivered primarily through external partners who had long-term relationships with the firm. Respondents from these firms stressed the need for customized but rapidly scalable offerings, reflective of their stage of growth. Career development concentrated on three needs: address employee concerns for work-life balance, attract high-performing employees, and secure key organizational talent. None of the respondents in these firms used metrics to evaluate the effectiveness of their outcomes.

### Forty Fortune 500 Firms

Respondents from the 40 Fortune 500 firms interviewed reported the most mixed composition of demand for career services. Moore terms this mature stage of the lifecycle "main street" (1995, 130). The majority of the firms (75%) at this stage of growth offered development services only to high-potential employees or employees in high-growth or high-demand roles. Less than 25 percent of these firms offered career development services to all employees. Becker, Huselid, and Beatty (2009) describe the former as a differentiated workforce strategy and the latter as an undifferentiated one. Firms providing widespread service offerings had strong organizational cultural norms around equity. As organizations reach this level of maturity, human capital needs are typically addressed by a range of providers: in-house organizational development and training departments, external business partners who have helped grow the firm, and firms of similar size and industry prominence as themselves but with specialized human capital expertise. While return on training investment was measured by a small number of these firms, most had not applied metrics to other human capital offerings.

Leadership development was the most important need expressed by these respondents. As a company matures, the growth rate slows and opportunities for advancement, particularly fast-track advancement, decline. As industry, product, and service lines mature, continuous realignment becomes the order of the day. In global markets, this often implies increased merger, acquisition, and divestiture activity. Because these firms tended to be large, career service offerings tended to be developmentally focused on high-potential employees and employees in high-growth or high-external-demand occupations. These offerings included developmental coaching, rotation assignments, employer-sponsored education, and employer-sponsored professional associations or other industry leadership participation. At the individual contributor level, the training department was most often tasked with filling all developmental needs. While this strategy is a cost-efficient means of bringing large numbers of employees to a standardized level of performance, it is rarely capable of tapping into the unique capabilities of each employee. Senior-level individual contributors are particularly underserved.

A significantly different approach to development was undertaken by a large, global technology firm. Tasked with using its significant training and development resources more effectively, Seagraves (2003–2006) developed an approach to evaluating return on investment (ROI) linked to changes in employee competencies. She benchmarked known competency gaps against the current training portfolio. This initial analysis indicated overinvestment in some areas and underinvestment in other key areas. An initial significant ROI stemmed from a reallocation toward the underinvested competencies. A second significant ROI came from developing and reinforcing desired manager and leader behaviors, including assessing manager progress in modeling and coaching these behaviors. Seagraves developed a predictive algorithm that indicated optimal development portfolio allocation with global, region, country, and team drill-down capability. The competency/development portfolio analysis enabled more targeted training, which resulted in $30 million annual savings.

## Two Firms Moving to Offshore Production

Among the 55 firms interviewed in 2004, only 2 firms, both in non-durable manufacturing, had reached the stage of employment decline.

Both firms were moving to offshore production, and development needs were focused on management and brand positioning in a global context. Career development was desired for high-level individual contributors and high-potential operations leaders. The organizations partnered with intercultural consulting firms to assess candidate likelihood of success, deliver intercultural training, provide family support, and develop cultural leadership competencies to ensure successful international assignments. Given the need to reduce staffing levels, career transition services were provided to ensure successful outplacement as well as maintain a positive brand image. Outcome metrics were not tracked within either of these manufacturing firms.

It is apparent from these examples that the business and organizational contributions from building workforce strength through career and workforce development can be substantial, and that there are significant opportunities to enhance the delivery or tracking of some initiatives. It is also apparent that the delivery approaches and business cases need to be tailored to the specific culture of each organization and its operating environment. Having examined the foundations of building workforce strength and establishing business and organizational relevance, in the next chapter we will examine the implications for working with different individuals in this rapidly evolving work world.

# CHAPTER 2

# Understanding the Needs of Different Individuals

*Rita Erickson and Michele McCarthy*

The world of work has changed dramatically in the last 40 years. The workplace is now more inclusive, global, and competitive. Consequently, it is increasingly important to build upon the strengths of each individual. The growing complexity of work combined with the accelerating rate of change diminishes the potential for educational institutions to be the sole source of workforce preparation. Lifelong learning is a requirement. This implies a willingness to risk, to initiate. Organizational survival depends on fully engaged, high-performing workers—employees who can stay abreast of changes in technology and business processes. Professionally guided career development and workforce planning are effective platforms for achieving this objective.

Professionally guided development may take many forms. This chapter begins by briefly introducing the role of the development facilitator. This is followed by a perspective on the need for a different development framework to address the needs of individuals from various populations and an overview of a proposed framework. The outline of the framework that follows shows how risk, initiative, feedback, and perseverance relate to organizational career development. Descriptions of components in the framework are followed by simplified case studies that highlight selected aspects. These case studies are used as examples of building understanding of the different perspectives people may bring to development, and supporting these individuals' forward movement. Brief summary points conclude the chapter.

Within an organizational context, the term career development is often used interchangeably with career management, career planning, or succession planning. In practice, a range of practitioners guide the efforts of organizational career development clients. These practitioners include career counselors, coaches, organization development practitioners, managers, trainers, human resource consultants, and recruiters. For the sake of simplicity, these individuals will be referred to as development facilitators in this chapter. These professionals bring different competencies to the process, and different likelihoods of succeeding with the clients they serve. For this reason, successfully staffing the development facilitator role is more highly correlated with the organizational culture and the needs of the targeted clients than with a person's prior title. Development facilitators often have diverse backgrounds from which they can draw expertise in addition to the specific knowledge, skills, and tools that exist within the professional and personal development arena. Their most relevant competencies, which are described in more detail in chapter 5, include content knowledge of the career field, effective individual and group interpersonal skills, and strategic understanding of workforce and organizational issues.

## THE NEED FOR AN INCLUSIVE FRAMEWORK

Career counseling or career guidance typically take place in educational institutions. Perhaps for this reason, the career field has generally evolved around the needs of upwardly mobile individuals. As the field has grown in scope and populations served, many new paradigms and theories have emerged that reflect the needs of underserved populations (Sue and Sue 2007). These theories are particularly helpful when working with clients in specific contexts. However, once individuals are employed in an organization, they enter into a shared experience and context. Development in a shared context requires thinking outside of a socioeconomic box that can define and confine individuals.

We reviewed more than 1,500 case notes spanning more than two decades of career development (Erickson 1989–2009). We reflected on coaching experiences with clients ranging from top executives in leading firms to unionized environmental service workers and those in many roles and levels between. Clients included national and international workers, Millennials to Traditionalists, and workers with GEDs to PhDs. We first sought commonalities rather than differences among these clients. We then looked for change levers, elements that accounted for "just-noticeable-differences" (Spencer and Spencer 1993, 7) between clients who were effective in reaching their goals and those who were less effective. Within the field of psychology, this critical distinction is referred to as the "difference that makes the difference" (Gordon and Dawes 2005). Viewing client experiences through the above set of lenses highlighted the importance of risk/initiative and feedback/perseverance in achieving successful outcomes. Evaluating challenges and opportunities through the risk/

initiative and feedback/perseverance lenses can reenergize clients who are stuck or free those who are caught within self-defeating cycles. Our purpose was to create an actionable framework for the development facilitator and the client. This framework is intended to offer perspectives to development facilitators and organizational career development clients at all levels and enable them to move forward on their paths.

## OVERVIEW OF THE THRIVER FRAMEWORK

The Thriver Framework is the result of this effort. The pattern that surfaced from the analysis underscored the importance of risk and initiative, feedback and perseverance. By combining these elements, four distinct groupings emerged: Open Road Ahead, Undercapitalized Talent and Passion, Shooting Stars, and Thrivers. This pattern is summarized in Figure 2.1.

The basic relationship will be explained first and then illustrated via composite case study examples. The case studies represent patterns of composite observations rather than specific individuals.

### Framework Definitions

The framework consists of two core themes, risk/initiative and feedback/perseverance. Initiative and perseverance are observable behaviors,

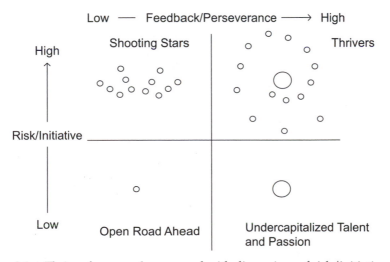

Figure 2.1.   Thriver framework expressed with dimensions of risk/initiative and feedback/perseverance. The circles in the diagram represent patterns of developing and integrating learning that are described in the later quadrants overview section of the chapter.

while the assessment of risk and the assessment of relevant feedback are internal judgments that influence behavior. We define risk as the perception of the uncertainty of an outcome. We define initiative as the willingness take action in the face of risk. The perception that a behavior entails risk drives or restrains the decision to take initiative. Perseverance is the willingness to maintain a course of action in the face of adversity. Based on our experience, we assert that perseverance is driven and supported by access to effective sources of feedback. As individuals assess risk, they make determinations about the likelihood of the outcome. The threshold that triggers initiative differs dramatically among individuals. Upon taking initiative, people seek feedback from sources they deem credible. Positive feedback increases their perseverance. This builds skills in calculated risk taking. Initiative increases. Negative feedback typically has the opposite effect, therefore diminishing the scope and scale of risk a person will embrace. The absence of credible feedback also inhibits perseverance.

Successful movement from one quadrant to another is a function of awareness, readiness, and resolve. The role of the development facilitator is to skillfully use her processes, tools, and models to elicit pattern awareness. As the elements of the underlying pattern clarify, the development facilitator and the client address them. Once the elements have been fully addressed, the development facilitator and client can craft a path forward. The rate at which this happens varies considerably from one person to another. From the perspective of the client, acknowledging the previous benefits and challenges derived from his thought and behavioral patterns concurrent with the present situation creates the bridge between awareness and readiness to change. The development facilitator plays an invaluable role in reflecting the client's beliefs and values. For example, a risk-averse client may need to acknowledge how caution has protected him or served him well in some domains while concurrently seeing the cost of this pattern in the present. Reconciling these differences brings the relevance of beliefs and values into conscious awareness. Once this awareness has been achieved, the client is free to tear the fabric of belief, and re-weave its threads in ways that better serve the client in the present. Another key role the development facilitator plays is to validate the client's experience and partner with the client to facilitate a more empowered sense of self. This results in resolve. Much that is surfaced here falls into the domain of counseling. These elements must be addressed within the ethical bounds governing the development facilitator's background, recognizing that referrals may be appropriate.

### Roles of Initiative and Risk

Individual initiative is often considered a precondition for successful development outcomes. Demonstrating initiative is contingent upon the ability to effectively assess risk, leverage talents, and facilitate outcomes against a given time horizon. The development facilitator and the client work together to understand the client's current assessment of risk while increasing her capacity to assess and deliver on risk. This means expanding the client's effective comfort zone. Assessment instruments such as the Strong Interest Inventory (Grutter and Hammer 2005) measure willingness to take financial and physical risk. Additional important dimensions that can be elicited in the developmental conversation process include interpersonal, intrapersonal, and intellectual risk (Erickson 2004). In practice, development involves taking risk in each of these areas. However, the particular developmental challenge undertaken may involve relatively more of one form of risk. Understanding how a client defines risk in these different areas creates a rich repertoire of potential experiences from which the development facilitator and the client can build developmental assignments.

### Roles of Feedback and Perseverance

Perseverance is the ability to maintain a course of action in the face of difficulty. This is significantly affected by feedback. Developmental conversations can reveal two important components. First, they may reveal how clients assign relevance to feedback from different sources. Second, they may reveal the intensity of the feedback needed to signal successful completion. When relevant, supportive feedback follows initiative then self-efficacy increases. Feedback comes from the work itself, the stakeholders, and significant others (Head et al. 1998, 625–38).

#### Types of Feedback

Feedback from the work itself is the clearest example. For some occupations this is the dominant form of feedback. Assembly work is a good example. The beginning and ending points are clear, as is successful completion. Certainly there is feedback from the manager and possibly from peers, but within the role, these are of relatively less importance. Feedback from stakeholders is the most important source of feedback in service and knowledge industries. Although the beginning point of the work may be comparatively clear, the ending point may not be clear, and much feedback is needed along the away to ensure a successful outcome. The most common stakeholders include clients, colleagues, managers, leaders, and boards of directors. Feedback from significant others is more about the role of work in the broader picture of our lives than about the nature of the work tasks and outcomes. Observations such as "you seem really happy now" or "you are really stressed" from spouses, family, and friends can significantly influence how people view their experience of work.

The relative importance of these sources of feedback varies considerably, both by occupation and by individual. Many clients come to career counseling because the source and frequency of feedback available from their work does not support their needs. Imagine the mismatch between the service-oriented call center representative who sees daily productivity statistics but never knows whether she helped her clients resolve their problems.

A simplified example may clarify these concepts. Successful sales consultants are characterized by their willingness to take considerable financial and interpersonal risk. Financial risk may be measured by the percent of compensation that is commission based. Interpersonal risk may be measured by probability of rejection. In order to increase her income, the media sales consultant may need to overcome latent negative self-talk. Successfully addressing internalized messages, their sources, and the ramifications elsewhere in her life is a form of intrapersonal risk. She must be willing to look inside herself. As she progresses to more senior levels with clients, both functional expertise and business acumen are increasingly threshold competencies (Spencer and Spencer 1993, 15). Acquiring and developing functional and specialized business mastery are basic forms of intellectual risk. Notably, it is the less common forms of risk taking, intrapersonal and intellectual risk in this example, which offer the greatest risk/reward payoff.

A variety of experiments and processes could be leveraged or designed to help the sales consultant integrate her emerging skills. For example, she may receive business acumen coaching. This may include training or mentoring in S.W.O.T. (Strengths, Weaknesses, Opportunities, Threats) analyses, scenario planning, or other types of strategic business planning (Schwartz 1996, 29–162). Upon completion, she may conduct research and present her findings in formats ranging from electronic presentations to more organic, white board–style presentations. Confidence would build iteratively as she moved from a more formal presentation with the content in the foreground to a relatively more informal presentation with the content in the background and her clients' needs in the foreground. To address the sales consultant's fear of criticism, the coach and mentor may play multiple roles, including those of her internal critics (Stone and Stone 1993), her clients, and their more supportive roles. It is essential that the feedback come from individuals possessing the domain expertise that will bestow credibility. Training and coaching provide the content while the feedback embeds the new content in the business context, resulting in both increased initiative and increased perseverance.

A key benefit to offering organizational career development is the potential of the organization to serve as a source of behavior-based feedback. When talent and reward systems are well designed and include clear role expectations, ongoing informal performance feedback, and periodic formal performance evaluation, then the organization represents an important source of work-based feedback. Coaching from skilled development facilitators can supplement this feedback. Organizational feedback may be biased or not provide a venue for acknowledging newly developing skills. Development facilitators may provide critical feedback that helps establish these emerging skills. This incrementally builds perseverance. Development facilitators can also empower clients to design and request more valuable forms or sources of feedback.

### Description of a Thriver

What is a Thriver? Thrivers are high in both risk and perseverance. Based on our experience with this framework, we believe that with awareness and support, anyone can become a Thriver. Their inner dialogues reflect beliefs in themselves and hope for their future. They are active authors in creating their compelling stories. This awareness empowers them to take risks in their preferred realms. Feedback from relevant others helps them assess the relative success of their actions. Risk, initiative, feedback, and perseverance combine synergistically to create momentum and a continuously evolving coherent sense of self.

## QUADRANT OVERVIEW AND MOVEMENT AMONG THE QUADRANTS: CASE STUDIES

### Open Road Ahead

Clients who are currently in the Open Road Ahead stage of development are both low in risk and low in perseverance. Represented by a single small dot against a large white field of unknown potential (Figure 2.1), clients presenting this way often are beset with a multitude of challenges. If these challenges have been life long or for an extended duration, it is likely that other life supports will need to be in place before effective career counseling can begin. Regardless of the initial reasons for these challenges, individuals in this quadrant are either fearful of taking risks or hold the self-assessment that they are unskilled in successfully executing in risk situations. Without willingness to risk, initiative is not possible. Without action, relevant feedback is typically absent for these individuals. Lacking this input, there is no fuel for perseverance. Without perseverance, the ability to maintain employment becomes increasingly challenging. These clients are more likely to be seen in a social service setting than in an organizational career development context.

Leveraging the framework allows us to see potential paths out. Eliciting the Story of Possibility or Impossibility highlights the client's beliefs and values. The Story of Possibility or Impossibility represents unarticulated beliefs and values creating real-world boundaries that no longer serve the client. These stories may also represent worldviews that run counter to Western corporate or organizational norms. The development facilitator can work within the client's current risk profile to create safe-fail activities.

Concurrently, the development facilitator and the client can identify sounding boards—understanding and knowledgeable individuals who can provide feedback that is relevant to the client at this stage of career development. Creating empowering communities of resonance, peers and mentors who understand the client's worldviews as well as organizational worldviews, is essential to moving the individual out of inertia and into a more rewarding life. This allows the development facilitator to meet the client where he is and bring him along to further growth.

### Undercapitalized Talent and Passion

Clients who are currently in the Undercapitalized Talent and Passion stage of career development are comparatively low in risk and high in perseverance. Effective, but with a small circle of comfort, individuals at this stage of career development are graphically depicted with a small but intact circle on a large white field representing their potential (Figure 2.1). The title Undercapitalized Talent and Passion was selected to describe these clients because they are not compensated for the additional value they bring to an organization. Many of these clients use their talents and passions in special projects, committees, or service roles within their organizations or communities. Passion is energy; it is the fuel that propels the talents. These additional talents are beyond the official scope of their present job descriptions. Explicit awareness of the value of these skills to their employer would bring greater compensation to the client and represent higher value added to the organization. Feedback from managers and colleagues indicates they see these clients as more talented than the clients claim for themselves. Common themes with these clients include first-generation status, security anchors, early negative experiences with risk taking, negative assessments about risk taking, or inexperience with risk taking. As intensely loyal employees, the challenge for these clients is the risk of being both undercapitalized (not fully leveraging their gifts) and overcompensated (job description versus the market pay rate). As a consequence, they are more likely to experience job elimination during company or industry restructurings. The tremendous opportunity for clients in this stage is fundamental self-evaluation leading to a realignment of capitalization and compensation. In the following case studies, Jessica represents an example of undercapitalized passion. Richard represents the dangers confronting talented individuals working in rapidly changing fields who surround themselves with too few and too narrowly focused sources of feedback.

#### *Parallel Train Tracks*

Jessica was a union steward for the Association of Federal, State and Municipal Employees (AFSME) union in the federal government. She had held a midlevel administrative assistant position for over 20 years, but she was embarrassed about this because she never sought nor was she given a promotion in these years. As a union steward, she enjoyed her leadership role as the go-to person when employees had legal questions or just needed encouragement and a listening ear. She was excellent at intervening in dispute resolution when that became necessary, and she was able to use the dispute resolution process to head off a potential griev-ance before it was filed. Jessica enjoyed assisting her employees to get what they needed. She liked the reputation she had of being someone they could call for support and guidance. Over the years she continued to do the midlevel administrative work that was required but never sought pro-motions because her focus was always on others.

After receiving career coaching, Jessica realized that she had become lulled into thinking she was active and progressing because she was help-ing others. She learned to reframe her activities as parallel train tracks, with one track helping herself progress in her career and the other track assisting the union members with their needs. Both tracks are equally im-portant. With regard to risk/initiative and feedback/perseverance, Jes-sica's turning point in career counseling was the realization of a pattern of equating progress in her career with being busy helping others. Jessica admits to some degree of magical thinking: "If I help others advance and coach them through difficult times at work, then someone will notice all my hard work, and I will be rewarded and compensated with a promo-tion." Jessica confused progressing others with advancing her career. She came to realize that this altruism and service to members was comfortable and familiar, but to do nothing but continue it would breed further frus-tration and resentment. Through career coaching, she was encouraged to reframe the situation and think of work activities as being on a parallel track, where she engages in activities that help others advance while also making behavioral choices that deliberately help her advance and qualify for promotions. The inner dialogue Jessica used that was keeping her stuck was this: "Helping others is helping me." This was simply not true, even though it gave her tremendous pleasure to see results this way. Her career was not moving forward in a way that was measurable for promotion.

The risk in Jessica's case was the courage it took to face a self-defeating pattern hidden behind her commitment to help fellow union members advance. According to Jessica, what finally broke the pattern was the image of the train track showing that she could do both: help others and help herself at the same time. Like many others with undercapitalized tal-ent and passion, she confused activity on behalf of others with activity that would benefit her.

### Market of One?

Richard was a computer programmer in a midsized West Coast town. He had been a dedicated employee of the same financial institution for over 25 years. A combination of high-level technical expertise, breadth of client knowledge, and superior problem-solving skills led to his guru status within the firm. Although he enjoyed mentoring and developing others, he did not enjoy the responsibilities associated with day-to-day supervision. Consequently, his firm's management track, the only advancement option open to him, was not an option he was interested in pursuing. For many years he enjoyed the challenge of custom programming and the respect earned from his unique knowledge set. Based on the framework described previously, for Richard a successfully developed and implemented computer program served as feedback from the job itself. Feedback from key stakeholders—his manager and his peers—convinced him that he was indispensable. He felt his future was secure. Then the acquisition was announced. New management communicated their intention to launch industry standard technology. Having never been exposed to these tools, Richard found himself doubly vulnerable, both underskilled and yet highly compensated.

As he entered the coaching process, he felt angry, betrayed, and obsolete. Over the course of coaching, it became apparent he had been an early shining star. His keen analytical skills had allowed him to excel in the realm of custom application, a world where few other developers survived, much less thrived. But this capacity had led to captivity. As the world of software development evolved into common languages and platforms, skills honed internally became increasingly irrelevant in the external market. In evaluating the scope and complexity of his work, it became apparent that he had been moving laterally for more than two decades. The variety of projects had concealed this crucial insight. Further, focusing his attention entirely inside the organization left him little time, energy, or inclination to stay abreast of changes within the broader software development field. Most developers are keenly aware of the technological trends and changes in the relative demands for particular skills. Richard's orientation toward learning and mastery was counter to the broader occupational culture.

This mismatch was addressed by crafting a development plan based on industry, occupational, and regional market research. This strategy quickly confirmed his precarious position and also motivated him to take action. His field research allowed him to see transferable technical skills and analogous development tools, which created a common reference language with his new manager. A custom development plan was created to leverage his analytical skills and put him on an accelerated advancement path. We took a calculated risk and computed a financial value for his legacy systems and legacy client knowledge. Client turnover among finance and insurance firms is significantly lower than overall industry averages, making this knowledge more valuable than it would be in other environments. A one-page business case spelled out the significant financial value of his client and systems knowledge as well as the value added from his targeted new role versus the investment in his development (customized tutoring as well as continued developmental coaching).

Within 90 intense days, Richard successfully completed the certification required for the new technical role in addition to demonstrating learning agility—and the company had capitalized on the hidden bonus of his client knowledge. The swiftness of the changes forced him to develop not only technical knowledge but also business acumen, an area he had previously considered unimportant. Additionally, the new skills opened up opportunities within the larger external job market. While he chose to remain with his company, he continues to advance his certification level, monitors industry trends, and remains an active contributor to an online user group. Most importantly, he has built a new feedback system based on internal as well as external industry relationships.

What levers moved Richard from the Undercapitalized Talent and Passion space into Thriver space? Richard's frame-breaking moment came as a result of the acquisition, which drove technology change. This external event necessitated the willingness to take intellectual and interpersonal risk. Richard and many others put themselves at risk when their only frames of reference became the company's strategy and internal feedback. Though he lacked a business background or understanding of company financials, he was willing to do the market research and take responsibility for co-creating the business case for remaining with the organization and developing. In his assessment, this represented not only significant intellectual risk but also significant interpersonal risk with his new manager. Career coaching significantly broadened his self-understanding, his technical frame of reference, and his market understanding. An unofficial survey was designed to solicit feedback from internal and external peers. This survey addressed wide-ranging competencies, including technical knowledge, global workplace effectiveness, and market awareness. Extending his intellectual risk taking and engaging in interpersonal risk taking ensured he remained on track. Soliciting internal and external feedback from sources he deemed credible was essential to keeping this Thriver in motion.

### Shooting Stars

Clients who find themselves in the Shooting Star stage have generally not yet discovered their passion or developed a career strategy. From the perspective of the Thriver model, they are high in risk but low in perseverance. Graphically, this stage is represented by a comparatively large dotted line ray, indicating incompleteness, against a relatively smaller field of potential (Figure 2.1). Shooting Stars change employers or occupations before reaching a significant level of mastery. Without a clear career direction, feedback comes from a variety of sources, and is rarely consistent or meaningful. Weakness in the feedback process inhibits perseverance. Lack of perseverance inhibits mastery. Not achieving mastery is the critical distinction between Shooting Stars and Thrivers, those who acquire skills, develop mastery, and continually evolve their career directions.

Most commonly, Shooting Stars have not done the work necessary to achieve career clarification. Most career counseling processes, tools, and assessments were designed to serve these clients. Less common, but possible, some Shooting Stars may also have an underdeveloped ability to assess risk. This may manifest as a lack of self-confidence or inflated confidence relative to their ability to implement their goals. Depending on the life stage of the client, codesigned internships, externships, temporary assignments, or field assignments may serve to hone the risk-assessing skill and thereby build both competence and confidence. In the case studies below, both Tom and Sharon had to break their familial stories and engage in intrapersonal and interpersonal risk in order to reach clarification and crystallization. Uncovering or creating relevant sources of feedback enabled Tom to align his wayward path and allowed Sharon to initialize a path and address her self-confidence issues.

### A Journey Full of Starts and Stops

Tom grew up the youngest son of four boys. His three older brothers seemed to know what they wanted to do in life, even from a very early age. Jim became a lawyer specializing in tax law. Daniel chose business, pursuing his MBA at Georgetown University. He was fortunate to land a job in new product development with Proctor and Gamble. Anthony, the oldest brother, followed in his father's footsteps and became an accountant with a top-notch firm, Ernst and Young. His mother did not work outside the home but was active as a volunteer for many charitable causes in their community of Philadelphia. Eventually, all the boys married and started their families. Tom married Ginny, a registered nurse who worked as a psychiatric nurse in a behavioral health organization in downtown Philadelphia. Tom worked part-time as a pharmacy technician and went to school full-time to be a pharmacist. After many years of this, he finally passed his state boards and began working as a pharmacist in another drug store. He wanted a fresh start from where he had been known as a pharmacy technician.

Six months into his new position as a pharmacist, Tom came home and announced to Ginny that he was tired of being a pharmacist and thought maybe he would enroll in an MBA program like his brother Daniel. He said Daniel seemed so happy at Proctor and Gamble. Plus it was a highly visible and prestigious company. Tom's plan was to work part-time again as a pharmacist now and go to school full-time. Ginny was explosive in her anger over this turn of events. She had delayed having a family for years while Tom finished his degree and was eager to conceive their first child. After much discussion, she finally came around, and Tom resumed his old lifestyle of working part-time and going to school full-time. This time he enrolled and was accepted into Strayer University's MBA program. College loans were growing. Years went by and still no family started for

Tom and Ginny. Tom eventually did finish his MBA at Strayer and took a job as a sales manager for new accounts at a pharmaceutical company. He worked for about a year when he decided to resign. Tom eventually started an Internet business selling sports equipment to young athletes, and he is happy to report that the business is growing. He is about to move it out of his basement and into a rented office space. Ginny eventually got her long-delayed wish for a family, and the couple is planning a second child. Tom finally found work that is satisfying—so far.

The initiative/risk and feedback/perseverance factors in Tom's case are as follows: Tom risked Ginny divorcing him over his lack of choosing one career path and sticking to it to begin paying off loans. Tom risked a great deal by changing his mind so many times about his life's work. Through career coaching, Tom learned it was a sense of newness, variety, and autonomy that were his career satisfiers and sustainers. He was happy working toward a goal, but once it was attained and the reality of the work revealed itself, Tom was bored, restless, and looking for the next challenge. This finally culminated in launching his own business. The feedback Tom received was in the form of demonstrated results for his efforts and his increasing sales. His need for variety was satisfied by the many different customers he assisted. What he sold them was in keeping with his values: these were products he would buy, so he was enthusiastic in his sales presentations. Watching his business grow financially and seeing it be directly influenced by his interpersonal effectiveness with potential customers provided rewards on financial and interpersonal levels. Being in his own business deviated from the pattern of holding a permanent job with benefits, which was central to the values held by his birth family. However, as coaching uncovered, these values were not Tom's drivers and motivators. He finally let go of a career story that had no resonance for him and stopped trying to be someone he wasn't. He accepted the fact that he held career drivers that were different from his family's values. Although he might share their desire for prestige, he also valued entrepreneurship, autonomy, and independence, which were not major motivators for his other brothers. Like many Shooting Stars, coaching helped Tom accept himself and his values. He put aside the feedback from sources whose values were not in alignment with his own.

### You First, Then Me

Sharon was part of a middle-class Southern family. She graduated with a bachelor's degree in fine arts in the mid-1980s. She married shortly after college and worked for five years in an unrelated field before beginning her family. As her family grew, her work declined in importance, and her family became the focal point of her energies. "Family comes first" was a common Sunbelt refrain. As her four girls began to leave the nest, she began to wonder, what next? Wanting both meaningful work and a meaningful relationship with her adult children, she felt caught between differing generational norms. At midlife, she came to coaching wanting clarity more than wanting options, wanting permission more than autonomy. It quickly became apparent that she had never chosen an educational path; rather, she had followed the paths of childhood friends. The familial and peer support for her decision to be a full-time mom reinforced her pattern of following others established earlier. As her daughters set out for college, she found herself revisiting her earlier choices. She wanted to be at peace with her past choices. She also wanted to learn a new pattern for decision making.

To honor her past choices, we mapped out her influencers, their messages, and the resulting decisions, and then ranked the importance of those influencers for congruence with her worldview at the time and with her present worldview. Physically ranking these by relevance allowed this client to see very concretely that she remained heavily influenced by individuals whose worldviews were now significantly different from her own. She needed to find a new community, a new reference group. Coaching provided her with permission and encouragement to experiment. Creating learning objectives and talking through her observations and experiences resulted in creating a framework and criteria by which she could make an informed choice. This approach not only helped build her calculated risk-taking muscle, but also highlighted areas where additional information or feedback would be vital to decision making. Between her growing self-understanding, her experiments, and the newly established feedback network, clear strengths and true passions began to emerge. With each successive experiment and subsequent feedback, her sense of her true self became more coherent. Sharon completed a second undergraduate degree and increased her community service work. She has established a small but growing creative consulting practice. Most importantly, she found a professional community that shares some of her values. Sharon's story is an example of building a community of resonance. Coaching allowed her to step into a participant observer role and benefit from community without losing her sense of self. She has begun to author her own story.

What levers does Sharon share with other Shooting Stars? Like many Shooting Stars, Sharon was caught between stories. She perceived significant risk in integrating these stories. On the intrapersonal level, she had not intentionally integrated the person she had been and the person she was becoming. On the interpersonal level, she feared that revisiting her choices would adversely affect key relationships. It took courage to reach the place where she could separate the value of the relationship from the value of feedback. Eliciting her stories, her influencers, and their feedback helped her honor her roots, build her participant-observer skills, and make grounded assessments of her paths thus far. This was a powerful process for helping Sharon create clarity in the present, and thus fully step into her own power. Once she had done so, she was free- to focus energy on the intellectual risk—a midlife return to a traditional college and the launch of her consulting business.

Understanding the broader picture and the details of what prompts a start and what triggers a stop is helpful when working with Shooting Stars. Even though the pattern may be different from person to person, the pattern is often consistent for a given individual. In Sharon's case, the start was always triggered by a friend's initiative—applying to college, enrolling in classes, and even launching a family. The stops presented when her self-confidence fell short of her ability to fully implement on the risk. Walking through this process with a development facilitator will help reveal generational, familial, cultural, religious, occupational, and gender patterns as well as developmental stage–driven changes not otherwise apparent. In Sharon's case, she realized familial messages, including those about the proper role of a woman of her circumstances, were further undermining her self-confidence. Awareness of underlying patterns allows clients to be authors of their own stories. As Shooting Stars complete this process, they literally fill in the blanks, and their sense of self becomes more cohesive. This cohesiveness propels them into Thriver space.

### Thrivers

Thrivers are high in risk and high in perseverance. We selected *Thriver* to describe this group because of their resilience in the face of adversity and their ability to see opportunity in change. Thrivers exist at all levels of educational attainment, in all occupational roles, and across all demographic groups. Graphically, they are represented by a tornado-like, increasingly upward spiral, within an ever-expanding white space of potential (Figure 2.1). They are the high potentials, the go-to people of their organizations. They lead or are key contributors on new initiatives, the hot projects. They have insatiable curiosity. As lifelong learners, they actively seek ways to acquire, develop, and master new talents. They have long-established patterns of taking and successfully delivering on risk. This iterative risk taking increases their ability to assess risks. The many facets of risk are analyzed and risk/reward ratios are computed, most often in an intuitive manner. Those in this group tend to build their own feedback networks, and they are quick to consider the source before internalizing feedback.

Thrivers are not born. Thrivers are made. To a degree, Thrivers are self-made, with tremendous support from colleagues, developmentally minded managers, friends, and family (Gladwell 2008). Astute and creative development facilitators can surface Thriver clients' realms of unconscious competence, enabling them to leverage their gifts not only in new ways, but also in ways that significantly increase their influence. Development facilitators also play critical roles helping Thrivers integrate their many experiences, thus finding their through-themes. Through-themes are deeply held values or beliefs that compel movement. Coaching can elicit these beliefs and values, and facilitate the development of an explicit vision or goal. Development facilitators also play a vital role in helping Thrivers integrate their many experiences, and in helping these clients achieve and maintain the balance necessary for sustained achievement. In the case studies below, Beth represents Thrivers who leverage existing resources and support within their milieu, while Bob represents Thrivers who create the resources and support that will enable them to thrive.

### Rushing up to Meet the Ocean

Beth is a union shop steward at a Virginia medical center. She chose to be a shop steward because it allowed her to grow her leadership and communication skills. Beth also has a need to serve and take care of others, so being a steward is a good fit. Whenever there are new employee development classes that are of interest to her colleagues or new policy changes that affect her group, Beth is the first to make others aware. She is also growing her own career by being enrolled in an associate of science (AS) degree program in nursing at Northern Virginia Community College. She is preparing to realize her long-time dream of becoming a registered nurse. When Beth was young, her maternal grandmother had lived with Beth's family. Her grandmother broke her leg and needed a visiting nurse to monitor her progress. The kindly visiting nurse was knowledgeable and gave comfort to the whole family. This experience provided the impetus for Beth to discover her calling.

After high school, Beth finished her certification at a local allied health school as a nursing assistant. She then got a job as a clinical assistant. All of this gave Beth the confidence to work steadily on her long-range dream of becoming a registered nurse. Especially helpful to Beth has been the availability of employer-based tuition reimbursement. Beth sees this as one of the advantages of being a union steward. Her position has helped her know what opportunities are surfacing in her organization and take advantage of programs that support her long-range dream. Beth serves as a role model for her colleagues because she lives what she teaches. In living her dream, she encourages others to reach for more in their careers by her enthusiastic example. Beth has a lot of energy and enthusiasm for her patients and for the union members she leads. Her friends say she is the type of person who not only seizes the day but also runs up to the ocean and embraces the waves with laughter.

In considering the dimensions of initiative/risk and feedback/perseverance, it is clear Beth benefited by career coaching in various ways. She was able to use her coach as a sounding board and a resource in applying for a patchwork of scholarship opportunities to lessen the financial burden of tuition and books. In addition, she took advantage of the tuition benefits her organization provided. For Beth, the feedback and personal support from her career coach were valuable because she was the first female in her family to seek education beyond high school. Beth's risk was intrapersonal. If she did not take advantage of the opportunities that were available to her, it would have had adverse consequences for her self-esteem. Beth doesn't like seeing opportunity go to waste.

In sharing her family background, Beth said two things motivated her to take risks and advance her career. She wanted to learn from the mistake her parents had made in failing to take advantage of their educational opportunities. The second source of motivation was her minister's inspirational message. This message was that she could be anything she set her mind to be. Beth chose to accept her mentor/minister as her most relevant feedback source at this time in her life. She is earning college credits toward an associate's degree in nursing. She also had to face being more highly educated than her parents by acknowledging that she was helping her entire family and not diminishing her parents' efforts and choices. She is able to leverage the risk she has taken before, so she layers or builds on the risk, and then she creates momentum for herself. The story she broke from was avoiding the limited career path of her parents, who had not pursued post–high school educations. The new story she built was to believe her mentor and minister that she could achieve what she wanted. This included taking advantage of her career coach's assessments to determine what path would be to her liking and give her the most satisfaction.

### Sharp Turn Ahead

Bob is a classic Thriver. Reared in a part of the country with little opportunity for advancement locally, he joined the military. His intelligence, initiative, and perseverance allowed him to advance to leadership levels. Prior to his retirement from the military, he sought guidance leveraging his talents, experience, and passions in a different line of work. Many clients bring more skills and talents to the table than they initially see for themselves. This was true of Bob. As a people manager for the last 20 years of his military career, he felt he had completed this portion of his work life and longed to do something different. Coaching revealed a desire to turn a lifelong hobby of car restoration into a second career. This would give him an opportunity to use his analytical skills in a creative endeavor with a defined end product. While he was confident of his mechanical engineering knowledge, he was concerned about the financial risk inherent in a new venture launch. The economic recession made this risk much more salient.

Coaching around transferable skills allowed him to see a much broader range of transferable skills and knowledge. With the more complete range of competencies and their relative strengths displayed, the full dimensions of risk can be evaluated more effectively. Most important in his particular case was the ability to anticipate, assess, leverage, and mitigate risk.

This is a core small business competency. He leveraged existing strengths while incrementally building competencies in new areas. As with all new ventures, whether a business launch or other significant role change, he assumed a variety of risks. While the financial risk is obvious, he also took on an interpersonal risk in forming key partnerships. One of these partnerships was not successful. He learned from this experience and put effective safeguards in place. He has always been known for his willingness to develop new solutions, a hallmark of intellectual risk. He also developed lifelong peer relationships with several of his strategic partners. Feedback from these external peers, in addition to feedback from his clients, served to propel his momentum past inevitable obstacles. Equally important, he had early and sustained support from his family. Over the years, he built a thriving practice with a regional reputation for excellence.

What levers make Bob a Thriver? As with all Thrivers, coaching helped Bob enhance his self-awareness, particularly in the domain of unconscious competence, and integrate that heightened awareness with his experience. The coherence, or the integrated sense of self, which emerges as a consequence of this process allows Thrivers to identify their most effective developmental routes, and plan for effective, aligned future development.

Another key trait of Thrivers is their willingness to take risk across many spectrums. This is often an unconscious competence for Thrivers. For this group, it is not about what is missing, but rather about eliciting the pattern and making it explicit. Coaching can help people generalize success and contextualize failure. Popularized by the work of Seligman (2006), the act of generalization allows the development facilitator and the client to leverage previously successful patterns into new domains. Essentially, this involves robustly transferring the core of what has made the client successful in many areas into a new area. Contextualizing failure focuses on understanding the discrete elements of failed endeavors. Our experience underscores the importance of two factors. The first factor is a high degree of specificity about the failed endeavor. This has the effect of quickly providing emotional distance from the failure. It is the emotional distance that allows the client to extract lessons learned. The second factor is making the critical distinctions between the spheres of control and influence, and acknowledging what is outside the client's sphere of control. When these two factors are combined, the client sees many factors that contributed to the failure and sees them in the context of the total experience. Appropriately embedding the outcome in the context effectively contains the damage. This high-level perspective allows clients to ascribe attribution in more objective ways. Empowered with knowledge, they continually expand the range and the level of risk they feel confident undertaking. Thrivers do not have exceptional, innate abilities to execute risk. They have an exceptional ability to learn from experience, adjust their behavior, and therefore increase the probability for future success. Coaches can help Thrivers be even more effective through the creation of strategic sounding boards. The composition of the board, nature and frequency of the meetings, and desired outcomes vary with the goals of the client. The coach is often an integral member of this board.

## SUMMARY

There are multiple routes to career success. There are wide ranges of career development, career planning, and career decision-making theories that provide valuable insight into the power of worldviews (Sue and Sue 2007). The Thriver Framework is not meant to supplant this body of knowledge. Rather, the intent is to provide development facilitators with a framework that is both concrete and intuitive, and most importantly, actionable. Our experience suggests it can help most clients move directly and comparatively rapidly into Thriver space. Revealing the structure of the framework with a client facilitates the creation of more effective development strategies. By narrowing the dimensions to risk, initiative, feedback, and perseverance, the development facilitator and client can focus the scope of their work. Viewing the client's experience through this lens will surface patterns not typically addressed in assessments, or in developmental or coaching conversations. The framework leverages the intuitive skills of the development facilitators and clients. They are encouraged to tap into their unique strengths when creating artifacts, whether elaborate spreadsheets or process maps, autobiographies, or other arts and crafts. Leveraging the client's innate creativity is an important part of the liberation that comes from employing the Thriver Framework.

The quadrant overviews and composite case studies, while simplified, are intended to give development facilitators core understanding. Clients in the Open Road quadrant will likely benefit from a multitude of support resources. Clients in the Undercapitalized Talent and Passion quadrant, who are eager and willing but with unharnessed resources, represent a hidden reservoir of ready organizational talent. Values and belief work serves to ground and then integrate the disparate experiences of Shooting Stars. When combined with relevant feedback, these clients may quickly become Thrivers. Thrivers, important contributors to highly effective organizations, represent the next generation of thought leaders or business leaders. Developmental facilitators can ensure that these high-potential contributors continue to expand their spheres of influence while insuring their sustainability. In a spirit of inquiry, we extend an invitation to development facilitators to explore this framework, knowing and honoring the catalytic roles facilitators play with clients. We offer this framework as a resource to spark movement and sustain momentum, a resource to help ascend a spiral of growth.

We move now from the individual client and development facilitator to system-level development resources. In the next chapter we explore linkages among organizations, educational institutions, and communities.

# CHAPTER 3

# Linking to Educational Systems and Community Development

*Nancy Atwood, Anna Domek and Richard Vicenzi*

One important aspect of workforce and career development is the linkage between organizations and educational institutions in supporting growing organizational needs for people with particular capabilities and skills. This includes equipping both those people new to the workforce and those with experience with needed competencies that evolve over time. This chapter explores building effective bridges from organizations to educational institutions, the value of experiential learning in partnerships between organizations and educational institutions, and one approach to creating internal learning within an organization.

The chapter illustrates the many benefits that occur when organizations and educational institutions partner. The first section of the chapter establishes a framework for this collaboration. This information may prove useful to those within an organization tasked with establishing strategies for employee development, or for individual employees looking to expand their professional horizons in a way that is beneficial to themselves and their organization.

The second section addresses the value of experiential learning in the context of partnerships between organizations and educational institutions. Those within organizations looking to attract the next generation of employees can use experiential learning partnerships to allow students to gain valuable, real-world education in their chosen field, and in the process attract highly qualified recruits.

The final section of the chapter examines strategies for developing intraorganizational development opportunities through mentoring. This strategy uses existing employees to support an organizational identity that promotes accountability and job satisfaction. It also allows employees to learn from more experienced co-workers in a safe and supportive environment—a useful approach for an organization seeking to reduce employee attrition and increase productivity.


## COLLABORATION BETWEEN ORGANIZATIONS AND EDUCATIONAL INSTITUTIONS

### Linking to Educational Institutions: Influence of the Work Environment

An organization that is mindful of future education and training requirements for its workforce has the opportunity to identify and develop ongoing relationships with educational institutions that are equipped to provide such learning. The factors that will play a part in determining the suitability of a training institution for a given organization relate both to the needs of the organization and those of the learner. As continuing education becomes increasingly necessary to stay current in many occupations, the role of the academic institution expands from simply preparing students to enter a given career to include the following factors as well:

- Keeping people current with technological advances and emerging cross-disciplinary factors
- Retraining learners in key skills as existing tools and approaches become obsolete

These components are driven in part by a rapidly evolving work environment. Disruptive technologies such as digital imaging, nanotechnology, cloud computing, and Web-based communications are creating new markets and marginalizing others. Availability of tools such as virtual storage, instantaneous communication, complex resource tracking systems, and peer-to-peer collaboration are revolutionizing how and where teams are able to work together, and who can potentially be a member of the team. No industry is immune to the implications of these trends.

An important, even critical, element in an organization's ability to succeed, or in some cases survive, in today's marketplace is the acquisition, accumulation, and use of existing knowledge assets, including the explicit and tacit knowledge of its employees (Nonaka and Takeuchi 1995, 49) within a system that promotes the creation of new knowledge. Workforce development, in this context, is challenged by attempting to anticipate an unpredictable future. It is estimated that over 90 percent of human learning has been acquired by people alive today, with the pace of that advance continually accelerating. For example, the number of scientific papers has doubled every 15 years since 1900, and the number of scientific journals has risen exponentially over time (Kelly 2006). However, much of this new knowledge is still in a conceptual stage, given the historic lag between invention and reduction to commercial practice (Hirooka 2006, 154–64). So in planning for future workforce requirements, it is possible that existing technological and social paradigms underlying many sectors—including education—will be transformed within a generation.

While recognizing the likelihood of significant future shifts, we begin the exploration of the links between organizations and educational institutions with what is known and understood today. Many factors are relevant to meeting the needs of both the organization and its employees, including- differences in the content and quality of various educational programs offered, formats and scheduling of programs, admissions timing, accessibility and entry requirements, and comparative cost and value. The attributes of educational and training programs, along with the characteristics of educational institutions, are our starting point.

## Identifying Institutions with Which to Develop Relationships

### What to Know about Accreditation

The range of educational offerings continues to increase rapidly in the United States, as will be apparent when we examine traditional versus nontraditional course structures. New and existing institutions have created courses and programs in a wide variety of occupational areas in response to the growing needs and desires of adult workers to enhance their skills or change careers. Some institutions have long histories of creating rigorous and high-quality learning experiences; others have little proven track record.

From an organizational workforce development perspective, linkages to educational institutions can address two primary needs. The first is planning for an adequate pool of appropriately trained workers in occupations that are central to the organization's current success. The second is anticipating and identifying sources for newly emerging skill areas that are likely to be critical for the organization's future success. Especially in emerging fields, validation of an educational or training program's ability to produce qualified talent through accreditation by appropriate educational or professional bodies is an important consideration. Educational accreditation is a third-party assessment process certifying that an institution meets accepted or official standards for training in either general or specific program areas. In the United States, it is a peer review process carried out by established commissions whose members define and maintain accreditation requirements. Educational accrediting bodies are themselves recognized as being reputable evaluating institutions by the U.S. Department of Education (2009) and the Council for Higher Education Accreditation (2009), a nongovernmental organization. In the U.S., there is no single, national accrediting body recognizing academic institutions. The primary accreditations at the community college, college, and university level are provided by six regional accreditors, depending on the location of the institution, or in the case of multiregional institutions, the location of its headquarters facility. Appendix A contains a partial list of accreditors in the U.S.

In some fields, for example radiology, completion of an accredited program is a requirement to practice. By screening institutions based on accreditation, it is possible to avoid exposure to diploma mill–trained personnel, who will likely lack the needed depth of learning (Council for Higher Education Accreditation 2009). Schools considered diploma mills make little attempt to meet minimum standards of training in their fields of instruction, and they require little or no rigor in the teaching or testing of students. Such diploma mills may enroll students based solely on their willingness and ability to pay.

*Traditional Versus Nontraditional Course Structures*

Traditional educational institutions provide classes in a structure with specific beginning and ending dates, usually based on a semester or quarter calendar. These schools typically require application for enrollment well before the first class and often have admission requirements that can include minimum GPA qualifications, test results, and other prerequisites. It is important for employees to be aware of these requirements because missing a deadline often means waiting several months for another class period to begin. Most community colleges, private colleges, and state funded colleges and universities have this traditional course structure.

There are a growing number of institutions appealing to increasing numbers of working people seeking additional educational opportunities. Some relatively new institutions, like the University of Phoenix, have grown rapidly. By making their course schedules more flexible, these institutions are more accessible to people with responsibilities that preclude engaging in a traditional educational schedule, including returning students older than the traditional college demographic. The National Center for Education Statistics estimated that in 1999–2000, 73 percent of all undergraduate students could be considered nontraditional. This report characterizes the traditional graduate as "one who earns a high school diploma, enrolls full time immediately after finishing high school, depends on parents for financial support, and either does not work during the school year or works part time" (2002).

Education course offerings provided by schools owned by for-profit corporations have grown rapidly. Revenues of for-profit, private degree–granting institutions almost tripled from the 1999–2000 academic year to 2005–2006 academic year. While the revenue of nonprofit, private, and public degree–granting institutions was more than 30 times greater than their for-profit counterparts in 2005–2006, revenue of the nonprofit and public institutions together grew more slowly, at 44 percent, over the same time period. (Digest of Education Statistics 2008). Within the for-profit educational institutions, there are many approaches to nontraditional scheduling, including one class at a time for one month; classes offered to morning, afternoon, or evening cohorts; choice of week night or weekend classes; hybrid classes composed of on-campus and Internet-delivered portions. A growing number of schools offer at least some portion of their courses online, including asynchronously formatted classes combined with discussion boards. In asynchronously designed, Web-delivered classes, students can attend class modules online at any time during a specified time period, and then make contributions to an online discussion moderated by the instructor.

### Variations in Admission and Registration Structures

Variations in admission and registration processes are also important considerations for organizations considering partnership with educational institutions. In the U.S., degree-granting institutions (as opposed to those granting diplomas or certificates) typically will require submission of standardized test scores from the American College Test (ACT) or the Scholastic Assessment Test I and II (SAT), often evaluated in tandem with high school or other previous grade point averages to meet admission requirements. Many schools may also require or strongly recommend other kinds of testing, for instance an English placement test or an entry-level math exam, depending on schooling already completed. Some schools require entering students to attend orientation sessions, meet with an academic counselor, and complete an assessment of capabilities for placement. Other programs require completion of specific prerequisite courses before application to the program. All of this can be time-consuming and affect the engagement process. On the other hand, some schools allow application for admission close to the beginning of the course sessions. These are important factors to consider in exploring partnership approaches, taking into account organizational and learner needs.

### Prior Learning Assessment Credits

Many schools accept credit gained through various prior learning assessment mechanisms (see appendix B). This allows students who have acquired knowledge in subjects other than through formal schooling to get credit for self-taught or home-schooled course work, independent study, cultural pursuits, travel, special interests, military service schools, or professional development. This credit can be achieved by passing recognized tests that various schools accept as demonstrating proficiency in a given subject at a level equivalent to passing a particular course in their curriculum, or by assembling a portfolio that demonstrates learning and is assessed by the institution.

Prior Learning Assessment (PLA) credits earned through alternatives to completing course work can reduce the time and cost of earning a desired credential up to a maximum number of prior learning credits determined by a particular school. Since institutions establish examination acceptance and course equivalency criteria, organizations forming partnerships need to consider the specific components of a given institution's approach. PLA credits can benefit employees and organizations in facilitating rapid advancement.

### Costs and Benefits of Educational Advancement

Affordability, potential career satisfaction, and additional earning power are aspects likely to be important to an employee considering returning to school. These factors will influence motivation and likelihood of completion. Analyzing the costs and benefits of a learning program to an individual is not simple because it can involve a number of intangible factors. Indeed, given the increasing cost of education, many people will be challenged to finance additional learning. From an organizational perspective, this means recognizing financial constraints for individuals and the value of providing financial support for continued learning. Tuition cost increases have significantly exceeded the rate of inflation over the past decade (College Board 2009). Meanwhile, wages for the typical American have stagnated. As measured by the Commerce Department, between 2000 and 2007 (before the financial crisis of 2008), the median income of American households, when adjusted for inflation, fell (*Washington Post* 2009).

College Board statistics (2009) indicate that, in 2008–2009, about two thirds of full-time undergraduates received some form of grant aid. The National Center for Education Statistics (2009) determined that more than 50 percent of full-time undergraduates borrow money to pay for education. Scholarships and grants exist at many levels, but they can be difficult to obtain and rarely cover more than a small portion of total costs. Consequently, most students use loans to finance college level, professional, or technical training. Providing financial support for continued learning is therefore an important component of an organization's workforce development approach in facilitating learning that will enhance productivity, address changing needs, and strengthen affiliation with the sponsoring organization.

## Questions for Employees to Consider

When working with employees about decisions to pursue education, it can be helpful to discuss a variety of financial and nonfinancial factors. The following questions can help facilitate this discussion:

- Is it necessary to reduce hours of current work time in order to accommodate class availability? What does this mean for lost income? What support might be available to address this?

- How much time is needed at a higher earning level to offset the costs of the educational program?

- Is there an internship, clinical experience, apprenticeship, or other training element that adds to the time before a credential is granted? If so, does a potential program provide placement possibilities?

- What resources and support does the institution offer students? Does the institution offer a high-quality library, access to and training in computer resources, clubs or interest-oriented organizations, internships, mentorships, career assessment and counseling, and exchange study programs?

- What other commitments—at work, at home, within the community—could affect the employee's ability to engage with time, energy, and focus in learning? Effective learning and assimilation require all of these. If there are such commitments, what adjustments to current lifestyle might be necessary?

The following questions can also be helpful in considering the longer-term implications and potential of a particular learning path:

- Is the occupation in demand currently in the organization, in the desired geographical area, or more broadly in the community? Is it expected to grow over the course of the education or training period?

- Is the long-term occupational path well aligned with individual aspirations and interests as well as with practical financial needs?

External market conditions can rapidly change the supply and demand situation for particular occupations and therefore affect compensation levels. Furthermore, compensation is strongly influenced by personal capability, the policies of a specific employer, and luck. As a result, a career based on intrinsic interests in the context of external opportunities, rather than one based solely on short-term external demand, is more likely to be fulfilling and sustainable. It is also more likely to bring financial reward because strong alignment with personal interests and aspirations translates to superior performance, which is rewarded accordingly.

### Establishing Relationships with Selected Schools

Educational institutions that market to the adult working population need to attract motivated students. Consequently, these schools are likely to be enthusiastic partners for employers with related workforce development programs. Introductory conversations with such educational institutions about relevant programs can often begin effectively with people in positions responsible for marketing to potential students. These positions include dean or assistant dean of programs or schools, department chair, admissions manager or advisor, career services director or manager, director of student services, program representative, outreach representative, or corporate or community relations representative. Often, schools will provide informational forums or presentations to groups of employees on company facilities. Many are willing to design cohort programs customized to company needs for the employee population given a guaranteed minimum number of participants. These classes may be delivered at company sites. Schools with corporate or community relations representatives are especially likely to offer such options.

Determining potential partner schools or training institutions can begin effectively with information gathered from the institution's Web site. Most schools have informative sites that provide excellent initial information on program areas, degrees and certificates, financial aid basics, important dates, and student support services. More detailed information can be found in the school's general catalogue, which is available online, or can be obtained from the school's admissions office. Further evaluation of a particular school's potential as a partner can be made through preliminary meetings with an appropriate member of the administration or outreach staff. Workforce development professionals who invest time in understanding educational institutions are likely to receive eager responses from schools. If nurtured over time, these relationships can benefit educational institutions, employees and employers alike—as all participants grow together.

## EXPERIENTIAL LEARNING

Another means of creating relationships between employers, employees, and educational institutions is through support for experiential learning. As educational institutions seek to develop a student body that will succeed in a competitive professional world, they can look to experiential learning to accomplish this goal. Experiential learning (or experiential education as it is sometimes called) is defined as a reflection on doing, in that people learn not just from reading or discussing a topic (as in classroom learning), but by actively participating in a field related to that topic. In career development circles, encouraging organizations to engage with students by providing them with relevant experience that supplements more traditional classroom education has gained new prominence, for it benefits both those learning within a field and organizations planning for the future. According to the National Association of Colleges and Employers (NACE) 2009 Experiential Education Survey of 174 different employers, "Employers sent a strong message: experiential education programs are valuable recruiting tools and their value is recognized by the organization" (1). For organizations, sponsoring experiential learning provides an excellent opportunity to help develop their future workforce by aligning with educational institutions in providing hands-on learning opportunities for students.

In this section of the chapter we explore:

- the benefits to organizations and individual participants of experiential learning;
- how an organization and an individual can create effective experiential learning opportunities; and
- the shared value to the community such experiences create.

## Benefits to Organizations and Individual Participants

### Benefits to Organizations

The process of creating, developing, and sustaining experiential learning opportunities offers numerous benefits for organizations. Organizations are given an early opportunity to train and observe those individuals who may become part of their long-term workforce. In addition, experiential learning can be the foundation of a lasting relationship between the educational institution and the organization, providing beneficial training and learning processes for students as well as a steady stream of potential employees for the organization. Organizations that offer experiential learning opportunities are creating a cost-effective screening program for highly qualified recruits. Furthermore, employers can develop students in critical areas to a needed level of competency. An internship (one form of experiential learning) can also function as an in-depth interview process prior to hiring. It is likely to reduce attrition as students feel a commitment to an organization that has invested in their development.

Experiential learning opportunities offered by organizations can take a variety of forms:

- Internships: academically related work experiences over a prescribed time period (typically a semester). They can be paid or unpaid, and may or may not provide academic credit for the student.
- Externships: similar to internships except they are shorter in length, typically lasting several days to several weeks.
- Cooperative education: paid, academically related work experience for which a student gets academic credit.
- Volunteering: unpaid work that may or may not be related to a student's academic field of study.
- Service learning: typically offered in conjunction with an academic class. This is a teaching method that involves students providing time and effort working with an organization as part of their class work.

These different types of experiential learning can accommodate diverse student and organizational needs. While the immediate benefit derived from experiential learning of creating a qualified pool of applicants is clear for organizations, a less obvious incentive for potential employers and educational institutions is the relationship created by establishing a program of experiential learning. Educational institutions know that their graduates will continue to receive hands-on experience in their fields. Employers know that students from these institutions meet entry criteria. Furthermore, students, staff, and faculty learn more about hiring organizations through the recruitment and experiences of students. If these experiences are consistently positive, there will be a continual referral of students to those participating organizations.

One example of this type of relationship is found in a successful internship program between a Sacramento area hospital and Sacramento State University. The hospital provides more than 50 volunteer internships in about 18 departments each semester. The students in these internship positions consistently provide the hospital with a dedicated staff, excited about hands-on learning within the healthcare field. The hospital provides the necessary experience for many of these students to succeed in applying to schools in competitive disciplines such as medicine, pharmacy, nursing, and physical therapy. Additionally, the hospital hires some of these students after they graduate. Furthermore, as a result of the internship, students at Sacramento State University learn more about the hospital and are predisposed to work there after obtaining further education.

### Benefits to Individual Participants

Krumboltz and Levin (2004, 5–7) argue that when a person purposefully engages in a variety of life opportunities that present themselves, this is likely to lead to an emerging career that is meaningful and fulfilling. Openness to possibilities can enable a person to embrace opportunities when they surface. For students, experiential learning is the beginning of this approach. While consciously engaging in different opportunities, the student can better understand the practical aspects of a chosen field, and his or her eventual role in it. The different types of experiential learning opportunities previously discussed all offer advantages for students. Students who use experiential learning are gaining practical experience, making important job contacts, and receiving training that will benefit them in a competitive job market. Additionally, students have the opportunity to apply skills and knowledge learned in the classroom to on-the-job experiences, helping them clarify interest in a particular career path. This allows them to test their career interests and gain a better understanding of their own skills and strengths.

Sometimes experiential learning that changes an anticipated career path is just as beneficial. For example, George, who had always planned to be a teacher, took a job one summer teaching low-income children. Although George enjoyed the interaction with these students, he realized that teaching was not a good fit for him. Instead, he was inspired to go into the political arena and work to help low-income children at a policy level. So, while George's experiential learning had a different outcome than he originally anticipated, it helped greatly in clarifying his professional goals and true passion.

Another example is a student from Sacramento State University, Allison. Unlike George, who changed an anticipated career path, Allison, with a double major in French and biology, did not have a clear idea of what she wanted to do in the future. After several career counseling sessions, some themes emerged as important, including a strong desire to work with people, an interest in working in different countries, and a wish to incorporate her love and knowledge of science. One field that seemed to allow Allison the opportunity to combine these interests was healthcare, but as a first-generation college student, Allison was unclear about what career paths were available.

Allison eventually decided to participate in experiential learning opportunities to explore the field of healthcare, including an internship at a local hospital and a part-time job at a dental office. As Allison spent time in these two places, she began to make contacts that helped clarify the nature of different paths she might pursue. She also clarified what would be needed to be competitive, including further education. Allison recently graduated from Sacramento State University and is applying for laboratory science positions while completing an application to pharmacy school. Her job and internship experiences opened her eyes to fields she had not previously considered, gave her contacts that helped her prepare to apply to pharmacy school, and most importantly gave her confidence as a first-generation student that she could succeed in ways she did not initially believe were possible.

## Creating Effective Experiential Learning Opportunities

### Structuring Experiential Learning from the Organization's Perspective

Employers can benefit greatly when they establish well-structured experiential learning opportunities. However, there are often questions about how to attract the best and the brightest students. The most effective experiential learning relationships include providing students with hands-on learning and increasing levels of responsibility over time. This needs to be a learning opportunity for students, not a delegation of tasks no one else wants to do. Students benefit greatly from a mentoring relationship with a supervisor, so identifying and carefully selecting who will supervise the student on a daily basis is important. The supervisor should review the student's progress, provide positive feedback, encourage dialogue by being willing to answer questions, and develop concrete objectives to measure progress. A critical, and often overlooked component, is having the supervisor provide adequate training so the student is clear about what is expected and how to meet these expectations.

### Structuring Experiential Learning from the Individual Participant's Perspective

The benefits to students and organizations using experiential learning are many. However, it is important for an organization to be open to opportunities presented to them by interested students. Most college campuses have a career center or internship office that provides students with information about available resources and opportunities. Many effective internship programs are competitive, and internship positions may be difficult for students to obtain. One way that a student might still take part in an effective experiential learning opportunity is by designing such an opportunity in partnership with the college or university and an organization. Often, a career counselor in the student's career center can assist the student in crafting a customized approach. Organizations open to such possibilities can gain access to students with initiative, drive, and an ability to solve problems in a unique manner. Characteristics that indicate a student's idea for a self-created, experiential learning opportunity merits attention include probing questions, a keen interest in the organization or the field, and a willingness to actively engage with an organization for mutual benefit.

### Shared Values Create Community

Experiential learning facilitates a bond between organizations and educational institutions that can provide the basis for long-term relationships. This bond grows stronger as more connections are established between students and an organization, and serves as the foundation for a pool of highly qualified recruits that an organization can draw from in future hiring. In addition to the obvious organizational benefit found in helping to train and prepare an organization's future workforce, there are larger societal benefits created. Students participate and learn about themselves and about different career paths and possibilities. They also gain valuable experience that helps them succeed in a competitive job market. Experiential learning contributes to allowing students, organizations, and educational institutions to work together in creating a productive society built on shared values and knowledge while meeting mutually beneficial goals.

## MENTORING ADULT STUDENTS AND CAREER SEEKERS

### Mentoring for the Changing Workplace

Another way that employees and employers can make use of educational opportunities within the changing workplace and adjust to a combination of economic, demographic, organizational, and societal change is through mentoring. Murrell (2009) defines mentoring as a process that involves cultivating and maintaining reciprocal relationships with the purpose of supporting or advancing an individual's career development. With flatter organizational structures and careers that change rapidly, the need for mentoring has increased. Additionally, many adults had little or no career guidance when they were in high school or college, and consequently seek such advice from their employers and professors.

In looking at both Levinson's Theory of the Seasons of Adulthood (Bee 1987, 70) and Erikson's Stages of Psychosocial Development (60), it is clear that having or being a mentor is necessary for certain aspects of growth. In Erikson's seventh stage, he proposes that in early and middle adulthood, choosing to be a mentor is one way to promote the feeling of supporting the next generation. Helping another person can make a lasting impression on the next generation and increase connection with others. In a dynamic workplace where employees are focused on maintaining certifications, licenses, and knowledge needed for their current positions, it is frequently overwhelming to think about exploring another's career. However, a mentoring relationship is an excellent developmental opportunity for all parties. Mentors may come from the current workplace, professional associations, previous employers, or educational settings. For educators, the mentoring relationship provides the opportunity to mentor as well as opportunities to strengthen ties (and increase knowledge) with business and industry and with students (mentees).

An example of a mentoring program that focuses on internal mentors was developed at Kaiser Permanente in the Pacific Northwest region. Although this program was developed for internal mentors, it would be equally applicable with external mentors or in a multicompany setting. The Leadership Diversity Development Program was developed by the organization to invest in its future leaders by preparing employees from diverse backgrounds for leadership positions within Kaiser Permanente. This program is an opportunity to assess and develop a cadre of highly talented employees from diverse backgrounds to help meet the organization's current and future needs. It helps create a more diverse workforce at senior levels, so that Kaiser Permanente reflects the diversity of its membership and communities. The program supports the advancement of traditionally underrepresented employees: women; people of color; people with disabilities; and those who identify as lesbian, gay, bisexual, and transgender or intersex. The program was created in 2006 guided by an internal consultant (Guinn 2009). Senior leaders and directors helped identity 30 exempt employees who attended an orientation to the pilot program. To be considered for the Leadership Diversity Development Program pilot, exempt employees had to have a bachelor's degree or have made significant progress toward a degree.

Other requirements included

- a demonstrated interest in growing their career at Kaiser Permanente;
- a commitment to being part of an 18-month program; and
- the support of their manager.

After an interview process, 20 participants were selected. The employees represented a wide range of years of service and work areas. The original goal was that at least two-thirds of the participants would receive a promotion or role expansion during the program, and that goal was met. Some participants were new to Kaiser Permanente, while others had many years of service. They came from a wide range of work areas, including ambulatory surgery, dental, laboratory and pharmacy services, finance, and nurse management.

The curriculum included the following components:

- Working with a mentor.
- Creating an individual development plan.
- Taking a battery of assessments at the start of the program. Along with the Myers-Briggs Type Inventory (Myers 1998), participants took an Intercultural Development Inventory to measure their reactions to cultural differences and a 360-degree evaluation, which identified leadership strengths and opportunities.
- Participating in leadership courses.
- Completing an action learning project. As the participants prepare for promotion or expanded roles and responsibilities, they are expected to engage in an action learning project to place their leadership training into context. It provides mentors an opportunity to see program participants in action as leaders.
- Attending a facilitated leadership workshop.
- Attending a monthly presentation or training session around a leadership topic. The monthly sessions involved a segment called "View from a Leader," where a senior leader spoke on a current issue.

Mentoring is the cornerstone of the program. Each participant is matched with a director or vice president who serves as a coach, role model, and confidante. Mentors are expected to help expand the program participant's network and provide career guidance. The added benefit for the relationship is that mentors can learn about diverse cultures and diverse perspectives from their program participant. People find out who they are as leaders, and they gain exposure to networks to which they wouldn't otherwise have access.

Here is an example mentor's perspective: "Kaiser now has nineteen new leaders who have finished the internship and who are...new leaders who are energized and enthused—and who know that Kaiser Permanente really believes in diversity...." Eighteen directors and vice presidents were recruited as mentors by the vice president of human resources and underwent training on mentoring. Their role was critical to the success of the program.

### Ambassador Program

Another example of a mentoring program is a peer-to-peer program. Although this provides mentoring opportunities, it also develops leadership skills based on experiential learning processes. The Ambassador Program was developed by the Workforce Planning Regional Team in Kaiser Permanente's Pacific Northwest region. This team is made up of labor and management representatives from many departments, who serve as an oversight committee. The team developed a program for current employees who wish to volunteer for recruitment activities, outreach events, and peer mentoring. These employee ambassadors serve as mentors and are able to work directly with their peers in a particular area of personal interest. For example, an employee who would like to share her love of her field or occupation can serve as a content expert at a career or job fair. The members of the workforce planning team develop strong ties with employees who participate, and employees are able to give back to their employer in meaningful ways. In addition to the workforce planning team's function of tracking changes in the workforce, and forecasting future employment and training needs, they also create a venue for employees to take on new and challenging volunteer responsibilities that translate to increased work skills.

What does it mean to be an ambassador? An ambassador is defined as a knowledgeable and experienced employee who serves as a trusted and caring resource to fellow employees as well as to the regional workforce planning team. An ideal ambassador is an employee who knows the company (and available resources) and is a respectful listener, one who exercises patience and has clear communication skills. Ambassadors may take on a variety of roles, including: providing informational interviews or representing Kaiser Permanente at speaking engagements, community events, job fairs, or outreach activities. Ideally, in many of these venues, the ambassadors will help mentees and peers by sharing their own employment experiences and educational and personal experiences.

Leaders of the regional workforce planning team actively promote the program and solicit applications from potential ambassadors. Mentees are employees who are referred to ambassadors by recruiters, managers, labor relations consultants, or counselors to gain information about a job, training program, or general career opportunities. To ensure a success-ful experience for both the ambassadors and their mentees, an orientation is provided for ambassadors by the co-chairs of the regional workforce planning team. The orientation includes exercises to maximize communi-cation skills plus an opportunity to develop a thorough understanding of company resources and leadership strategies. During their assignments, ambassadors receive ongoing direction and support from the workforce planning regional team. To assist the co-chairs with appropriate place-ments, participants in this program submit a form to the workforce plan-ning co-chairs to indicate their interests.

Through these activities, ambassadors develop peer relationships based on employment, academic, and social interests. They support employees in making successful transitions to, and within, Kaiser Permanente and serve as information agents for the company while fostering their own and their mentee's commitment to the organization. Additionally, they have an opportunity to apply leadership and public relations principles covered in their orientation. The Ambassador Program also provides opportunities for the organization to link with educational institutions. As educational requirements for careers change, it is vital to have mem-bers of the academic community serve as resources to ensure that infor-mation shared by ambassadors is accurate and representative of future educational directions.

### Does the Type of Mentoring Make a Difference in Career Development?

The purpose of a mentoring program is to encourage employees to effec-tively manage personal changes and take initiative in their transitions through life events as independent adult learners. In order to create a successful envi-ronment where this is possible, mentors need to have strong communication skills; broad knowledge of their area of expertise; accurate knowledge of certification, education, and licensure; and knowledge of career paths within the organization. With this background, mentors are able to

- support mentees in reflecting on future career paths and educational devel-opment components;
- guide mentees through in-depth review and exploration of their interests, abilities, ideas, and career beliefs;
- review individual choices based on sound knowledge of options and resources;
- help clarify perceptions about possible paths forward through listening responsively and asking open-ended questions;

- provide constructive feedback;
- express confidence in mentees' decisions; and
- encourage mentees' ability to develop talents and pursue dreams.

Career paths are no longer a steady upward progression driven only by an individual. Instead, they include experience interspersed with learning, and they are built on a foundation of interdependence as discussed earlier in the book. Mentoring programs are an excellent way to provide support in this emerging work world to benefit both individuals and organizations.

When individuals, organizations, and educational institutions create long-term relationships focused on professional development that involves experiential learning and mentoring, employers and employees alike can derive substantial benefits. Mentors benefit organizations and mentees in a variety of ways:

- Creating valuable relationships that support individual development and career growth
  - Enhance mentees' understanding of the social and political dynamics within an organization
- Creating opportunities to build relationships inter- and intraorganizationally, and between industry and educational institutions.
  - Enhance shared knowledge, organizational understanding of educational resources, and workforce flexibility

## CONCLUSION

Organizations focused on strengthening their future workforce can benefit from the processes, partnerships, and relationship building described in this chapter. These include external partnerships with educational institutions and development processes such as experiential learning and mentoring. A common theme is that of establishing long-term relationships focused on the needs of all participants. The avenues explored in this chapter directed to promoting workforce and career development are intended as examples of the many opportunities that exist for creative partnering and relationship building. Having established a foundation for building workforce strength in the first section of the book, we will now explore implementation in organization settings.

# PART II

## Implementing in the Organization

We need to find a place where we are safe.
We walk into that which we cannot yet see.
 —Elizabeth Alexander, "Praise Song for the Day:
 A Poem for Barack Obama's Presidential Inauguration"

# CHAPTER 4

# Creating Value with Workforce Planning and Development

*Bob Redlo and Ron Elsdon*

A number of years ago, there was an advertisement making the rounds that showed a small, enthusiastic team in a start-up business. The team had just introduced a new product and was watching a computer that showed sales as they happened. The sales meter on the computer began to advance slowly at first; then, to the team's consternation, it began to accelerate furiously in response to an avalanche of orders. The team was unprepared. One of the chapter authors remembers well being part of a tremendous team introducing fiber products to the market that were embraced enthusiastically by customers. Again, the meter was spinning furiously as customers tried to secure product. And they were not happy when supplies were limited. We hear stories of emergency rooms in hospitals overwhelmed by patients needing treatment, faced with long hours of waiting. Conversely, we see examples of organizations, such as the major U.S. automakers, burdened with excess capacity and more employees than they need. Each of these cases illustrates the challenges of anticipating future workforce needs and having the right resources and team in place to address them. Each of these cases underlines how value can be created if such resources are balanced correctly. This is the domain of workforce planning and development, and it is the focus of this chapter.

Workforce planning is a systematic approach to understanding future needs so that steps taken now, through workforce development, ensure that future capabilities are there when needed. Several components fit under the umbrella of workforce planning:

- Characterizing the organization's current workforce
  - For example, defining existing capabilities by key functional area,

operating segment, nature of the relationship sought with individuals, and demographic (e.g., location)

- Projecting how current workforce trends will likely influence future workforce composition
    - For example, exploring the implications of different attrition rates on future hiring and capability needs
- Based on primary targets the organization has adopted, defining and prioritizing core capabilities and relationships sought with individuals by workforce segment at various points in the future
    - For example, analyzing to what extent changing role requirements will affect strategic, conceptual, and technology skills needed versus more routine processing skills
- Identifying gaps between future needs and current workforce projections and defining how to eliminate those gaps
    - For example, examining the right balance between redeployment and hiring, or defining the focus of learning processes needed to build critical skills
- Tracking progress and adjusting as needed
    - For example, monitoring workforce trends continuously to guide needed changes

Workforce development is a response to the workforce planning process. At an organization level, it can be described by the four options shown in Table 4.1, which are not mutually exclusive.

**Table 4.1.  Different approaches to workforce development**

|  | *When* | *Why is it typically done?* | *How is it typically done?* |
|---|---|---|---|
| Redirect organization | • External shift <br>• Losing competitive position | • Survival | • Top down |
| Reorganize | • Emerging/ changing skill/ ability needs <br>• New leadership | • Channel skills <br><br>• Politics | • Organizational assessment <br>• Top tells the middle what to do to the bottom |
| Buy talent | • Out of ideas <br>• Crisis <br>• Growth | • Quick <br>• Available | • Cast the net |
| Build capabilities | • Clear direction <br>• Growth | • Align aspirations, skills <br>• Realize potential | • Focus on individual development and performance, workforce planning and development |

The first option is that of redirecting the organization, typically driven by a major external shift. Examples include Microsoft's (late) adoption of the Internet as central to its strategic direction, and the adoption by fast food chains of more healthy offerings in response to changing consumer sentiment. Redirection can also be imposed when an organization is losing its competitive position, for example, U.S. clothing manufacturers or software developers struggling to compete against low-cost operations in emerging economies and, as a result, shifting their sources of production or design to other countries. Redirection is often driven by survival needs and is usually a top-down initiative.

The second option is that of reorganizing. This can be driven by emerging or changing skill and ability needs. In many areas, ranging from movie production to healthcare recordkeeping to airline reservations, advancing technology and communication capabilities have fundamentally changed production or transaction processes. New skills can be created by reorganizing to channel existing capabilities in new directions, often guided by an organizational assessment. Sometimes, unfortunately, reorganizing is driven by political considerations when a new manager brings political allies into the organization. In these cases, the process can be one of the top telling the middle what to do to the bottom.

The third option is to attempt to buy talent. We saw this frenzy unfolding in the dot-com days when lavish signing bonuses were common in the technology world, and tenure with high-tech organizations dropped to an average of about 18 months as people job shopped continuously. Buying talent is typically viewed as a quick fix to solve a crisis, sometimes caused by rapid growth. It requires that people with needed skills are available, which is questionable. People are usually sought by casting a broad net, using costly brokering processes such as executive search.

The fourth option is that of building capabilities. This requires clarity of direction and senior leadership invested in committing time and energy to the building process. It often occurs in a growth environment although it is integral to the sustained success of any organization. For example, healthcare organizations that link their community and student outreach efforts to hiring, integration, and development are creating a sustainable future workforce. Building capabilities requires continued realignment of people's aspirations and skills with organizational needs. This means having systems and policies that support such realignment, for example, removing barriers to, and enabling, internal transfers. It is through the building process, and integrating individual development and performance and workforce planning and development, that the potential of each person in the workforce can find expression, resulting in productivity benefits. Organizations seeking long-term prosperity adopt this fourth workforce development practice of building capabilities as a central strategic approach, augmented as needed by the other approaches.

In practice there can be varied organizational stances to workforce development as follows:

- Ignore
  - This is the going-out-of-business approach. There is little or no investment in building workforce capability. This approach may be adopted on the basis of perceived low risk in the short term; however, it creates huge risk in the long term.
- Haphazard
  - In this case, workforce development occurs sporadically according to the whim of the moment. Examples include adoption of the latest management fad, or viewing development as an employee perk uncoupled from organizational or individual imperatives. It depletes resources and contributes little.
- Short-term performance focus
  - This approach focuses only on short-term organizational results. It is driven by tactical outcomes and generally alienates the workforce, leading to rapid, acrimonious departure of people. An example would be the venture-backed company that demands excessive work hours from employees while providing negligible support for their development.
- Long-term development focus
  - This is a partnership between the organization and the individual, addressing strategic outcomes for both. It is a balance of giving and getting, and it generates long-term, sustainable success. DuPont's successful reinvention almost every 30 years, for about 200 years, is a demonstration of this approach.

A number of factors influence how an effective workforce planning and development effort can be best structured for a given organization. They are as follows (with examples):

- Organizational values and operating approach
  - A large organization with a highly participative culture may incorporate workforce planning and development as additional means to build consensus, explicitly acknowledging this aspect by focusing on reducing barriers within the organization and encouraging movement. On the other hand, a small organization relying on specialized skills, and challenged to secure such skills, may emphasize individual relationship building.
- Needs and attributes of different workforce segments
  - An organization seeking to build extended relationships with a segment of the workforce may tightly integrate workforce planning and development into managers' goals and objectives to emphasize their importance. Conversely, an organization that outsources many functions may include the system implications of outsourcing in

workforce planning but leave development of individuals to the outsourced entities.

- Rapidity of change
  - Organizations operating in high-technology areas may need to build workforce planning and development functions with short time horizons, for example, months. On the other hand, public sector organizations, where change is constrained by policy considerations, may build the workforce planning and development focus around major policy change points.
- Importance of cumulative learning
  - Organizations that are building significant accumulated learning, such as in drug discovery, likely need to address extended time horizons. Workforce planning and development processes then focus on securing staff continuity and strong affiliation over many years.
- Availability of key skills
  - Organizations needing capabilities that are not readily available from conventional educational channels may focus significant workforce planning and development activities and resources on building internal learning processes.
- Leadership capabilities
  - For those organizations with senior leaders having insight into, and understanding of, the importance of workforce planning and development, primary emphases of the workforce planning and development activities can be on implementation and sustaining support. Those organizations with senior leaders still building such understanding will likely need to dedicate significant time and resources to defining and communicating the benefits of workforce planning and development.

Acknowledging and addressing these factors make it possible to tailor the implementation approach to each organization, recognizing that this will need to address several aspects:

- Outreach and hiring practices
- Integration processes
- Provision of support for individual development
  - Career development
  - Educational resources
  - Shared interest communities or affinity groups
  - Online performance, development, and succession planning systems
- Proactive processes to support people in transition
- Resources to guide system-level workforce development

Implementation also needs to acknowledge demand and supply considerations both inside and outside the organization (Ruse and Chapman

2009). These include external political, environmental, social, and technological changes that affect demand for people in particular occupational
areas; population demographics and competitive factors that address
external supply; organizational culture, strategy, and structure as they
affect internal demand; and demographics, movement, and performance
attributes of the employee population as they affect internal supply.

Having framed the context within which workforce planning and
development take place, we will now look at an example. The organization from the healthcare sector is Kaiser Permanente, one of the largest
healthcare providers in the U.S. with more than 167,000 employees, over
14,000 physicians serving almost nine million members in eight regions
of the U.S. Kaiser Permanente also has one of the largest and most successful labor-management partnerships in the U.S., with a national
agreement covering over 100,000 staff members in over 32 local unions.
While workforce planning and development at Kaiser Permanente are
important for the entire workforce, this example will describe one aspect:
workforce planning and development for the labor union–represented
population.

## MAKING THE CASE FOR TRANSFORMING
## HEALTHCARE AT KAISER PERMANENTE:
## WORKFORCE PLANNING AND DEVELOPMENT

### Shelley's Story

Shelley is a medical assistant with 15 years experience at Kaiser Permanente (KP). When Shelley made the decision to return to school, she was
recently divorced, raising three children, and had just purchased a house.
Clearly, she would need to be creative and committed to achieve her goal
of becoming a marriage and family therapist. From the beginning, she
had two advantages that are important ingredients in a development program. She was able to take advantage of evening classes that minimized
disruption of her work schedule, and she had an understanding, supportive manager. Education provider flexibility and management support are
essential ingredients to successful workforce development.

Shelley was able to leverage KP tuition reimbursement to defray a substantial part of her education costs. She was also a recipient of a scholarship from her union. Furthermore, a stipend program from one of KP's
Taft-Hartley trusts was available to provide her with income replacement
one day each week during her internship period. Thus, Shelley achieved
her goal of completing her graduate degree and internship, making it possible to pursue career advancement within KP, while the organization was
able to retain an engaged and committed employee to serve members.
Here is Shelley's perspective: "Kaiser's workforce development program
gave me the flexibility and resources to improve my life."

## Healthcare Landscape

Shelley's success demonstrates how one person benefits from workforce development resources and support. Similar examples cascading across the organization bring strengthened workforce capability and needed flexibility that lead to increased performance of the organization. Let's step back to understand the setting within which this takes place for KP. Since KP operates exclusively in the U.S., the U.S. economic and healthcare infrastructure provide a primary context for KP's workforce planning and development activities, recognizing also the growing importance of global workforce and economic influences. In moving through the 21st century, healthcare reform will play an important role in the success of the U.S. economy. In 2009 healthcare costs are projected to account for 17.6 percent of U.S. Gross Domestic Product (Kaiser Family Foundation 2009). This places significant competitive pressures on organizations operating in the U.S. that will intensify if healthcare costs continue to increase. A shift from employer-paid health plans to employee-paid health plans will result in a similar outcome. Future cost increases in healthcare that mirror experience since the 1970s are unsustainable because they would exacerbate this situation, contributing to continued high unemployment, reduced spending, and a weak economy. The U.S. healthcare system will be under considerable stress in the future as it responds to such challenges and opportunities. Since the majority of healthcare delivery costs are associated with personnel costs, as indicated by KP internal information, workforce planning and development within healthcare become critically important both for organizations operating in the healthcare sector and for the national economy. The importance of the healthcare sector as a major employer is underlined by a Bureau of Labor Statistics prediction (U.S. Department of Labor), that between 2008 and 2018, the healthcare sector will generate more jobs than any other sector in the U.S. Demographics of an ageing population drive this trend, which is further complicated by continually increasing technical sophistication of healthcare delivery.

Workforce planning and development are crucial to the success of long-term healthcare reform and delivery. Efficiencies in chronic care management and availability of new technology will require that workers possess new and enhanced skill sets. Economic pressures will drive healthcare providers to accelerate the redesign of work processes. These are challenges throughout the U.S. as well as globally. Solutions will require the development of centralized programmatic approaches implemented to meet regional needs. Properly trained workers are critical to meeting the changing needs of healthcare delivery. This is highlighted during periods of economic challenge and change. How healthcare institutions develop and deploy their workforce policies, practices, and programs will to a great extent determine the level of

Table 4.2.   Changing nature of healthcare in the U.S.

| Today | Tomorrow |
| --- | --- |
| Acute treatment | Chronic prevention and management |
| Cost unaware | Price competitive |
| Professional prerogative | Consumer responsive |
| In-patient | Ambulatory: home and community |
| Individual profession | Team |
| Traditional practice | Evidence-based practice |
| Information as record | Information as tool |
| Patient passivity | Consumer engagement and accountability |

their success in this dynamic environment. In the two decades after 2010, the U.S. healthcare system will likely adjust as shown in Table 4.2. Successful healthcare organizations will understand this transition and create strategies to respond.

### Workforce Planning and Development for the Labor-Represented Population at Kaiser Permanente

In this environment, KP recognized the importance of workforce planning and development as major components to strengthen its healthcare delivery system and promote world class excellence in healthcare service and quality at affordable rates. Workforce planning and development take place in an integrated program based on a strong labor-management partnership. This is reflected in the goals adopted in the most recent (2005) national labor agreement for workforce planning and development:

- KP will have the most stable, highly skilled, and highly trained workforce in the healthcare industry by:
  - Developing workforce skills to meet future healthcare needs
  - Achieving regional retention and reduced turnover targets
  - Motivating the workforce through career advancement and increased mobility
  - Ensuring employee career alignment with KP strategic goals
  - Making KP the best place to work
  - Reducing outside labor costs

In implementing workforce planning and development, KP describes three integrated program components: workforce planning, workforce development, and workforce resources.

*Workforce Planning*

Workforce planning is an engine that drives workforce planning and development success at KP. The workforce planning program includes these elements:

- Needs assessment

An assessment is conducted annually that measures vacancy rates and, through surveys of regional management and labor leaders, identifies critical positions by region. Results are communicated within the organization (using online tools) to assist employees in understanding key occupational areas of need for which they might seek training. In deciding the path forward, employees are supported by career counselors. The results of the needs assessment are important in supporting individual job security while addressing organizational needs.

- Gap analysis

An analysis is conducted annually to characterize supply and demand, and gaps in all job classifications. This information is necessary to help in defining critical positions in each region. The analysis includes the availability of labor, both internally and externally, in each geographic area in which the organization operates.

- Workforce dashboard

A workforce dashboard provides real-time electronic access to key data for managers and labor leaders at any location at KP. The data includes the following:

  - Demographics (e.g., retirements)
  - Recruitment data (e.g., vacancy and turnover rates)
  - Retention data (e.g., career mobility and transfer rates)

This newly developed tool allows national or regional trends to be identified and tracked in real time, previously a difficult manual operation with limited access. Data is available by job classification, with the dashboard providing consistency in all regions, and it is easy to maintain.

- Job forecasting

A forecasting model is under development that will use existing workforce dashboard and assessment tools along with an external education database to determine supply of labor. This will be integrated with financial and business planning scenarios, capital expense and expansion plans, and new hospital and medical center staffing projections. Incorporating the anticipated influence of technology will provide an assessment of anticipated staffing changes over a 5-, 10-, and 20-year horizon.

- Staff planning and projected staffing levels

Staff planning and projected staffing levels are additional crucial components of workforce planning. Staffing plans in each department and regional medical center are integrated into the needs assessment and gap analysis. These plans take into account census data and analysis of hospital scale and services.

- Strategic education plans aligned with regional business strategies

Each geographic region at KP completes an annual business plan, agreed upon and supported by regional and national leadership, which defines organizational goals and priority business initiatives. Education and training initiatives support the business plan as well as the integration and alignment of workforce planning and development with business operations.

- Exit interviews and new hire interviews

Confidential exit interviews of staff who have left voluntarily and confidential interviews with staff recently hired are conducted by a third party. These interviews provide information about the reasons for departures, and perspectives staff have about their employment experience that offer opportunities to reduce attrition.

- Evaluation and metrics

Ongoing monitoring of workforce planning and development provides the basis for continually improving effectiveness. Metrics include surveys and third-party interviews among managers, labor leaders, and participants in the education and training programs, in addition to tracking measures such as attrition rates, career mobility, and vacancy rates.

*Workforce Development*

The second key ingredient in KP's workforce planning and development program is the workforce development component. This includes both in-person and online support services. The four most important aspects are as follows:

- Career counseling services

Evidence from internal evaluation processes demonstrates that personal career counseling combined with online career services provides the most effective assistance to staff. Career mobility is complex with numerous options and directions. Resources and benefits can be difficult to locate and understand. Career counseling services enable individuals to link their career aspirations to critical job classification areas. This is an important contribution of the workforce planning and development function. The investment in career counseling is central to making KP programs a success. Career counseling services include personal, confidential career counseling available at any time in each KP region. Third-party career counselors are well trained and aware of the most recent information about career mobility at KP. They have access to workforce dashboard information and understand internal as well as external educational opportunities in each geographic region. Career counselors provide individual services and group seminars as well as advice about training programs linked to organizational needs and individual regional interests.

- Career paths

Career paths have been developed on national and regional levels to broaden understanding of career mobility. These are displayed on a career planning Web site. Over 60 critical positions at KP have been analyzed covering nursing and allied health (e.g., imaging and laboratory) job classifications.

- Alignment with recruitment

Workforce planning and development must be aligned with recruitment for maximum effectiveness, linking critical position needs to staff training and recruitment. Recruiters can access both internal and external candidates, which provides operating economies as the cost of filling positions internally is much lower than the cost of external hiring.

- Career planning Web site

A career planning Web site is an important component of workforce development at KP. This Web site, which can be accessed by employees at KP or from home, provides a broad range of career-related information. The access portal and login process allow for tailoring to the individual employee. The site includes specific union information, information about regional career paths and benefits, and links to regional educational opportunities from local colleges and online training programs. The Web site has six distinct links that are critical to success. One link lists the career counselors in a given region, outlines available career services, and allows individuals to make career counseling appointments. A second link provides information about the employee's union affiliation and union. It also provides information about union benefits or scholarships, and how to apply for those benefits. A third link provides information about career paths and career mobility. Career paths are diagrammed, and they include comprehensive information about specific positions. A fourth link provides updated information on critical positions at KP along with video vignettes from employees describing their daily experience in these positions. A fifth link provides success stories of employees progressing with their career mobility The final link provides further information about benefits and resources available to each employee in the region. Employees may apply for benefits directly from the Web site.

### Workforce Resources

The third ingredient of the workforce planning and development program is the ability to provide workforce resources. These resources are provided through the career planning Web site. They include the following:

- Tuition reimbursement. Employees are reimbursed for tuition and books as well as being reimbursed for continuing education units that are required for their profession. Tuition reimbursement ranges by region from $600 to $2,000 annually.

- Education leave. Most union members at KP have education leave that may be up to four weeks per year. This leave can be used flexibly in daily or weekly increments.

- Student financial aid. Student financial aid from external sources, whether from government or other sources such as loans and aid from educational institutions, is integrated with the employee's benefit package.

- Scholarships. Scholarships to support career mobility are offered by the unions and by individual programs within KP. In addition, KP has a number of organizations and associations, (e.g., African American, Hispanic, and Asian) that offer scholarships for education and training.

- Individual stipends for career development. Stipends are available to union employees that include up to eight hours of supplemental wages per week, with a maximum of $8,000 in one program over a two-year period. Employees must reduce their work schedule in order to receive this supplemental wage. This benefit is well used as it allows employees to complete educational programs that advance their development.

- Group stipends for cohort training programs. Group programs such as those for progression from medical assistant to licensed vocational nurse or radiology technician, or from licensed vocational nurse to registered nurse, are also well supported by KP's workforce planning and development program. Group training programs are normally initiated in KP's regions and are supported by individual unions as well as by operational and HR leaders in the regions.

- Educational partnerships and grants. Educational partnerships and grants, as available from government sources, can provide additional support for career mobility. These funds are usually matched with workforce planning and development resources to supplement existing resources for employees.

- Forgivable loans. Forgivable loans help ensure that employer or union investments provide benefits to the organization. The forgivable loan is similar to the group or individual stipend; however, if an employee leaves within a defined time frame, the forgivable loan must be repaid.

### The Creation of the Labor-Management Trusts

The workforce planning and development efforts are supported by two Taft-Hartley education trusts (Taft-Hartley Act 1947) that KP founded in 2004 and 2005. Taft-Hartley trusts were created in 1947 to provide direct benefits to employees through joint and equal participation of labor and management. The KP trusts have equal representation from labor and management. The trusts are separate legal entities created between the unions and the organization. The KP trusts sponsor both cohort and individual training programs, and provide funding for individuals for items such as books and tuition. They also support career counseling and the development of online career related resources. Resources and programs from the trusts include the following:

- Career preparation services
- Nurse education
- Professional and technical education
- Customized education and training
- Individual and group education stipends
- Redeployment and transitional support

### Integrating Workforce Planning and Development into the Organization

The integration of workforce planning and development into the operational performance of the organization is essential to the success of the endeavor. Workforce planning and development at KP include leadership involvement and executive support at the national and regional levels. Each of KP's eight regions has its own workforce planning and development team that meets regularly to discuss and implement workforce development activities, such as training programs, to strengthen the workforce. Chapter 9 provides an in-depth example for these activities in one of the KP regions. Each region develops an annual education strategy aligned with the regional business and operational strategy. Quarterly meetings between regional leaders, labor and management representatives, and national workforce planning and development staff help maintain alignment and identify changes as needed. These include reviews of training programs in each region and sharing of best practices and programs. For example, the Southern California region established an online nursing program that was then shared with other regions. Similar programs were developed for nursing specialties, medical terminology, and imaging.

Workforce planning and development also acknowledge and act within a framework of operational agreements and operational change. For example, in order to ensure labor participation in its workforce planning and development efforts, KP established an Employment Security Agreement (E.S.A.) that allows frontline staff and labor leaders to participate in workforce changes without fear that job elimination will occur. This agreement outlines a specific understanding that if a job is eliminated because of technology, or because of a process improvement, employees will have a minimum of one year of training, supported by KP, to qualify for another position. An application of the agreement arose with respect to KP's transformation of its paper record systems to an electronic medical records process over a five-year period, involving thousands of employees. Workforce planning and development processes were instrumental at regional and national levels in providing training and education opportunities during this transition, and in securing needed workforce flexibility. Numerous upgrades and transitions occurred with the participation of labor and management through workforce planning and development. As a result, employee satisfaction, as demonstrated by annual surveys, steadily increased during a period of extensive workforce transformation.

### Looking to the Future

Given the fundamental shifts occurring in the healthcare landscape in the U.S., the challenges of healthcare reform in the 21st century will require that workforce planning and development are coordinated across multiple healthcare providers as well as aligned with educational institutions and regulatory bodies. This coordination can provide the basis for a common healthcare curriculum across educational institutions in tune with new technology and delivery systems. In this case, healthcare providers would partner with educational institutions to support development of the new healthcare delivery systems that will require new workforce skills and flexibility.

One example is KP's exploration of grant funding for a 21st-century healthcare initiative. This proposal, if funded, would create a three-year project partnership among various KP entities, University of California–San Francisco Center for Health Professions, California Primary Care Association and its community clinic members, California Association for Public Hospitals and associated clinics, the California community college system, and local workforce investment boards. The project is outlined in the following two sections.

*Project Problem Statement and Proposed Solutions*

As the population ages, the prevalence of chronic diseases such as diabetes and heart disease continues to rise. The current healthcare workforce may not be fully prepared to provide population care and panel management within the current healthcare infrastructure, particularly if the number of under- and uninsured continues to increase.

- Fifteen-minute office visits are not sufficient to provide proactive, preventative care.
  - Solution: train medical assistants, licensed vocational nurses, registered nurses, and other clinic staff using a specific protocol to optimize every patient encounter through panel management
- Healthcare providers are adversely affected by staff shortages, high-volume patient visits, and limited resources.
  - Solution: increase clinic efficiency and workflow by training clinic staff to delineate roles, work as a coordinated team, use technology effectively, and optimize provider support
- Lack of access to high-quality interpreting services in a healthcare setting is an underlying cause of healthcare disparities for patients with limited facility in English.
  - Solution: train qualified bilingual staff and healthcare interpreters to provide linguistically and culturally competent care in order to assist in decreasing racial and ethnic disparities
- The need for certain allied healthcare positions is projected to grow rapidly through 2018.
  - Solution: increase the supply of adequately trained personnel for high-growth healthcare positions such as medical assistants, licensed vocational nurses, and healthcare interpreters by funding community college programs for incumbent, dislocated, and unemployed workers

*Project Goals*

- Use a proven protocol to train 5,500 incumbent medical assistants, licensed vocational nurses, and other clinical staff in California on panel management and chronic disease care.
- Contract with 8 to 10 community colleges to build a new supply of adequately trained medical assistants and licensed vocational nurses.
- Expand the base of qualified bilingual staff by at least 1,500 employees. Add four to five healthcare interpreter certificate programs to build a career pipeline for approximately 100 bilingual incumbents drawing from a pool of dislocated and unemployed workers.

Anticipated outcomes are summarized in Table 4.3.

In addition, the KP workforce planning and development organization is joining with other provider organizations, associations, and coalitions

Table 4.3.   Anticipated outcomes from a proposed grant-funded program

| *Healthcare system outcomes* | *Patient outcomes* |
| --- | --- |
| • Increased pool of adequately trained and diverse healthcare workers | • Increased access to physician and healthcare team through multiple points of contact (pre-visit, office visit, post-visit) |
| • Efficient use of technology | • Improved healthcare outcomes through prevention and case management |
| • Proactive office encounters | • Adoption of healthy behaviors |
| • Increased staff satisfaction and reduced attrition | • Improved patient satisfaction |
| • Multiskilled staff within appropriate scope | • Access to quality interpreting services |

to address workforce planning and development needs associated with healthcare reform. Examples of partnering organizations include the California Hospital Association, the California Health Workforce Alliance, and other coalitions that call for educational reform and more resources to meet the demand for healthcare staffing in the future.

### Future Challenges

Workforce planning and development will become more important in the coming 10–20 years in healthcare. Demographics of the KP workforce bear this out. The average age of staff in many critical positions is over 50; the average age of clinical laboratory scientists in hospital and medical office settings is over 55. With economic growth in the future, vacancy rates will increase in critical positions, including nursing, clinical laboratory scientists, respiratory therapists, and highly skilled imaging positions. In addition, numerous physicians choose to practice in specialty areas, leaving a void in the number of primary care physicians. Yet, in the future, with a likely emphasis on six major chronic conditions, and the need to provide healthcare coverage for those currently uninsured and underinsured, the need for primary care physicians will increase. This will place an additional strain on educational institutions already challenged by budget restrictions.

### Response to Healthcare Challenges through Workforce Planning and Development

Given this environment, workforce planning and development within KP have the following strategies to meet future healthcare challenges:

- Create pipelines for tomorrow's workforce, equip KP staff with tools to enhance flexibility while meeting transformational challenges, and expand access to college prerequisite classes for those who will become tomorrow's registered nurses and allied health workers.

- Use workforce forecasting tools and other metrics to estimate workforce needs and gaps.

- Expand career counseling to better enable people to navigate through the changing healthcare environment.

- Deploy programs to meet critical needs: nursing, laboratory, imaging, and other allied health occupations.

- Become a thought leader in healthcare workforce education. Partner with community colleges and policy makers to improve employees' access to high-quality training and education.

- Create a culture of lifelong learning. Emphasize the need for all employees to continuously develop throughout their careers, facilitating a successful response to changes in healthcare delivery.

KP's approach to workforce planning and development offers insights into how a program can be implemented in a high-performance organization. This includes integration and alignment with operations, finance, and information technology functions; involvement of frontline staff in decision making; securing adequate funding and executive sponsorship; demonstrating strong value contribution; and partnering with other entities such as educational institutions, healthcare providers, and government agencies. In the next chapter we will explore a specific component, namely designing, developing, and measuring effective career development processes and systems, an important component of workforce development.

# CHAPTER 5

# Designing, Developing and Measuring Effective Career Development Processes and Systems

*Rita Erickson and Ron Elsdon*

"Our organization is being acquired; our new owners will be in place next month." The CEO's words to the assembled staff of a high-technology organization sent shivers of apprehension through the room. He paused for several seconds then went on. "Now you have a sense what it feels like to face this prospect. In fact, next month we will be making the acquisition. We will suddenly have a much larger workforce. Our success depends on how well we come together as organizations." This paraphrase of an actual situation described by a colleague shows the CEO beginning to build a shared basis for a difficult, critical transition ahead. Successful long-term integration of these two organizations will come when people see a path forward for themselves. Workforce strength means making this path forward possible and visible for each person, and career development is central to achieving this objective.

This chapter explores how to create effective career development processes in organizations. We first acknowledge the driving forces for implementing career development processes and then explore the context within which career service delivery takes place from the perspective of different organizational cultures and delivery structures. We then examine the implications for implementation, including which services to deploy, what skills are needed, and how progress can be measured. We also provide an overview of some factors affecting launch of the services.

## DRIVING FORCES

As the skills needed to deliver products, services, and information become more complex, as mentioned in the introduction, and the growth rate of the workforce in developed countries continues to decline (see, for example, M. Toossi 2006), the challenge of establishing and sustaining the needed workforce becomes acute. For many organizations this is a primary driving force for implementing career development processes: to secure needed capabilities. In other cases competitive pressures and a changing environment drive a need for enhanced productivity. At one time this was addressed primarily through economies of scale. However, in an environment where innovation and flexibility are primary sources of competitive advantage, productivity gains come from the ingenuity and commitment of people, rather than from scale. Ingenuity and commitment grow with development of people. Studies by Elsdon, Inc. show that, on average, people self-assess that they only operate at about 60 percent of their full potential. Securing the remaining 40 percent is a primary source of competitive strength, and it can be accessed through career development. The growing complexity of workforce skills also increases the value contributed by each person, and as a result, it increases the cost to organizations when people leave. Exit interviews conducted by Elsdon, Inc. across a broad range of sectors have shown that a primary reason people leave organizations is lack of development opportunities. Career development addresses the need for support in this area and can therefore play an important role in limiting attrition.

So there are a variety of factors that, either singly or in combination, can prompt an expressed organizational need for career development. These factors, whether addressing securing needed skill sets, enhancing productivity, or reducing attrition, speak to the long-term health and vitality of organizations and to the strength of affiliation and sense of fulfillment for those in them. Not surprisingly, these factors are influenced by the organizational culture within which such development takes place. The organization and workforce culture also significantly affect the nature and structure of career services delivery, and that is where we begin.

## UNDERSTANDING AND WORKING WITH DIFFERENT ORGANIZATIONAL CULTURES

### Individual Perspective: Role of Career Anchors in Influencing Career Services Delivery

The salient role of Career Anchors in creating and sustaining demand for career development services is apparent in 2004 interviews and surveys conducted by Erickson (2004). The results from these in-depth, structured interviews with career counselors, coaches, human resource consultants, and organization development leaders in 40 Fortune 500 firms were described in chapter 1, and these results underline the importance of aligning the capabilities of development facilitators, as described in chapter 2, with the needs of the client population.

The work of Schein (1978, 2006) led to the Career Anchors framework, which is based on more than three decades of occupational self-concept studies. Career Anchors result from the interaction between a person's values and needs and the work context. As individuals explore new roles or settings that compromise their needs or values, they find themselves pulled back (anchored) into more congruent work (Schein 1978, 125). The occupational role does not determine the anchor. Rather, it is the intention, the underlying needs of the individual, the occupational reinforcers the individual seeks, and what these reinforcers ultimately allow that determine the individual's anchor.

Schein posits eight fundamental Career Anchors: technical/functional competence; autonomy/independence; security/stability; entrepreneurial creativity; pure challenge; lifestyle; service/dedication to a cause; and general managerial competence. A brief explanation of each anchor (Schein, 2006) and the implications for the skills needed to facilitate individual career development follow. The examples are based on Erickson's career coaching work with individual clients between 1989 and 2009.

Individuals with technical/functional anchors are fundamentally attracted to the content of their work. The largest of the eight groups on a percentage basis (Schein 2006, 8–11), these individuals are mobile and represent the dominant occupation within their respective industries. Examples include engineers within research and development firms or accountants within financial services firms (Erickson 2000). Intellectual challenge is the reward they seek. Rather than title, rank, or other external measures of influence, their goals are generally to achieve higher levels of complexity and novelty within their area of specialty. Dual career tracks (functional as well as managerial) are essential to attracting and retaining the best among them. Education and continuous professional development are essential to securing increasingly challenging assignments. Individuals with technical/functional anchors greatly value expertise and competence, and readily partner with those they feel are equally or more competent in a domain in which they find themselves lacking.

Individuals with autonomy/independence Career Anchors need to feel as though they are masters of their own destiny (Schein 2006, 16–19). They thrive on setting their own standards and owning ultimate accountability and responsibility for their work. They tend to gravitate to occupations that lend themselves to self-employment or independent contracting arrangements. Medical doctors, consultants, and professors are common examples. Less interested in upward mobility than their technical/functional colleagues, they tend to be interested primarily in executive development coaching or other practice-building-related coaching. They seek honest, direct feedback as well as sounding boards to hold them accountable for fulfilling a larger vision. Coaches and consultants are often particularly effective with autonomy anchored clients.

Individuals with security/stability anchors tend to gravitate to large, well-established firms (Schein 2006, 17–18). They operate under the assumption that the organization's current lifespan is a predictor of its future success. They value the prestige associated with the firm and derive a sense of pride from being an employee of IBM, for example. Of the eight groups, individuals with security anchors are most sensitive to the context of the work. Generally long tenured within their organizations, what matters most to them are positive relations with co-workers, pleasant working conditions, and traditional benefits that mitigate risk. Individuals with security anchors tend to work for government, quasi-government, or industry sectors where mean tenure is significantly above average. This group forms a significant percent of the employees in most large firms. These individuals rarely anticipate or proactively prepare for change. As a result, they need significant support in all facets of change management, ranging from understanding the changing business context to laying the foundation for success in a new role. Upfront effort in the realm of work values, interests, beliefs, and self-confidence will significantly enhance their ability to successfully adapt to the changing work environment and continue to add value to the organization. Well-rounded career counseling skills, including current knowledge of the world of work, will best serve a career counselor working with this group.

Entrepreneurial creativity is the fourth anchor. Individuals expressing this anchor are fundamentally driven by the need to create an enterprise (Schein 2006, 19–20). Once the challenge of creating has been accomplished, the individual is compelled to move to the next pursuit: the business is sold to a manager while the individual moves on to another opportunity. These individuals value professional development expertise, business acumen, and mentoring-like relationships. Successful executive coaches and branding strategists have the greatest likelihood of success with this group.

The pure challenge anchor characterizes the individual who thrives on continuously proving his mettle (Schein 2006, 22–23). Within the business world, these individuals are most often found in strategic consulting firms such as Booz Allen Hamilton or McKinsey & Company. Self-described adrenaline junkies, these individuals must continuously test themselves at ever higher levels of challenge. Given the insatiable desire for proving oneself common to these individuals, it is not surprising to learn that consulting firms were among the first business organizations to offer organizational career coaching. Understanding the worldview and drive of individuals with this Career Anchor is essential to establishing rapport and credibility. The ability to build customized coaching strategies that will effectively serve the individual and the organization is essential to an effective relationship.

Lifestyle anchors are becoming increasingly common as dual-career families are becoming the norm (Schein 2006, 23). Among married couple families, both husband and wife worked in just over half of the households in 2007 and 2008 (U.S. Department of Labor 2009a). Individuals with this anchor seek out employers who emphasize family-friendly or work-life balance attributes in their culture. Numerous best places to work books, magazines, and Web sites cater to this growing market segment. This group is particularly sensitive to nonpecuniary benefits such as flexible workplace, flextime schedules, and access to other resources that allow them to juggle work, home, leisure, and eldercare responsibilities. Increasing numbers of these individuals have migrated into full-time positions in the corporate world. The dual-earner subsegment of this anchor highly values career counseling and coaching as they typically want the best of both worlds: challenging and meaningful work along with family and leisure balance. The counselor's creativity, abilities to coach for clarity and crystallization, and organizational awareness combined with the client's willingness to take risk typically yield positive individual and organizational outcomes. A variant on this type of career counseling will become increasingly important to organizations as individuals want to contribute to their organizations in meaningful ways that are less time-intensive as they age.

Service anchors define individuals who want the expression of their values to be central to their work (Schein 2006, 21). These individuals may work in traditional helping occupations (e.g., nursing, various human resource roles) or in any job in which they self-define the primary characteristic of their role as helping others. Working in for-profit as well as nonprofit entities, these individuals seek broadening spheres of influence and greater autonomy. Individuals with these anchors often reach out to career counselors early in their careers because they feel disconnected from their occupational peers. Career counseling plays a pivotal role in eliciting their values, and connecting these values to a mission and vision for their lives. This is foundational for clients with service anchors. Once this has been accomplished, the counselor and client can conduct values-based research in the world of work.

Individuals with a general managerial anchor express analytical competence, interpersonal competence, and emotional competence (Schein 2006, 11–15). They most value increasing levels of, and scope of, responsibility, and are performance and results driven. They are highly motivated by traditional perquisites of success. Like entrepreneurs, they feel it takes one to know one, and establishing credibility as a coach or career counselor is often contingent on having a similar or higher level of success than the client. Most often this is a description of an executive coach or consultant.

The preceding observations suggest that optimal outcomes result when the needs of the target clients and the skills of the person facilitating development are well aligned. Depending on the population served, this may mean staffing an organizational career development initiative with career counselors, coaches, organization development practitioners, human resource consultants, those with leadership experience, or recruiters. Ideally, an individual facilitating development will bring multiple aspects from his educational and work background. Such alignment establishes credibility and serves as the foundation for building trust. For example, software developers with dominant technical/functional anchors may expect those facilitating their development to understand the content and the context of their work (Erickson 2000). This implies a basic understanding of the role progression within the industry, as well as a rudimentary understanding of the different programming platforms and different programming domains (e.g., application level or operating systems level). They will also expect their development facilitator to have this knowledge prior to engaging with them. For the development facilitators in this example, this is the threshold level of competency necessary to establish credibility. For clients with a technical/functional anchor, subject matter expertise, status or other indicators of thought leadership within the career development field are essential for moving the relationship to one of trust. Having explored how predominant individual values influence the delivery of career services, we will now examine the organizational perspective.

### Organizational Perspective: How Business Need and Career Anchors Influence Approaches to Career Services Delivery

Organizations may choose to offer career development services in order to secure a competitive advantage, enhance productivity, maintain a market leadership position, attract high-potential talent or an in-demand core workforce, minimize attrition, or redeploy valued employees affected by organizational restructuring. The business case for this is explored in more detail in chapter 1. The review in the preceding section of values that influence career drivers for individuals underscores the need for a customized approach to designing, developing, and delivering career development services. A list of key competencies for the facilitation of individual development sets the stage for exploring the approaches of using either internal or external resources for delivery of career services. These approaches bring differing competencies, involve differing time horizons, and imply differing levels of organizational commitment.

#### Competencies Needed to Facilitate Development

Regardless of the approach used, the necessary skill set for those facilitating individual development needs to be defined. Career counselors, organizational development, and coaching professionals often have diverse backgrounds from which they can draw expertise in addition to the knowledge, skills, and tools within the professional and personal development arena. Given this breadth of expertise, staffing a career development initiative should primarily reflect the needs and expectations of the targeted clients rather than be constrained by the occupational titles of those facilitating development. The earlier description of Career Anchors can assist in matching the skills and backgrounds of the development facilitators with the client population served. In general, the broader the occupational composition of the organizational career development initiative, the broader the skill set required for successful implementation. The most relevant competencies for those facilitating development include the following:

- Change management (including managing personal transitions)
- Strategic partnering skills
- Global cultural understanding
- Understanding of personal leadership styles
- Knowledge of career development theories, frameworks, and processes
- Knowledge of effective approaches for engaging with individuals in career coaching and counseling
- Knowledge to build resources (e.g., employer-specific skill assessments, frequently asked questions, job aids, or educational databases)
- Understanding of organizational culture
- Understanding of power and influence
- Understanding of group dynamics
- Knowledge of strategic planning
- Knowledge of instructional design
- Understanding of adult learning strategies
- Effectiveness in group training delivery
- Knowledge of talent acquisition, management, and development
- Understanding of job analysis
- Knowledge of career pathing

## Staffing Career Development Initiatives Internally

Four of 40 firms surveyed by Erickson (2004) experimented with staffing the career development initiative internally. Two of these firms relied on senior-level recruiters to fulfill this primarily developmental process, while the remaining two firms used former functional subject matter experts who had become in-house trainers. In all four cases, the primary need was to enable current employees to navigate quickly within the firm. In the two firms that used senior-level recruiters, these recruiters knew the functional skills needed in targeted positions, which made them effective career developers in the short term. Their knowledge of the organization, departmental culture, and hiring managers' leadership styles allowed them to quickly engage with employees who knew precisely which skills they wanted to acquire and where they wanted to transfer. However, despite years of organizational knowledge and often a decade or more of successful recruitment and placement, these same recruiters were not successful in effectively developing employees in the organization. Self-reported obstacles experienced by the recruiters included employee concerns about confidentiality, lack of understanding or clarity about the firm's organizational strategy, unclear expectations about future development paths on the part of the managers and employees, and most importantly, lack of knowledge of how to support people in their career development.

Interviews with these recruiters revealed that the terms career advancement (promotion), career management (mobility), and career development (coaching to integrate self-knowledge, education, and work context) had been used interchangeably in communications. This was a significant factor in creating different expectations among various sponsors. In particular, Human Resources was expecting to use promotions as the measure of career advancement, without regard for developmental interventions. Middle managers, as sponsors, expected to see individuals acquire skills as the primary measure of career development. Director-level managers, as sponsors, expected to see individuals acquire greater business acumen contributing to their longer-term career mobility. The recruiters' actual focus on supporting internal navigation with employee-driven skill building enabled individuals to move successfully laterally or advance one promotional step. This satisfied the Human Resources criterion for success, which was the only overtly expressed goal for the initiative. However, employees did not build the foundation for continued advancement along their paths (career development) or build an understanding of the business, which was essential to broader movement (career mobility) within the firm. Thus, the initiative failed to meet the unexpressed criteria for success of the managers and directors. In both of these cases, single occupational groups (engineers and developers) were served. Although these initiatives were intended to serve as pilots for broader future occupational inclusion, failure to define and align organizational objectives at the onset of the pilot resulted in cancelling the pilot after one year.

The two cases involving in-house trainers were beset with analogous issues. The trainers had significant functional depth of knowledge but little organizational knowledge or knowledge of individual development. Even though the trainers were effective in developing rapid skill-building offerings, they did not address the whole person—the critical interests, values, and strategic career planning components. Many key components were not addressed in these narrowly focused initiatives. While activity-level data (e.g., program participation) was favorable, successful placement into new roles was less successful. Training, because it is a popular form of employee development, had been confused with more broadly based career development. As in the previous two cases, narrowly defined departmental goals were achieved, but neither the individual client nor the broader organizational needs were surfaced, much less addressed. Within a year, both of these pilots were reabsorbed into the broader training divisions.

### Building Career Development Initiatives with External Resources

The second approach is partnering with an external provider to deliver services. There are varying types of partnering possible with external providers. One approach is for an organization to purchase a fixed or customized basket of services. For the sake of simplicity, this will be called the buy approach. This limited form of partnering is useful for a variety of event-driven services, including outplacement, exit interviews, and alumni management. The partnership, which may include long-time vendors and preferred providers, is limited because there is a clear boundary between the organization and the consulting firm. As a result, the bilateral flow of information between entities also tends to be limited, as is access to organizational sponsors.

Staffed with organization development consultants, career counselors, and trainers, this limited partnering approach is effective in helping many involuntarily transitioning employees. Confidentiality is assured. A variety of business partnerships, nonprofit organizations, and joint ventures between community colleges and private industry councils employed this approach in the wake of the 1990–1991 recession. The limited partnering relationship decision is driven by the length and quality of the vendor's relationship with the Human Resources department, service delivery capability, and the skills fit of the consulting firm's staff with the needs of the targeted population. Many of the outplacement firms have built effective, long-term relationships with organizations to provide transition services, but they have not manifested significant success in extending services into the developmental segment. Staff and management of client organizations continue to see these firms as outplacement providers and are concerned about the perceived message that partnering with these providers would send. None of the firms Erickson interviewed in 2004 used this form of partnering to provide career development.

The second form of partnership is more strategic. In this approach, the consulting firm embeds resources within the client organization. This means the development facilitators deliver workshops, career counseling, and coaching services with an understanding of the organization's human resource strategy, its career paths, and its role competencies. Because this involves building a shared understanding of the environment and the services to be delivered, this type of collaboration represents a higher level of organizational commitment. Staffing is accomplished primarily through career counselors, many of whom routinely offer virtual or in-person training to supplement individual counseling. Delivery through a third party ensures both neutrality and confidentiality, two critical elements correlated with long-term success. Offering the services through the employer is a tacit endorsement of these services and a manifestation of organizational commitment. The contextual knowledge gained through onsite work enriches the quality of counselor-client engagement. Kaiser Permanente, a leader in the managed healthcare industry, serves as a robust and current example of this approach as described in chapters 4 and 9.

This in-house partnering approach allows the career counselors to readily leverage their counseling competencies as they master the nuances of the client's organizational culture, role competencies, and career paths. In the short term, there are two learning curves counselors must master. The first is building an understanding of the specific job paths within the client organization. Since many organizations employ competency-based career ladders, this challenge is often quickly mitigated. For organizations that do not use competency-based approaches, counselors must build an understanding through job analysis. The second learning curve involves mastering the nuances of the espoused versus the enacted culture of the organization. While this is a longer learning curve, it puts the counselor in the same position as any recently on-boarded employee. Ability to assess and act on this information generally resides in the organizational development function within the organization. Optimally, there is an informal relationship between organizational development and career development as many synergies arise from their complementary knowledge. Because change is an individual decision, whether it is career advancement or the desire to redeploy internally before, or in conjunction with, organizational restructuring, the counselors' intrapersonal and interpersonal understanding makes them optimally suited to meet a wide variety of needs over the longer term. Indeed, data from the 2004 research indicated that firms using this approach had higher client usage rates, significantly greater longevity (several contracts had been in place more than a decade), and higher client satisfaction rates.

Organizations specializing in career development consulting generally employ a variety of career development or organizational development frameworks, and have the capacity to generalize knowledge gained from pilots to broader-based, organization-level initiatives. There are boutique firms that specialize in different aspects of the career development process, specialize within a market space (for example professional services), or leverage expertise within a firm. They tend to partner with a small number of customers over a longer time horizon and offer a variety of development-related services.

*Comparison of Approaches*

A comparison of the in-house, limited partnering, and strategic partnering approaches yields interesting insights and underscores important implications for career development initiatives. Internally staffed initiatives can be effective when the need is narrowly defined, the target is a small and homogenous employee population, and the timetable is aggressive, for example one year or less. When staffed with skilled professionals whose competencies can satisfy the immediate need, defined tactical goals can be successfully accomplished. Unit or departmental support may suffice for this type of engagement. Yet the conditions that enable short-term success sabotage the ability of these internal initiatives to be successful over a longer time horizon. A key reason the four internally staffed initiatives failed was because they lacked the breadth of knowledge and skills necessary to meet expectations. The absence of a framework, a robust needs analysis, or career development knowledge would have made expanding these pilots extremely difficult.

The second approach, limited partnering, affords some benefits. A key advantage from the organization's perspective is on-demand access to highly skilled professionals who are needed only on an intermittent basis. By engaging in long-term relationships with the same providers, the organization minimizes internal time and resource commitment while maintaining desired levels of service for employee groups, for example, transitioning of former employees. As with the internally staffed approach, organizational commitment is generally confined to the human resources function. The intended time horizon for these initiatives is intermittent over several years. Generalizing the initiative across the organization may not be a goal for these engagements. Attempts to extend service offerings may meet internal organizational resistance. For example, Erickson's interview data with more than 80 decision makers in 40 Fortune 500 firms indicated that these firms were reticent to use branded outplacement firms for development purposes. All respondents indicated their firms used different vendors for outplacement, career development, and leadership development.

The strategic partnering approach most effectively combines internal knowledge with specialized external expertise. Employees benefit from developmental coaching and consulting from highly skilled professionals. The organization benefits from leveraging this external expertise within the context of the organization. Organizational commitment may extend beyond Human Resources and include senior leaders as a shared business context is created. Frameworks and processes are sufficiently robust to generalize the initiative across the organization. The development or customization of client-centric processes, tools, and service offerings increases the alignment between individual development and organizational strategy. When this alignment is an explicit goal of the career development initiative, it is more likely to bring organizational benefits (Elsdon 2003, 147–57). This may represent a new frontier in organizational career development. None of the 40 firms contacted in Erickson's 2004 study had attempted to use this approach.

## DEFINING AND IMPLEMENTING CAREER SERVICES

Having examined the organizational context for implementing career services, and the implications of different structural approaches, we will now look at components that are part of this delivery. Although the specific components chosen, and how they are delivered, will depend on the organization's objectives and culture, there are some general principles to consider:

- Blending individual and group delivery
- Integrating in-person and virtual delivery
- Addressing institutional support from managers and the organization
- Building a repository of career-related knowledge
- Linking to educational institutions
- Identifying and securing the skills needed for implementation

Each item brings specific choices and opportunities as follows.

### Blending Individual and Group Delivery

On the one hand, decisions people make about their career development are intensely personal, balancing multiple individual life choices and values. Examples include the balance between income and time commitment, or the balance between living in aesthetically pleasing locations and having access to employment opportunities. On the other hand, choices about career development take place in, and intersect with, multiple communities, including those of family, organization, or professional institution, inherently recognizing the importance of interdependence introduced in chapter 1. Furthermore, natural personality attributes may lead to a preference for a more reflective, personal engagement in career related discussions, a more communal discourse, or an integration of the two. Consequently, both because of the nature of career-related decisions and varying personal preferences, delivery of career services needs to support an individual in more contemplative aspects as well as with communal engagement.

In doing so, there are a number of factors to consider:

- Responsibility for career development resides primarily with the individual, supported by managers who ideally will listen and encourage, and supported by the organization that provides a framework and resources within which development occurs. The authors have observed that feedback from clients receiving career services strongly reinforces this division of responsibility. Such a division of responsibility requires an approach that honors and encourages personal decision making within a supportive organizational framework.
- Widely varying rates of career change need to be accommodated, from the immediacy of rapid redeployment to gradual reassessment of direction and

purpose, recognizing that emotional intensity will vary significantly according to the nature and rate of change.

- The organizational culture and the predominant attributes of the workforce as outlined earlier in this chapter need to be taken into consideration.

With this in mind, effective delivery of career services is built on a foundation of experienced career counselors/coaches providing individual interaction and group facilitation. These individual and group sessions cover a wide range of content areas, from building self-understanding with the use of appropriate assessment instruments (a comprehensive review of such instruments is provided by Whitfield, Feller, and Wood 2009) to helping individuals progress in an organization. A blended approach that combines group delivery with individual preparatory or follow-up sessions can provide an effective combination. One challenge that may arise is the need to balance a focus on building career development skills with organizational imperatives for general skill development, for example communication or leadership skills. Protecting scarce career delivery resources, while honoring such additional organizational needs, requires ongoing adjustment and judgment.

### Integrating In-Person and Virtual Delivery

In-person delivery of career counseling services is particularly effective and efficient when the served population is readily accessible. When geographic reach is broad, for example with international locations, virtual delivery can provide a sound complement. Virtual approaches can include the use of delivery platforms such as Go-to-Meeting or Go-to-Webinar that allow visual and audio connection, in addition to providing for recording of events that can then be accessed at any time. Blending both direct and virtual contact also allows participants to select an approach that best matches their availabilities and preferences. Virtual tools complement, rather than replace, in-person interaction. Meister and Tonkin's 2009 study confirms a preference of the generations active in the workforce today, including Millennials (born between 1977 and 1997), for learning though direct personal contact, either in individual or group settings.

### Addressing Institutional Support from Managers and the Organization

While acknowledging that the primary responsibility for development is with the individual, we also emphasize that managers and the organizational support infrastructure are critical elements in encouraging both initial participation in career development activities and continued engagement. Incentives for managers to support the development of their direct reports can include incorporation of development of others into performance objectives and performance management processes. This demonstrates that the organization values such activities. Also important is educating managers about how to have effective development conversations. This includes how to listen well, how to access resources and build links in the organization, and how to construct a meaningful development plan that acknowledges individual aspirations, is linked to organizational realities, and includes appropriate development activities. Career counselors can play an important role both in coaching managers in their development activities with direct reports, and in helping individuals understand and navigate around structural barriers to development in the organization, where they exist.

Providing organizational support means allocating needed resources for career services, eliminating parochial perspectives that create internal barriers to individual movement, and providing access to information about openings and opportunities. It may also include implementing one of the many online performance, development, and succession planning systems (for example, see Business Decisions Inc., http://www.business decisions.com/) that assist people in identifying competencies needed to pursue a particular path.

### Building a Repository of Career-Related Knowledge

Career services provide a valuable window to opportunities in the organization and resources that are available internally and externally to support development. This information is often effectively delivered through an internal Web site such as that described in chapter 4. It is frequently linked to other Human Resource departmental information systems, with the Web site including resources such as the following:

- Financial support resources for educational activities
- Access to assessment instruments
- Access to networking and mentoring resources
- Descriptions of career paths
- Compilations of related Internet resources
- Availability and access to stipends that support time spent in educational activities
- Information about relevant educational institutions

### Linking to Educational Institutions

Educational institutions support development in a variety of contexts:

- Traditional academic credit programs
- Continuing education activities that may lead to certificate programs

- Academic credit programs through assessment of prior learning and practical experience
- Recognition of accumulated knowledge through testing processes

Career services can be an effective window and then a bridge to educational institutions. Important roles include information gathering and dissemination, making personal contacts, and providing approaches such as an online portal connected to an educational institution and tailored to employees of the organization. More information about the relationship between organizations and educational institutions is provided in chapter 3, recognizing that engagement in educational activities can occur individually or through cohort programs developed by an organization.

### Identifying and Securing the Skills Needed for Implementation

Successful implementation of organizational career services requires a combination of career counseling and coaching capabilities for both individual and group delivery as described earlier in the chapter; organizational savvy and interpersonal skills to understand, interpret, and address organizational needs; project management skills to guide overall direction, establish a supportive environment, and ensure that learning transfer occurs; and skills to create a support infrastructure that facilitates communication and provides the ability to effectively and efficiently track progress. This is a broad-ranging scope of capabilities that includes interpersonal and communication skills, content know-how, and technical capability. Identifying responsibilities and skill needs for the roles of career counselor/coach and project manager and for the activities of infrastructure development and customer relationship development provides additional insight.

- Career Counselor/Coach
  - Career counselors/coaches need to bring expertise in these areas:
    - Program design and development to build the content and information base to deliver services. This may include gathering and organizing information about learning and development resources, analyzing and synthesizing information about career pathways, reaching out to external partner organizations, and partnering internally to develop Web-based resources and workshop content.
    - Individual career counseling/coaching and workshop facilitation. This includes administering career-related assessments, providing confidential support to clients in wide-ranging career-related development areas, providing clients with support during transitions, supporting clients in leveraging opportunities and resources, facilitating workshops, and contributing to the development and monitoring of metrics.

- Ongoing organizational needs assessment and partnering. This includes creating and administering processes to determine and prioritize organizational needs related to career services, building and maintaining relationships within the organization, and planning and facilitating outreach activities to engage clients and enlist support from managers.
- Career counselors/coaches need a minimum of several years' experience to build these needed skill sets, coupled typically with an advanced degree in career development, counseling, or a related field. They also need to possess computer literacy, strong communication skills, and organizational skills given the many interfaces that need to be maintained. Prior experience in a business or organizational setting is a major asset.

- Project Manager
  - Project managers need to bring expertise in these areas:
    - The ability to recruit, lead, train, and inspire the career counseling/coaching team. This includes strategic insight to understand and anticipate organizational needs related to career services; interpersonal skills to build and deepen relationships; in-depth knowledge of the career field to provide informed guidance to the team; analytical skills to contribute to metrics deployment and interpretation; and communication, organizational, and technical skills to guide the team and facilitate transfer of learning.

- Infrastructure Development
  - Infrastructure development includes the ability to deploy online database systems to capture broad-ranging metrics that guide the evolution of career services, provision of a communication infrastructure to support information capture and content transmission and delivery, and support capabilities to address administrative aspects.

- Customer Relationship Development
  - Whether career services are delivered by a third party, an internal group, or a combination of both, they are delivered for a customer within an organization having performance expectations and objectives. Establishing multiple, effective communication channels to initially define delivery expectations, track and communicate progress, and adjust and evolve as needed are important elements in ensuring successful ongoing delivery.

Bringing these skills together to add significant value, in a manner that is fulfilling for those involved, is supported by the identification and adoption of effective metrics to measure and inform progress.

## MEASURING PROGRESS

Sometimes myths shroud metrics, perhaps suggesting that they are the domain of esoteric specialists with mysterious brews of boiling metrics pots. Nothing could be further from the truth. Metrics are readily accessible to all; they are simply measures that show progress. They are simple, natural extensions of organizational processes based on logic and common sense. They help guide decisions. With career services, measuring progress informs both client interactions and value contributed to sponsoring organizations by addressing questions such as the following:

- How are career resources used, and what adjustments might be needed?
- Who is engaging with the services, and how does this match workforce demographics?
- Why are people engaging, and what does this mean for future program emphasis?
- What actions are people taking, and how do those actions match the objectives of the services?
- How do people perceive the effectiveness of the services, and what does this mean for the future?
- What are career services outcomes, what is the value contribution and how does this compare to costs?

Insights gained from answering such questions, linked to the driving forces for establishing career services, are critical in securing ongoing support for needed resources. For example, an earlier study (Elsdon and Iyer 1999), which examined career services at Sun Microsystems, demonstrated significant financial benefit to the organization from reduced attrition, one of the driving forces for providing career services. This was an important factor in deciding to continue service delivery. Today, online databases simplify the gathering of information about service delivery from widely dispersed geographic locations. They also make timely access possible. Such measurement, applied to career services, is built on the following core principles:

- Measurements are timely and, where possible, continuous.
- Anonymity of client participants is protected.
- Measurements are linked to key organizational outcomes.
- Measurements provide the ability to look back in time, describing what has happened, and to look forward to predict and prescribe what will happen.
- Measurements are tailored to the needs of the intended audiences; for example, they might address a particular geographic region when provided for local staff, or they may be aggregated for those with overall program responsibility.

In looking at structuring measurements by examining recent practice, it is helpful to first establish an organizing principle, as shown in Figure 5.1, so there is a structure into which the measurements fit.

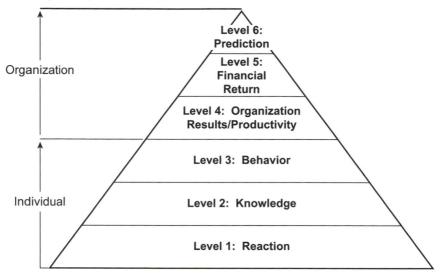

Figure 5.1.   Framework for characterizing measurement

   This figure is based on a four-level measurement framework outlined by Kirkpatrick (1998), extended to a fifth level by Phillips (1997), then to a sixth level by Elsdon and Iyer (1999), and applied to career services here. The first three levels address measurements focused on the individual, where level 1 measures individual reaction and planned action (sometimes know as a smile sheet) to a particular development activity; level 2 measures changes in knowledge, skills, and attitudes, for example, how to interview effectively; and level 3 measures changes in behavior, for example, engaging in educational programs.

   Levels 4, 5, and 6 are focused on the organization, with level 4 addressing organizational results such as productivity or reduced attrition; level 5 addressing financial return by comparing benefits to costs; and level 6 addressing prediction, the anticipated influence of future resources committed on future performance. Gathering and interpreting measurements is more complicated at higher levels as many factors in addition to career services can influence organizational outcomes. However, the higher levels of measurement are of most interest to senior leaders in organizations, and not surprisingly, in most organizations, information is sparse at these higher levels (Phillips and Phillips 2009). Addressing levels 4–6 includes comparing movement for people who have received career services with movement in a reference population (peers who have not received career services). This movement can be internal to the organization (e.g., developmental transfer, promotion, functional switching, redeployment), or external (attrition). Additional measures relate to changes in satisfaction and wage progression. The value created by the delivery of career services can be compared with costs of delivery to calculate financial return. Further perspectives on building such a framework are provided in the chapter 9 case studies.

In examples from recent practice at Elsdon, Inc., measurement of levels 1–3 occurred through four primary processes using online information gathering systems:

- Activity tracking by career counselors/coaches with respect to their time distribution, and their involvement in outreach and workshop engagements

- Measures of individual career counseling identified by career counselors/coaches to characterize attributes of individual clients and sessions. They include client demographics, reasons for client participation, and the actions that result from the sessions

- Client surveys, where direct quantitative and qualitative feedback is gathered from clients receiving individual career counseling/coaching, about the value of the sessions, knowledge gained, and the actions and behaviors that result

- Workshop feedback, where direct quantitative and qualitative client feedback is gathered about the workshop experience, its value, and its contribution to knowledge gained and behavior change

Figure 5.2 illustrates an example of activity tracking and client perspectives for career services delivered by Elsdon, Inc.

The top left chart shows the percentage of time spent in various activities by a career counseling team of nine full-time equivalent career counselors (at full staffing) each week from project initiation in June 2007 to September 2009 (the project is ongoing). Individual career counseling and group workshops accounted for the largest share of time, increasing from the early stages as the project became more established. Information gathering and outreach were particularly significant in the early project stages and continued to be important throughout. Significant time was spent in orientation and learning in early project stages, with the time needed for this activity declining as the focus moved to service delivery, although recognizing that learning is always present. Program administration, planning, and involvement in organizational workforce development committees increased from the early stages as the career counseling activity became integrated with ongoing workforce initiatives. Transfer of learning within the career counseling team was a consistent emphasis.

The benefits of these time investments are seen in the growing strength and capability of the team as illustrated in the chart at the upper right. This shows the results from client surveys, administered on a quarterly basis. These surveys are with clients from a broad range of occupations who first engaged in career services during each quarter shown. The surveys contain quantitative questions on a seven-point scale (seven is the most positive) as well as qualitative questions. Client satisfaction

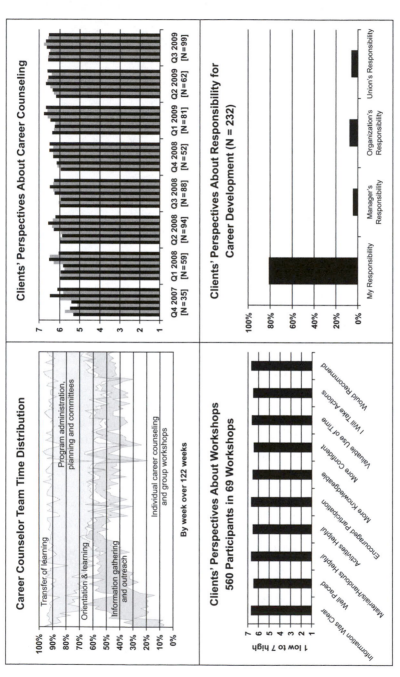

Figure 5.2. Examples of career counseling activity and client perspectives. Each sequence of bars in the upper right chart contains the following nine elements as client responses to survey questions, from left to right: 1. Services met my needs; 2. Helped me develop new ideas and options; 3. Career counselor knowledgeable about external resources; 4. Career counselor knowledgeable about internal jobs; 5. Career counselor knowledgeable about internal resources; 6. Career counselor knowledgeable about career planning; 7. Career counselor was supportive and encouraging; 8. Career counselor understood my needs; 9. Readily able to schedule appointments

indicators increased significantly over time, from an already initially high level, consistent with the career counselors' increasing depth of knowledge about the organization. The scores also became more consistent over time across the different elements. The strongly positive responses speak to the effectiveness of career services delivery, which was particularly encouraging given that the responses were obtained at a relatively early stage in the career counseling relationship with individual clients. The survey responses also point to areas of learning opportunity about jobs within the organization that help guide counselor development activities. Qualitative client comments reinforced the positive, quantitative feedback. Similar positive responses were evident from client evaluations of workshops. Aggregated responses from workshops are shown in the lower-left chart. The chart at the lower right shows how people assigned responsibility for their career development distributed among four categories: personal responsibility, manager's responsibility, the organization's responsibility, and the union's responsibility (this was a union-represented group). Personal responsibility dominates, an observation that was consistent across multiple quarterly surveys, underlining individuals' commitment to leveraging the resources of career services.

Figure 5.3 shows additional examples of client and career counselor perspectives about individual career counseling sessions.

The top two charts show direct client feedback aggregated from quarterly surveys, with the reasons clients seek career counseling (top left) and the effect of career counseling on clients' career views (top right). Clients were coming to career counseling primarily for developmental reasons as opposed to dissatisfaction with their current positions. In this case, career counseling was an investment in the future of the individual and the organization. As a result of receiving career counseling, clients reported being significantly more encouraged about their ability to pursue career opportunities within the current organization, find and pursue a career path, and engage in educational activities. Many reported themselves to be more confident in their current role. The career counseling process is supporting clients in strengthening their beliefs about their ability to engage successfully in their career development. This benefits both the individual and the organization.

The lower two charts speak to the paths forward clients take. The chart on the lower left shows the actions and outcomes clients self-reported in quarterly surveys. Clients' substantial interest in exploring opportunities within the organization, accessing educational programs for development, increasing satisfaction in their current roles, and interviewing for, and securing, new positions is noteworthy. The chart on the lower right is based on career counselors' observations about clients' paths forward from the final of a number of follow-up sessions. The paths forward chart underlines the effectiveness of the career counseling process in supporting clients' progress, particularly within the organization. All this information,

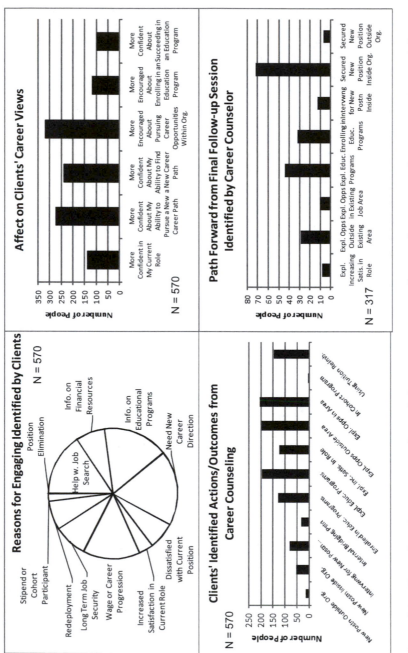

Figure 5.3. Examples of career counselor and client perspectives: why people engage with career services and the outcomes they experience

and additional metrics, are used for ongoing career counselor development and for communication with the sponsoring organization about career services and client perspectives. Now that we have examined the rationale for career services and aspects of implementation and tracking progress, it is helpful to look next at an overview of launching the services.

## OVERVIEW OF CAREER SERVICES LAUNCH

Prior to launch, building stakeholder consensus about the value of career services is an important step. Examples are addressed in chapter 9. Launching a career services initiative typically requires coordination across multiple groups within the organization and with service providers. It also involves building infrastructure to design, deliver, and communicate the availability and attributes of the services. The scope and scale of delivery influence the nature of this stage; for example, a simultaneous launch in multiple geographic regions is more resource-intensive than a single launch in one location. Regardless of complexity, the launch process can be considered in three phases: planning, design, and delivery. Each benefits from a detailed launch plan including milestones, timing, and responsibilities. Examples of components in each of the three phases are as follows:

### Planning Phase

In the planning phase the implementation timeline is finalized with each of the launch locations (if there are multiple locations), addressing the following elements:

- Identifying potential career counselor candidates, building as appropriate on prior contacts
- Liaising with launch locations to identify infrastructure needed—office and support facilities and services
- Clarifying the specific needs of each launch location to be addressed during delivery
- Establishing a draft implementation timeline for each launch location

### Design Phase

In the design phase, the elements needed to deliver career services are put in place. They include the following:

- Hiring career counselors for each location.
- Assembling materials to support the career counselors in their service delivery, for example, workshop materials. A shared online resource system can greatly facilitate provision of such delivery tools.

- Finalizing assessment materials to be used by the career counseling team, including online access as needed.
- Developing the foundation for metrics and reporting, including creating online systems.
- Instituting the needed infrastructure at each launch location (e.g., office space and computing equipment).
- Establishing administrative processes for transactional needs (e.g., expense and payment processing).

### Delivery Phase

The delivery phase involves the provision of services that include the following:

- Delivering individual career counseling on a confidential basis
- Finalizing and delivering group workshops on key topic areas
- Establishing needed repositories of information
- Participating in workforce planning and development activities
- Contributing to the design of online career resources for employees
- Building relationships with management and labor contacts to clarify and address evolving needs
- Building relationships with community and professional groups regarding educational opportunities
- Finalizing and implementing metrics and reporting, and capturing shared learning across locations (if there are multiple locations) to continuously enhance delivery
- Promoting career services and providing assistance in outreach activities to engage employees

The details of the launch process will vary by organization and launch location. Such customizing is an important step in securing ownership and support at the local level. As the launch unfolds, additional components will surface and need to be incorporated, including implementing and tracking individual educational and occupational profiles. A successful launch also involves continuing to reach out and engage those who can benefit from the services. In the next chapter, we explore such outreach and promotion, as well as additional aspects of implementation.

# CHAPTER 6

# Implementing and Carrying the Career Development Message

*Amy Lichty and Darlene Martin*

People in organizations want to make a difference by contributing their capabilities to the mission of the organization. Jaffe, Scott, and Tobe (1994, xiii) point out that people want more than higher pay and greater benefits; they want work that is meaningful and rewarding in a personal sense. Gallup's research on employee engagement found that newly hired employees are "enthusiastic, committed, and ready to be advocates for their new employer" (*Gallup Management Journal* 2002). The research also found that beyond the first year, the longer employees stayed, the less engaged they became. The opportunity in implementing a career development effort is to recapture this initial energy and desire to contribute in a way that allows each person to develop to their fullest potential. The value of career development is in helping employees align their talents with the organization's purpose.

This chapter will examine how to reach out effectively to people within an organization to communicate the benefits and value of career development processes, and it will explore the opportunities and challenges that accompany implementation. Engaging people in career development conversations means establishing a reason why this is important; sustaining their interest means creating ongoing individual value. The chapter will also address the needs of managers who carry both personal career development aspirations and the responsibility for supporting others in their development. With this in mind, we will examine a conceptual framework, how to apply this framework to career development in an organization, and how to assess progress.

## CONCEPTUAL FRAMEWORK

Valuable concepts taken from positive psychology will be introduced as they relate to organizational career development. Positive psychology is the study of human strengths and virtues (Sheldon and King 2001). It emerged out of the awareness that normal human functioning cannot be explained from a purely deficit or problem-focused frame of reference. The study of positive psychology, from which employee engagement and the strengths revolution emerged, looks at what makes people flourish in successful learning and workplace environments (Buckingham and Clifton 2001; Harter et al. 2006).

### An Appreciative Approach

When faced with an organizational problem that needs to be solved, what do most managers and employees typically do? Operating from a deficit approach, the natural response is, "Let's fix what's not working!" The repair tool kit consists of a four-step process:

1. Identifying the problem
2. Uncovering the cause
3. Defining alternative solutions
4. Creating an action plan

An alternative is the appreciative approach, which also has four stages (Elliott 1999, 3–4):

1. Appreciating the best of what is
2. Imagining what might be
3. Designing what could be
4. Delivering what is desired to be

Which approach is more compelling in the context of employee performance and development? To answer that, ask an employee to reflect on her professional development experiences. Was she motivated to develop a critical competency when her manager seemed to only point out what she was doing wrong? How was it different for that same employee when she was working for a manager who appreciated and acknowledged her natural talents and then challenged her with assignments where she could apply those talents? Although drivers of increased contribution vary, findings from past studies indicate that managers fall short in encouraging and rewarding their employees' use of talents (BlessingWhite 2008, 2). It is in strengthening the processes for development support and encouragement that there is much opportunity.

*The Positive in Action*

The appreciative approach, based on positive psychology, has been applied extensively to organizational consulting. This approach works under the assumption that in every organization something works. Change can be fostered by identifying what works and doing more of that which works (Hammond 1996). An appreciative approach has also been applied to professional and career development (Buckingham and Clifton 2001; Schutt 2007). The following example is a case that highlights the value of this approach in building workforce strength.

In an aerospace company, a midlevel manager asked an internal career consultant to deliver a briefing about career services; he wanted his employees to take responsibility for their development. When asked what he wanted as an outcome, it was a workforce that was growing and developing in ways that would enable people to deliver the unit's business goals. Knowing that the answer wasn't as simple as a presentation (an advocacy approach), the consultant asked the manager if he would be willing to gather his managers and over 200 employees and ask them (an inquiry approach) what would need to be present to better enable them to deliver the unit's goals. The employee input was then organized by themes and shared with the management team; then, a plan was designed that captured what was desired going forward.

When that manager first approached the career consultant, he was looking for a quick fix to concerns expressed by employees and for his desire to improve productivity. He discovered that he needed to listen—to his employees and his own leadership values. It changed his perspective about how he wanted to improve his unit. As a result, he inspired his management team to take ownership for creating an environment that encouraged employee participation in goal setting, professional development, and shaping their careers. Gallup Organization research (*Gallup Management Journal* 2002) substantiates that managers can increase employee engagement by first developing a strong relationship with them, which includes improved communication. Managers must also create opportunities and remove obstacles so employees can concentrate on what they do best. This includes building their talents into strengths by developing the skills and knowledge needed to contribute. Peter Drucker, in an introduction to the idea of appreciative inquiry, states it as "The task of organizational leadership is to create an alignment of strengths in ways that make a system's weaknesses irrelevant" (qtd. in Cooperrider and Whitney 2005, 2).

*Establishing Resonance*

Whether it's a senior executive communicating the company's strategy, a manager aligning the team's goals, or a Human Resource professional implementing a workforce development effort, it is important to pay attention to whether or not the message being sent creates resonance. Resonance, as applied to organizational dynamics, is defined by Cox and Liesse (1996, 40–43) as shown in Figure 6.1.

Rhetoric, on the left in Figure 6.1, is what is said and essence, on the right, is what is done. Cox and Liesse indicate that the greater the overlap between the two dynamics or circles, the greater the alignment of authenticity, and the more an organization can leverage its capacity to achieve. In organizations, resonance ideally occurs on multiple levels. For example, on a policy level, are human resource systems established to implement an organization's rhetoric to grow talent from within? If management states that an organization grows talent from within but external hires fill 30 percent of management and leadership openings, there is a mixed message. To create greater resonance, management would need to reevaluate and better align employee training, tuition reimbursement, leadership development, performance management, and career development policies and systems to help internal employees advance. On a leadership level, does a manager show sincere support for growing talent from within, or does a manager merely demonstrate required action? Notifying employees of job opportunities might exemplify required action, whereas sincere action might be characterized as reviewing the career goals of each employee and sponsoring advancement within each employee's profession or the organization.

Opportunities for building resonance can be found by regularly scanning for prospects to match the organization's essence—what is done—to

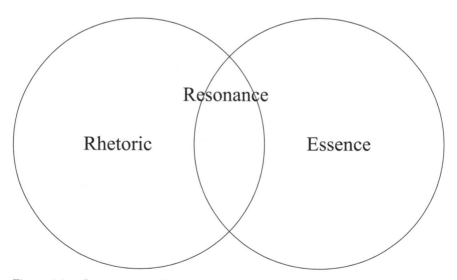

Figure 6.1.   Components of resonance

the organization's rhetoric—what is communicated. The aerospace manager scenario mentioned earlier is an example of someone who was building resonance around contributions and professional development with his employees. Complementary to this, also related to advancing a career development effort, is identifying those managers whose natural approach to development (essence) is consistent with the development agenda (rhetoric). In one division of this same organization, a career development consultant built a working relationship with a midlevel manager who was known as a development champion. This manager wanted to map the development planning process, hold her managers accountable for development conversations, and track the progress of employees' development plans in her unit. Because of their working relationship, the career consultant was asked to be a key member of the project team chartered to design the process and the computer system needed to support development. When the system design was sufficiently advanced, it was presented at a senior staff meeting, resulting in a decision to implement the system division wide. The company president then learned about the endeavor and wanted to know if it could be applied company wide. Expanding resonance for development can be as simple as recognizing those leaders who show sincere support for growing talent from within and marketing their success as a best practice for the organization.

## OPTIMIZING THE EFFORTS

Four important methods for optimizing organizational career development efforts will be covered in this section:

- Align agendas
- Communicate the value of career development
- Work with resistance
- Build strategic partnerships

### Align Agendas

An important step in ensuring that a career development effort succeeds is aligning career development goals with organizational priorities. In the context of the appreciative approach, each goal can be considered as an ideal state. In creating a plan for the future, it is also helpful to understand the real state or current performance level, and then determine which organizational priorities can be influenced. This is followed by assessing the current strengths of the career development effort and defining how to build on them to move to the ideal state. Amplification of the strengths creates synchrony between the real state and ideal state.

The following is an example of this process.

*Organizational Priority:* Increase capabilities to compete effectively

*Career Development Alignment Goal:* Leverage organizational knowledge to increase responsiveness

*Specific Actions:*

1. Modify and re-launch a mentorship database for just-in-time, short-term, mentoring focusing on transfer of knowledge through an expert connection

2. Expand a virtual career center by creating an online library of the center's physical self-development resources, categorized by the organization's critical competencies

3. Implement an online multirater competency assessment with intact work groups as a way to align individual development goals with the unit's team goals

A similar strategy can be applied to fill gaps wherever the ideal state and real state are different. In another example, one way an internal career consultant addressed this in an aerospace company was to recognize a need to help managers communicate organizational priorities and establish performance goals with their employees. This complemented the individual development process. Accomplishing an organization's critical priorities is dependent on commitment by employees at every level. "While goals must flow through the organization, they can't be communicated in the same way to everyone" (Haughton 2004, 6). In the example, there had been no prior forum for managers to explain unit goals to all employees.

A goal alignment workshop was developed by the career consultant that covered the following topics:

- Overview of the goal alignment process
- Review of the organizational priorities for the year
- Manager's presentation of the unit's goals in relation to the division and organization goals
- Discussion of what individual contributors can do to influence the unit's goals
- Review of how to write S.M.A.R.T. (Specific, Measurable, Achievable, Results-oriented, Time-bound) goals
- Timeline for submitting individual contributor goals

Prior to the workshop, the career consultant met with the manager and discussed how to translate the unit goals into objectives for the unit. The manager's presentation and the discussion that followed helped build common understanding. The workshop design also included a breakout exercise for employees to brainstorm what they could do to contribute to those objectives, reinforcing this as a team effort. Whether it is an individual contributing to the team's goals, career development staff contributing to the organization's goals, or unit goals linking to organizational priorities, the appreciative approach builds upon strengths, while reducing gaps, and in so doing moves the organization toward an ideal state.

### Communicate the Value of Career Development

With an overload of information in the workplace, it is critical to find innovative ways to communicate the value of career development efforts. This begins with determining the career development brand. Branding includes the qualities that will draw the target audience, in this case employees and managers, by creating a connection with them. While management will want to know the practical benefits such as reduced attrition of valued employees, branding is also about making a visceral connection. Bedbury points out that "the most successful brands consistently evoke positive feelings over time" (2002, 15).

Branding the value of career development includes the following components:

- Take an inside view
- Take an outside view
- Use multiple methods and media
- Follow up with tangible deliverables

*Take an Inside View*

Creating a career development brand begins with taking an inside view. What does the career development effort stand for or represent? What are the benefits of career development that others need to understand? In an aerospace company, the philosophy for professional development was a commitment to encouraging employees to grow and develop in ways that would contribute to, and maintain, high performance levels. To increase competitiveness in a global market, the organization needed employees who were continuously expanding the breadth and depth of their skills and talents. Professional development became a cornerstone of the business strategy; it was based on a shared responsibility for development that involved employees, their managers, and the organization.

*Take an Outside View*

Taking an outside view means defining who the customers are as well as their unique needs. By identifying gaps, it is possible to determine what the organization does best and how career development can address what is missing. The employees of the aerospace company, through an employee opinion survey, indicated that the organization didn't provide sufficient opportunities for them to develop their careers. Addressing both the needs of the organization and the employees, the brand position for the Professional Development Center (PDC) was defined as follows:

1. Helping employees become self-directed and grow in ways needed by the organization
2. Supporting managers in the development of employees
3. Implementing organizational systems that reinforce the selection, development, and retention of employees and contribute to the company's success

All marketing materials, including the logo, were designed to convey the synergy between the organization and employees. Literature that distinguished the roles and responsibilities for each stakeholder also emphasized the intended message of shared partnership.

### Use Multiple Methods and Media

Once the brand is created, it is essential to use multiple methods and media to inform people and make certain the effort succeeds. For example, to attract attention and let 9,000 employees know about the PDC, the company president and other prominent supporters were videotaped. Then video kiosks were built and rotated from building to building, allowing the message to reach all employees within a relatively short period of time. In addition, briefings were delivered to managers at all levels because their buy-in and support was an essential ingredient of the overall success of the professional development effort.

### Follow Up with Tangible Deliverables

A major communications initiative must be followed with tangible deliverables; examples in this case included lunchtime workshops, individual career counseling, the PDC library, and professional development available to all employees at their desks through the PDC Online (the virtual center). These deliverables need to address the most effective ways to connect with people. For example, in a study on a related topic, when employees were asked to rate the helpfulness of various career resources, the top six, in order of preference, were career coaches/consultants, career coaching training for managers, training/workshops, temporary assignments/secondments to a position, job postings, and assessments for development planning (BlessingWhite 2007). Interviews conducted for this study further revealed the theme that advice and insights, not information by itself, provided important career influences.

It is critical to capture early successes so employees can answer the question, "What's in it for me?" Posting success stories on the Web site, hosting brown bag sessions, and using an e-newsletter are examples of using varied media. Since people have different learning styles, some employees will benefit from touching a keyboard, others will seek information by talking with people, and still others will want to read about successes. In one ongoing career services project conducted by Elsdon, Inc., word of mouth was the most significant means by which people learned about the service, accounting for 33 percent of the responses from 473 clients over eight quarterly surveys. Word of mouth continued to grow in importance over time, averaging 30 percent in the first four surveys and 38 percent in the second four surveys. Continued emphasis on communication, advertising, and word-of-mouth information is needed to make brand value pervasive in an organization.

The following are strategies to keep an organization informed about a career development initiative:

### Phase 1—Implementation

- Design marketing materials consistent with brand—posters, brochures, postcards, flyers, give-away products
- Hold a kick-off event—advertise via video kiosks, mass email announcements, and marketing materials
- Develop and deliver briefings for executives, managers, and employees
- Create the basics of a career planning Web site—include the Web address in all advertising materials

### Phase 2—Growth

- Produce an annual report for executives and managers
- Hold a company-wide career development event
- Partner with Human Resources and other departments for outreach events
- Create new briefings for executives, managers, and employees to address progress and enhancements
- Expand the career planning Web site—hold information sessions to describe new features
- Contribute articles for a company newsletter
- Deliver programs to internal employee groups

### Phase 3—Maintenance

- Continue the strategies implemented in Phase 2
- Send informational emails to target groups—for example: career development practices for managers, study strategies for employees using tuition reimbursement programs

- Create an exhibit booth to promote services and programs—take this to locations and buildings where employees work, exhibit at events such as internal conferences
- Publicize new programs

Promoting the career development effort includes communicating the business case, educating stakeholders about the process, and publicizing the services and products. This is a continual process, not just an event (Leibowitz, Farren, and Kaye 1986, 241–54). An ongoing marketing strategy will attract more participants, create greater stakeholder engagement, and strengthen the organization's commitment to career and workforce development.

### Work with Resistance

No matter how much is communicated about the value of career development, there will be those who will resist the introduction of something new. Kotter and Schlesinger (2008, 2–5) found that the four most common reasons why people resist change are as follows:

1. Not wanting to give up something of value
2. Misunderstanding the change and lack of trust
3. Conviction that the costs outweigh the benefits
4. Low tolerance for change

Nevis (1987, 60–61) points out that there is much ambivalence regarding change in any system. Knowing how to approach those who resist is critical to engaging the organization. When the ambivalence is seen as normal, then there can be great value in heightening awareness for the individual or organization of the forces for and against the change. When there is resistance to the career development effort, it is important to understand what people are thinking and feeling rather than ignoring that resistance. The goal is to help resolve the dilemmas that underlie the ambivalence. This applies both to implementing an organizational career initiative or career progress at the individual level.

Let's look at this first from an individual perspective. "To engage people in a joint inquiry at such times is to enact one of the most powerful forms of participation" (Nevis, Lancourt, and Vassallo 1996, 100). Joint inquiry begins with listening. Until the origin of resistance is understood, an individual may remain stuck in a pattern of attempting rather than progressing. For example, a person knowing he cannot progress in an organization without more education, and yet is resisting going back to school, may unconsciously be frightened of the prospect of attending school. Understanding this and working toward bringing awareness about the ambivalence can help an individual work with, rather than against, his resistance.

Kegan and Lahey (2001, 84–92) identified the subconscious conflict as a competing commitment that is inconsistent with the stated commitment. They recommend taking steps, such as the following, to create a break-through:

1. Diagnose the competing commitment. This is what the employee is doing or not doing to keep the stated commitment from being realized. For example, in the case of the individual just mentioned, instead of applying to a bachelor's degree program, he continued to apply for positions that did not require a degree. The undermining perspective was a fear of not being smart enough to pursue a degree program. The competing commitment was not pursuing something if he thought he might fail.

2. Identify the big assumption. This can be discovered by creating a sentence stem that inverts the competing commitment, then filling in the blank. An example of a sentence stem the coach might ask is, "If you pursue something you think you might fail at…" Client response may be, "People will think less of me."

3. Question the big assumption. The intention is to help the person become more self-aware in the context of the big assumption without challenging the assumption. A valuable discussion is to have the person talk about how the big assumption developed and then explore the effect of believing in the big assumption.

4. Test and consider replacing the big assumption. By analyzing the circumstances leading to the assumption, the person can test the basis for it and experiment with behaving differently. For example, as a way of testing the big assumption, the individual signed up for a community college course in an area of interest. Afterward, he discussed this positive experience and discovered that the big assumption could be changed.

This approach is consistent with Beisser's (1970) paradoxical theory of change, which asserts that one must fully experience what is before recognizing all the alternatives of what may be.

Just as we need to listen to the individual, there is also a need to listen to the collective organization. Is there an underlying resistance that needs to be surfaced? Elsdon points out that leaders and human resources professionals need to listen "to the voices of the organization to gain an understanding of individual needs and the general themes that arise from these needs" (2003, 70). Organizational listening brings to light problems and opportunities; this is a requirement for designing interventions that will enhance organizational effectiveness and strengthen affiliation with each employee. An organization that has supported the education of employees in the past only to have star performers leave may show resistance toward career development efforts, particularly when reducing attrition of talent is a key organizational priority. Organizational listening, via employee surveys, can provide one component of this listening process and help define the basis for action. For example, an employee opinion survey helped an aerospace organization discover that people wanted resources to help them manage their careers. In a survey conducted two years following implementation of a career development initiative at that organization, the perceived value of the career development services and resources showed a significant increase (Lichty 2000). The career development effort made substantial gains in helping employees highlight their skill sets and grow their careers in the organization. Consequently, this organizational asset was featured as a key element of the recruitment strategy.

In their work on the theory of reasoned action, Ajzen and Fishbein (1980) suggest that behavior is affected by mind-set and the belief that positive results will occur. If this premise is put into practice, then framing attitudes about career development appropriately can contribute to greater individual and organizational acceptance. Below are examples of positive framing for career development services.

### Positive Framing for Career Development Services

Here are example components:

- Employees have greater self-awareness and are more informed about the organization.
  - They make better job choices.
  - They know how to identify organizational trends and career implications.
- More employees are in jobs that are a better fit.
  - They are more engaged; their interests match the characteristics of the position.
  - They are more productive; their skills match what is required to perform the work.
- Managers who develop their employees will attract good people.
  - Managers can build a reputation for investing time in employee development.
  - Employees will be drawn to the positions these managers oversee.
- Organizations that provide career development services create a workforce responsive to organizational and market changes.
  - Employees learn that career mobility goes beyond vertical promotions and includes enrichment in current positions, lateral moves, and the ability to position themselves for emerging opportunities.
  - The organization develops the reputation that it is a great place to work because there are opportunities for growth and development.

The organization, managers, and employees need to hear what can be achieved with successful career development services. Remembering the purpose of organizational listening as that of building understanding and consensus for action, career initiatives that emerge out of identi-fied needs are most likely to contribute to individual and organizational success.

### Build Strategic Partnerships

Our final method for optimizing the career development effort involves building strategic partnerships. For a career development effort to suc-ceed, relationships must be established at all levels and throughout the organization. The following approaches will be reviewed:

- Engage stakeholders at all levels
- Establish calculated trust
- Be present and available

#### Engage Stakeholders at All Levels

Engaging stakeholders at all levels was accomplished at one aerospace organization by inviting employees to help launch the organization's new Professional Development Center (PDC). Approximately 100 volunteers served on six committees and managed everything from designing the physical center to identifying and purchasing the multimedia library resources, creating an electronic library check-out system, developing the virtual center, handling contracts, and formulating a marketing plan. These volunteers came from many functions of the company, including facili-ties, business, engineering, information systems, and Human Resources, and from many levels, including administrative, professional, technical and managerial. The involvement of these volunteers not only produced innovative results, but the volunteers also became influential proponents of the PDC. When the PDC wanted to host a Professional Development Day, those volunteers were already supporters, staffing booths for their respective divisions and encouraging employees to attend. Over the years that followed the implementation of the PDC, the volunteers' names sur-faced frequently in relation to new projects and endeavors, reinforcing the value and importance of their early involvement.

#### Establish Calculated Trust

Calculated trust occurs when the displayed behavior of one person mirrors the behavior desired by another (Haughton 2004, 13). Examples of behaviors that lead to calculated trust include sharing the same val-ues, having the experience of being listened to, or speaking the same language. While most people prefer to spend time with others like them-selves, establishing relationships with those who are dissimilar requires more proactive strategies (Hill 1996). The three actions that the most successful professionals do to build relationships are as follows (Andreas and Faulkner 1994, 141–58):

1. Determine the goal for the relationship. For example, a goal for a relationship with a midlevel manager would be to have a positive experience that results in an invitation to conduct a briefing at a staff meeting.

2. Establish nonverbal rapport. Any behavior that can be observed can be matched, including facial expression, rate of breathing, voice tone, tempo, and pitch. Matching occurs naturally when two people are in rapport, and it can be used to consciously establish or increase rapport.

3. Produce positive feelings in others. The concept behind this step is that each of us represents something to others in their lives. In addition to deciding what kind of positive influence a person wishes to have on others, those good feelings must also be associated with the person's professional competence. Rapport alone will not sustain a relationship; being able to deliver on commitments is essential to long-term rapport.

Consider the following example that took place in a healthcare organization. A career consultant was about to deliver a workshop about exploring personality attributes to a team of nurses, when the clinic administrator preempted the meeting with news that staff hours were going to be reduced due to the economic recession. Can you imagine how little engagement there would have been if the program had been delivered without taking into consideration the emotional impact of the news? Rapport was established by acknowledging what was happening and focusing on the concerns in the group. Rather than delivering the workshop as planned, the consultant redesigned the exercises to help participants process the news while learning the intended concepts. By the time the meeting was over, the nurses had begun to make sense of the change as well as how their personality styles influenced their perceptions and decisions. The administrator was pleased that he was able to engage in discussion with the staff and better understand their concerns. Everyone was aligned. The career consultant had established enough calculated trust to lay the foundation for future individual, team, and organizational consultations.

### Be Present and Available

Engaging employees and managers in the career development process begins with being present. As mentioned earlier, outreach, marketing, and advertising are needed, including newsletters, brochures, business cards, and flyers, but the real connection is made one-on-one. Making assumptions that people will just come when a program is offered will not work. This statement is particularly true in a healthcare environment where work patterns can be unpredictable. Participation by healthcare workers in career-related activities may be delayed because of patient needs. In many organizations, especially in a healthcare setting, staff members have time-dependent responsibilities that must be accomplished. This can limit time availability for career-related activities. Organizational policies may need to be developed that encourage employees to take advantage of career resources available to them at work. A method used at one healthcare organization was to deliver services to employees at their work sites through career counselor visits. This approach consisted of regular counselor visits to each facility. It required flexibility and planning by the career counselor along with support from management. In this method of engagement, the career counselor visited each facility once a month. These visits were planned in advance, and a flyer was sent to the facility to advertise the visit. Each visit began by the career counselor making career rounds in each department to remind employees that the counselor was available for the day. Sometimes individual consultations were scheduled; at other times, a lunch time workshop was offered. There were also time slots reserved for drop-in appointments. Being present at the facility made it more likely that staff would take time to engage the counselor in discussions about career needs.

One area of flexibility needed for site visits has to do with time. In standard career counseling situations, the career professional might expect to have at least 45 minutes or an hour to meet with an individual. However, working in a medical facility means that there may be only 10 or 15 minutes available to talk with someone. Just a brief conversation can lead to emails, phone calls, and additional scheduled visits. With marketing in mind, the counselor or mentor can leave a brochure that provides a list of topics for a career discussion, including career exploration, back to school planning, updating a resume, and interview preparation.

By traveling with a laptop computer, the career professional can receive a draft resume, review it between appointments, and later meet with the employee to discuss recommended changes. Being at the medical facility does not mean that the counselor will experience down time between appointments; in fact, it is an excellent use of the counselor's time to work on special projects. Having openings on the career counselor's calendar makes it easier for employees to engage in just-in-time appointments. Being present at the facility also serves as a visual reminder of the services.

The site visit works best if the career professional remains attentive to what is happening in the facility. By checking in with the clinic administrator, the counselor can make adjustments if there is an emergency or if the facility is extremely busy. As the career planning visit becomes both accepted and expected, this creates an anticipation of services among the staff and inquiries about the timing of the next visit. The career development process is kept alive throughout the organization and is accessible to everyone. An added bonus to this approach is the opportunity to develop career champions among employees. These are staff members who see the value in career development and quickly inform others. If these champions know when a visit is planned to their facility, they will encourage others to take advantage of the services offered. This is one of the quickest ways to integrate career development into the mainstream of the organization.

## OPENING DOORS THROUGH MANAGERS

Although engaging clients in the career development process is a key goal, the path is made easier when managers are also engaged. Engaging managers in the career development process is both difficult and rewarding. While career professionals will be excited about career development, others in the organization may need to be convinced of its value. This section addresses the following topics related to engaging managers in the career development process:

- Will career development cause employees to leave? What's in it for me as a manager?
- Readiness to engage in change

Managers can be the best allies or present major barriers depending on how they perceive what is offered. The benefits of career development in an organization are many: improved decision making, enhanced self-esteem and confidence, clarified career direction, increased dedication to a job, and purposeful goal achievement. Such benefits lead to a more productive organization (Simonsen 1997). However managers may not be aware of these aspects.

### Will Career Development Cause Employees to Leave? What's in It for Me as a Manager?

Enabling managers to understand and embrace positive results that occur from a career development program helps move the employees and the organization forward. However, the message can be derailed by communication difficulties and skepticism. For example, if a manager feels that such a program might cause a good employee to leave, this can produce fear and anxiety. A question that may surface for managers is, "What if they engage in career planning, and they leave?" This question should be, "What if they are unhappy in their work, and they stay?" Ignoring the career needs of an individual in the organization may mean losing high performers while retaining those who are less effective. Productive, motivated workers are those most likely to look outside if they perceive a lack of internal opportunities. This is a strong argument for a career development program in the organization, and one that is particularly relevant to managers.

Consider the new manager who has just started to adjust to the responsibilities of a supervisory position. How might that manager react to adding a new career development program? Will it be just one more thing to oversee? The seasoned manager may also resent the introduction of a career program. If she knows little about career development, then she may feel threatened by lack of knowledge of the subject. Since the ability to regulate emotions may not be readily accessed by some managers, these emotions could be expressed in various ways: anxiety, anger, resistance, need for control, or passive/aggressive behaviors (Cherniss and Goleman 2001, 35). Anticipating how managers might react and being ready to respond is essential to engaging them.

### Readiness to Engage in Change

One way to approach the challenge of readiness to engage in change is to look for champions. As with the employees, management champions are the early adopters who are not coming from a place of fear. Early adopters have long been considered innovators or visionaries. The early adopters are those who see the benefits of a new product or idea (Rogers 1962). When the Nielsen organization devised a survey to identify early adopters for marketing purposes, they were able to measure related attitudes, finding, not surprisingly, that early adopters are both drawn to new ideas and energized to tell others (Wilke and Sorvillo 2004).

Early adopters of career development recognize an opportunity to support employees in progressing and enhancing alignment with their work. They are open-minded and can quickly see the benefits of a career development program. Early adopter champions will spread the word about the program. It is important to invite these champions to meetings, give them marketing materials, and ask them directly to help spread the word. Champions can come from different functional areas or groups and may exhibit a range of personal characteristics. Here are some examples.

### *Introverted Champion*

The quiet, introverted champion can be just as effective as the outspoken early adopter. One such person, an assistant facility manager at a healthcare organization, serves as an example of a quiet champion. She began early in the process to recommend that her employees take advantage of career development planning. She engaged her staff individually and identified those people who were motivated to move forward. A pharmacy technician was the first client. Because of the small size of the facility, the manager recognized that the pharmacy technician could not advance without leaving the facility. The technician was an excellent employee, one of the best. When the manager heard about the career development program, she immediately suggested that the pharmacy technician use the service. The employee received various career services—career coaching, resume writing, and interviewing skills—and was immediately hired at a larger pharmacy within the organization where the volume of work was as great as the opportunity for growth. The fact that she would lose one of her best workers to another facility did not concern the manager. She recognized the value of the program and of helping one of her staff grow and reach her career goals. She continued to be a quiet champion for career development and recommend the program.

### Extraverted Champion

Of course, the extraverted champion is also a huge asset. This manager can spread the word far and wide. It is important to make sure he has advertising aids and contact information because he will want to let many others know about the career development services. It is also important to be sure he has current and correct information. He can bring some of the more reluctant managers along. It is important to stay in touch with this champion, and share successes, so he remains current and engaged.

### Reluctant Adopter

Conversely, there are managers who are uncomfortable with the introduction of a career development program in the organization. These reluctant adopters may be afraid that a career program will upset the balance in the department (Gardner 2006, 99). They may see the program as a threat to their authority, or to the smooth running of their departments. They may even see it as something that could negatively affect their upward mobility. These managers may feel overwhelmed by the idea that they now have to concern themselves with not just their career development but the career development of others. Acknowledging their resistance and clearly outlining and explaining the positive benefits are important steps (129). As with the champions, reluctant adopters will react in different ways according to their personalities.

- Extraverted reluctant adopter. The extraverted reluctant adopter may openly question and express criticism about a new program. A clear understanding of the business case will help alleviate the extraverted reluctant adopter's fears. One success measure for managers is low attrition in their work groups. Upper management has an important role in reassuring the extraverted reluctant adopter that as employees move and progress, this will be reflected positively in the manager's performance appraisal and professional growth.

- Introverted reluctant adopter. Probably the most important person to identify is the introverted manager who does not understand or agree with the addition of the career program. She can be highly detrimental. She may be the one who quietly sabotages the program. It may take time to identify such a person who works quietly behind the scenes. One-on-one face time and proof of success can help to engage this person. Pairing this person with a quiet champion can also be highly effective.

In summary, managers need to hear that a career development effort will help them move toward their own career management goals as well as advance the objectives of the organization and the careers of others. The next section provides perspectives about growing and developing a career services initiative.

## GROWING AND DEVELOPING CAREER SERVICES

Once champions are identified and employees actively use the career services, what then? For a successful career development effort to move forward it must sustain energy, grow interest, and be inviting. New offerings are needed to continually engage employees and provide organizational value.

The following example shows how this evolution occurred in one healthcare organization and energized one aspect of career services delivery. Lunch time career workshops were not attracting employees as expected; employees were frustrated at having to use their free time. Participants would arrive late or leave early. With only 45 minutes available, little could be achieved. After discussions about this dilemma with the Human Resources director, a decision was made to include the career planning workshop as a part of regularly scheduled course offerings. Employees could sign up for the career planning workshop through the organization's in-house training system and request time off for training without using personal time. The structure of the career workshop was changed to incorporate all of the 45-minute modules into one 6-hour session. The response was strongly positive both in terms of participation and feedback. Indeed, a number of participants contacted the career counselor after the workshop for additional individual sessions. The structural change in delivery helped ensure the growth of the effort and further legitimized the need for, and an appreciation of, career development in the organization. The organization benefited from more informed employees with a clearer vision of how their knowledge, skills, abilities, interests, and values complimented the needs of the organization.

Growing programs, offering workshops, and seeing clients are important aspects of career services delivery. Another important aspect is integrating career services so that it contributes to an organization's business objectives. To integrate career development activities into an organization, offerings need to be developed in light of business objectives. Following are examples of building such connections.

### From Growth and Development to Integration

One of the major organizational goals of a career development initiative may be reduced attrition of employees through enhanced affiliation. This means supporting employees' growth in their current positions or supporting their progress to other positions. Where there is such a desire to grow employees internally, a plan is needed to facilitate the transition from rhetoric (talk) to essence (what is done). For example, at a healthcare organization call center, a team of individuals convened a work group for the purpose of equipping people with the skills needed to manage their careers and progress in the organization. The team's approach included defining career paths with identified skills corresponding to each level of progression. This process offered the organizational benefit of equipping people with an understanding of the capabilities required to fill needed positions, while addressing individuals' career aspirations.

An important consideration in growing employees from within is providing alternative career paths, such as administration and management, to complement those in a particular functional discipline. One component of such a managerial track is training in leadership skills prior to assuming such responsibilities (Rosenbluth and Peters 2002, 71). An example of such a program exists in the public health system. The director of one of the larger public health agencies in the southeastern U.S. recognized the need to develop future leaders. These leaders could come from many disciplines, for example doctors, nurses, clerical staff, technicians, and Human Resources. Potential leaders were offered the opportunity to take 12 leadership-based classes over the span of a year. This leadership academy provided skill building in areas critical for a new manager, including time management, project management, communication, team building, supervision, diversity, and the roles and responsibilities of leadership. After the first year, some individuals moved into management positions within the organization. Echoing the Cox and Liesse approach mentioned earlier in the chapter (1996), the organization was able to take the desire to develop and promote leaders from within (rhetoric) and provide training and support (essence), thereby promoting managers from within and expanding the resonance and authenticity of the organization.

## PRESCRIPTION FOR SUCCESSFUL IMPLEMENTATION OF CAREER SERVICES

Successfully implementing and carrying the career development message means communicating the benefits and value, and the opportunities and challenges, inherent in such a program. The checklists that follow can be used to guide and assess progress in implementation at various levels in the organization. Table 6.1 summarizes information for the executive and organization policy levels; Table 6.2 provides a summary for the frontline manager and individual contributor levels.

These checklists can provide a foundation for establishing goals and objectives in implementing career development processes. They are coupled with identifying champions to support the path forward, and with creating an image of success or mental rehearsal (Andreas and Faulkner

**Table 6.1. Checklist to guide and assess progress implementing career services for executive and organization policy levels**

| Executive level | Doing this well | Need to enhance this | Planning to do this |
|---|---|---|---|
| 1. Leadership communicates expectations for career development to managers and employees. | | | |
| 2. Leadership creates resonance by actively supporting the career development effort, for example, ongoing communications, briefings, and events. | | | |
| 3. Leadership models the desired behaviors by holding career discussions with direct reports. | | | |
| 4. Leadership values managers who develop their employees by recognizing their efforts. | | | |

| Organization and policy level | Doing this well | Need to enhance this | Planning to do this |
|---|---|---|---|
| 1. Career development is linked with other HR systems, for example, performance management, tuition reimbursement, recruitment, and affiliation building. | | | |
| 2. There is a commitment to grow employees internally. | | | |
| 3. Employees' education goals are integrated into staffing plans. | | | |
| 4. There is an ongoing marketing and communication strategy that builds understanding and enthusiasm for career development. | | | |

**Table 6.2. Checklist to guide and assess progress implementing career services for frontline manager and individual contributor levels**

| Frontline manager level | Doing this well | Need to enhance this | Planning to do this |
|---|---|---|---|
| 1. Managers are provided the skills to hold career discussions with employees that focus on current job development and future goals. | | | |
| 2. Managers engage in career planning and development with their direct reports. | | | |
| 3. Managers use assignments to provide learning and development opportunities. | | | |
| 4. The management team incorporates the outcomes of career discussions, including target goals and development needs, into staffing and training plans. | | | |

| Individual contributor level | Doing this well | Need to enhance this | Planning to do this |
|---|---|---|---|
| 1. Employees are provided access to career development tools and resources, including workshops, individual career counseling/coaching, and Web-based resources. | | | |
| 2. Employees have access to position descriptions, critical competencies, career paths, and job requirements; these tools are integrated into the career planning process. | | | |
| 3. Employees have written career development plans that allow for enrichment in their current positions when movement is not the goal. | | | |
| 4. Employees are given the opportunity to assess their manager's people development skills. | | | |

1994, 143). This mental rehearsal includes emphasizing the people and relationships needed to move forward effectively. Moving forward with a career development initiative is an opportunity to build competencies that include organizational consulting; human resources systems integration; training; career counseling and development; and administration of related resources, projects, and services. In building these competencies and delivering the services, workforce capability and flexibility are materially strengthened. This chapter has addressed organizational aspects of career development initiatives; in the next chapter and section, we will explore career development from the perspective of the individual, and the building of organizational support for mutual benefit.

# PART III

## Working with Individuals in Organizations

Treat people as if they were what they ought to be and you help them become what they are capable of being.

—Johann W. von Goethe

Remembering the stable where for once in our lives
Everything became a You and nothing was an It.

—W. H. Auden, "For the Time Being: A Christmas Oratorio"

# CHAPTER 7

# Acknowledging and Addressing Components of Career Fitness

*Michele DeRosa and Cynthia Brinkman Doyle*

Whether employee, contractor, or would-be entrepreneur, any member of the workforce must continually ask, "What do I need to be doing to be effective and viable in my work roles and sustain my career fitness?" Several factors contribute to career fitness from mind-set to skill set and from awareness of trends to readiness for transitions. In this ever-evolving world of work, the prevailing attitude must be one of being eager to stay and prepared to go. There are many indicators that support this realistic and proactive approach to career fitness.

From a macro perspective, the days are gone when workers experienced a single career using a static or narrow skill set, one company with the guarantee of upward mobility, an implied contract offering lifelong employment, and a countdown toward traditional retirement. Many strong influences affect our work lives today—technology, globalization, and pluralism, among others—creating both uncertainty and opportunity. From a micro perspective, employees may be making decisions about their careers with limited information: about the tasks and environments related to specific occupations; about the time, availability, and cost of training; about what skill sets and roles organizations consider to be critical to success going forward; and about the organizations' requirements for moving into those roles.

This chapter focuses on employees in organizational settings, offering a contemporary skill set essential for career fitness, a framework for understanding the natural cycle of career fitness, and strategies for organizations to assist employees in cultivating a mindset and developing a tool kit to be eager to stay and prepared to go. So, what does it look like when employees demonstrate being eager to stay and prepared to go, and what role does the organization play? Employees take primary ownership of their own career management by initiating the process and seeking out resources to assist in sustaining individual career fitness. It is to the benefit of organizations to offer internal resources that address these career fitness skills and influence the direction of employee career development, which might be viewed as the organizational contribution to individual career fitness. It is the intention of this chapter to discuss these individual career fitness skills and the strategies organizations can use to promote, develop, and strengthen these skills for employees. The framework for the chapter is as follows:

- A Contemporary Skill Set for Career Fitness
- Cycle of Career Fitness
- Shared Roles
- Connecting Stages of Career Fitness with Engagement Strategies

## A CONTEMPORARY SKILL SET FOR CAREER FITNESS

Though career management skills can be grouped in many ways, the following categories address the critical components for being eager to stay and prepared to go, as well as emphasizing the connection of these skills to workforce capability and flexibility. These categories also provide employers with a holistic framework or a sampling of activities to use in designing career development processes and programs. They include the following:

- Ongoing Assessment of Self and the Organization
- Awareness of the Influence of Trends
- Tools of All Trades
- Planned Happenstance

### Ongoing Assessment of Self and the Organization

Individual assessment generates valuable data for targeting and refining career direction. It illuminates the innate talents and developed skills an employee brings to the workplace and clarifies what is most important for work tasks and environments to be satisfying, or fulfilling. It also provides language an employee can use in promoting herself in the competitive marketplace, internally or externally. Important aspects of this skill set include these:

- Understanding the organization's culture and direction

- Assessing values and skills, and knowing how they align with the organization's goals
- Initiating feedback and development discussions
- Conducting effective career information gathering.

### Understanding the Organization's Culture and Direction

An aspect of being eager to stay is to know what is important to the organization, and then how an individual's role contributes to organizational goals. A solid understanding of how it's done around here better enables the identification and mining of development opportunities and navigation of a satisfying career path. Employees value organizations that use varied channels to communicate frequently about current priorities and direction. Storytelling and modeling of desired behaviors by leaders further assist employees in grasping and appreciating the current climate and ongoing culture.

### Assessing Values and Skills and How They Align with the Organization's Goals

It is important that employees take a periodic check of their values and interests to ensure continued alignment with the organization's focus and direction. In addition, a frequent skill review is necessary to stay on track with evolving industry standards as well as organizational priorities. Individuals can do this by meeting with a career counselor or using related Web sites, for example O*NET OnLine Help: Skills Search (http://online.onetcenter.org/skills/), http://www.authentichappiness.sas.upenn.edu/Default.aspx, www.quintcareers.com, www.skillscan.net, and www.strengthsfinder.com. Employers may also offer assessments related to competencies deemed valuable or necessary to the success of the organization; for example, visit http://www.shrm.org/TemplatesTools/AssessmentResources/SHRMTestingCenter/Pages/main.aspx, www.lominger.com, www.cpp.com, and www.envisialearning.com.

### Initiating Feedback and Development Discussions

The strategy of talking with supervisors, mentors, and trusted others about career interests is often a critical step for moving forward. Career conversations can go in several directions: increasing satisfaction in current role; building skills for future roles; exploring internal opportunities; testing the realities and trade-offs of a career change; and learning others' perceptions about strengths, reputation, and areas for improvement. From an organizational perspective, supervisors and managers will need career coaching feedback skills if employees are to be held accountable for initiating development discussions.

*Conducting Effective Career Information Gathering*

Making informed decisions as well as preparing for the next career steps depend on gathering and analyzing data from a variety of sources. Internal job qualifications and descriptions provide excellent data for assessing individual strengths and skill gaps as well as gauging what positions are critical to the organization. Recruiters and professionals in the field can also provide timely and targeted information, while shadowing and volunteering provide real-time observation or hands-on experience. Career decision making, networking, resume writing, and interviewing will all benefit from encouragement in spending time and energy on effective information gathering using resources such as www. online.onetcenter.org, www.rileyguide.com, and professional association Web sites.

## Awareness of the Influence of Trends

Staying alert to external factors also contributes to career fitness. Monitoring shifts in industry and business trends supplies critical data for making informed and timely career decisions. Important aspects of this skill set include the following:

- Keeping up with global business and industry trends
- Developing business acumen: knowing about the business of the business
- Recognizing, learning from, and leveraging diversity
- Anticipating change and managing transitions.

*Keeping Up with Global Business and Industry Trends*

The title of Thomas Friedman's book *The World Is Flat 3.0* (2008) may seem like a throwback, but in fact describes a future that is here now— global, Web enabled, and in constant flux, allowing for immediate communication and connection without geographic boundaries. Business being conducted globally affects individual employees in many ways, through for example, virtual communications from an international top management team, outsourcing of manufacturing and customer service, increased opportunities for assignments in different countries, and partnering on projects with international colleagues solely via technology. Acceptance of this reality and engagement in related activities will serve employees well in weathering potential career crises and in identifying and embracing development opportunities. For example, at a recent presentation by a talent management team from Zurich Farmers Insurance, geographic mobility was identified as a nonnegotiable consideration for someone to be included in the organization's leadership talent pool (Vanitzian and Croci 2009).

*Developing Business Acumen:*
*Knowing about the Business of the Business*

Employees need to know, and be able to articulate, how their daily work contributes to the organization's goals. Further, understanding of the functions that are needed for the organization to operate successfully enables employees to explore an array of career options within the organization and contribute most effectively. A good example of an employer making this information available is Kaiser Permanente's labor management partnership, which offers half-day workshops for employees on the company's financial and operational structure and diverse marketing channels (www.lmpartnership.org).

*Recognizing, Learning from, and Leveraging Diversity*

Many organizations today are rich with diversity. Workforce capability and flexibility are enhanced by a respect for differences in cultures, generations, learning styles, and abilities. Diversity within a team can add alternative ways of perceiving and approaching projects and challenges, enhancing the potential for creativity and innovation. One approach to foster diversity is reverse mentoring, in which younger employees mentor experienced leaders based on the strengths they bring to the professional relationship. Two such examples include Unilever USA's pairing of talented information technology staff to help senior leaders recognize the value of, and effectively use, technology (http://www.careerinnovation.com/upload/assets/CiDigitalGeneration-UnileverCaseStudy.pdf), and Thomson Reuters's program to encourage candid discussions so that executives will effectively incorporate diversity into their daily business (http://careers.thomsonreuters.com/LifeAtThomsonReuters/Default.aspx?id = 128). In addition, AOL offers an online tool called the Culture Wizard to strengthen employees' interactions with colleagues and customers from around the world as well as prepare them for international business travel and assignments (http://corp.aol.com/careers/career-development).

*Anticipating Change and Managing Transitions*

"We are not free to choose to avoid dealing with change," advises Max DePree, former CEO of Herman Miller (DePree 1992, 83). He continues, "The only thing to decide is how to deal with change once you create it yourself or once you find it staring you in the face" (83). Acknowledging that change is the most reliable constant is a necessary step to navigating the uncertainty of today's world of work. Then it is about developing the attitude and related skills that allow individuals to minimize the almost predictable angst while continuing to move forward. Changes in the external environment lead to feelings associated with internal transitions: loss, fear, confusion, and skepticism. Being flexible and alert to new possibilities allows for awareness of both the risks and the opportunities inherent in change and transition. This is a concept Gelatt and Gelatt (2003) refer to as "a paradoxical principle" encouraging a "both/and" vs. an "either/or" perspective (95). Employers can assist individuals in effectively dealing with organizational change in ways that range from frequent communications to supporting wellness activities to activities that strengthen employee engagement.

An example of strengthening engagement is Kaiser Permanente's support for employee participation in unit-based teams to address issues and implement improvements within departments (www.lmpartnership.org). The Southwest [Airlines] Way is about employees having "a Warrior Spirit, a Servant's Heart, and a Fun-LUVing Attitude" with related behaviors clearly articulated "to help us be a safe, profitable, and fun place to work" (see http://www.southwest.com/careers/culture.html). Additional suggestions about employee engagement are provided by Kaye and Jordan-Evans (2008).

### Tools of All Trades

Today, working smart is more valued than working hard; this means making timely and consistent contributions to an organization's goals and priorities. Many tools and strategies exist to enhance the ability to work smart, regardless of occupation or industry. Adding these to a professional tool kit will benefit both employee and employer. Important aspects of this skill set include the following:

- Staying on top of technology
- Managing projects or actively participating on project teams
- Honing customer service skills
- Engaging in lifelong learning

### *Staying on Top of Technology*

Whether a native of the digital age or an immigrant to it, computer skills are mandatory to function effectively in most work environments today. Organizations can offer basic computer training to employees who lack these fundamental skills, for example, keyboarding, understanding Windows, navigating the Internet, accessing email, and creating documents and spreadsheets. Training in more advanced computer skills and applications depends on the needs of the organization and the interests of the employee, including creating charts, tables, and graphs; designing and facilitating webinars; conducting specialized research; and leveraging social networking sites. For instance, Berkowitch, Kreitzberg, and

Kreitzberg (2009) assert that "smart organizations are using social networks for recruiting, marketing, and more . . . particularly relevant because they are cost effective and produce rapid results."

## Managing Projects or Actively Participating on Project Teams

With work increasingly driven by project accomplishment rather than routine task completion, knowledge of the elements of project planning is particularly valuable. Organizations can provide varying levels of exposure to resource allocation, project planning, and timeline and progress monitoring, either in relation to a specific project or as a discrete skill set. The Project Management Institute offers related training, events, and credentials (www.pmi.org) as do many university extended education programs.

## Honing Customer Service Skills

Most jobs require some competency in customer service, working either with external clients, internal clients, or co-workers—or all three. Elements of excellent customer service include, but are not limited to, active listening, problem solving, effective response, empathy, and efficiency. Hiring for strengths in these areas along with offering training, shadowing, and mentoring are ways an employer can develop employees while fostering outstanding customer service for the organization. Berry (1995) provides sound insights in this area.

## Engaging in Lifelong Learning

Learning is no longer relegated primarily to kindergarten through age 18, but is now more appropriately characterized as kindergarten through age 80 and beyond. Lifelong learning includes continuing education, professional development, self-study, and on-the-job development. Successful executives report that their most effective learning is gained from hands-on experience, other people, and formal training, in that order (McCall, Lombardo, and Morrison 1988). Employees need to stay attuned and take advantage of development resources offered by their organizations. Organizations that value employee development often provide a combination of learning components and resources that include tuition reimbursement, technical training related to the business, skill-building workshops, career coaching, and mentoring.

## Planned Happenstance

One career fitness strategy today is described by Mitchell, Levin, and Krumboltz (1999) as Planned Happenstance. This means being aware of chance happenings as they relate to career progression, even learning to create them, and then leveraging the opportunities that are presented. Planned happenstance enables an individual to proactively deal with workplace uncertainty and draws on the skills of curiosity, persistence, flexibility, optimism, and risk taking. Important aspects of this skill set include the following:

- Acknowledging uncertainty and embracing a both/and philosophy
- Discovering opportunities to connect, collaborate, and influence
- Demonstrating curiosity, persistence, optimism, flexibility, and risk taking
- Seeking growth experiences
- Envisioning varied roles

### Acknowledging Uncertainty and Embracing a Both/And Philosophy

By avoiding an either/or philosophy that excludes options prematurely and constructs arbitrary boundaries, it is possible to stay flexible and open to possibilities, enabling a both/and mindset. This serves individuals well in adapting to the reality of a constantly changing environment (Bright and Pryor 2008).

### Discovering Opportunities to Connect, Collaborate, and Influence

Development opportunities often result from building on networking relationships and connecting with others in person or electronically (Dikel 2009). Moving forward in a career involves sustained, solid performance, yet performance is often a necessary but not sufficient condition. Other factors include reputation and visibility. So supporting employees in related areas is important for the organization, for example, joining and participating in professional groups; requesting feedback from others; offering to be part of project teams; becoming a mentor or a mentee; participating in seminars, workshops, and conferences; and making presentations or writing for Web sites and journals. Organizational support can take various forms. For example, AOL offers business resource groups and employee interest groups to enable colleagues to meet and connect (http://corp.aol.com/careers/career-development). Funding can be made available for professional memberships, meetings, or conferences. Mentoring programs can also address this important career fitness skill.

### Demonstrating Curiosity, Persistence, Optimism, Flexibility, and Risk Taking

Curiosity, persistence, optimism, flexibility, and risk taking are skills associated with Krumboltz and Levin's (2004) concept of planned happenstance, employed to explore and evaluate opportunities, deal with related challenges, and take full advantage of planned as well as chance events. In today's dynamic and uncertain world of work, employers can reward this contemporary combination of qualities that assists employees to accept change and sustain productivity (Krumboltz and Levin 2004; Sharf 2005).

### Seeking Growth Experiences

Experiences that provide professional or personal growth do not always mean advancement; they do always mean learning and development. Ongoing development of knowledge and competencies, connecting with others, and being flexible and open to possibilities often result in opportunities and benefits that are unanticipated (Bloch 2005).

### Envisioning Varied Roles

Being clear about what is important through understanding of personal values, evolving interests, and preferred skills is important at each stage of the career path. This is supported by stepping outside occupational stereotypes and gathering knowledge of career options. The metaphor of a career ladder is no longer the only viable option; instead, think garden lattice or chessboard or ocean waves, all of which allow for movement in many directions. Upward movement in title, responsibility, accountability, and pay represents only one option. Movement across, around, or down, or working for an expert in a field, may offer excellent learning options and the opportunity to renew professional passion, facilitate a career change, or enable a necessary lifestyle shift.

Elsdon (2003, 40–41) summarizes well the intent of this section when he encourages employees to "know yourself, keep learning, stay flexible, champion change while searching the horizon, and dare to dream." So, with this contemporary skill set in mind, the next step is to look at the cycle of career fitness.

## CYCLE OF CAREER FITNESS

There is a cycle and associated components that are important in maintaining career fitness. Just as neglecting components of physical fitness can cause problems, such as obesity, illness, or untimely death, neglecting components of career fitness can derail a career through stalled progression or lack of mobility. The cycle of career fitness for purposes of this chapter includes the following components: Understanding of Self, Opportunity Identification and Exploration, Direction and Decision, Negotiating Favorable Entry, Integrating and Excelling in New Situations, Maintenance or Sustainability, and Transition.

## Understanding of Self

The first step in the cycle of career fitness is having a clear understanding of self. This understanding assists individuals in engaging in careers that fit their skills, values, interests, and personalities. It can become a foundation for realizing career satisfaction and achieving superior performance.

### Skills

Skills are developed and honed in a variety of settings that include work, volunteering, and educational and leisure activities. Transferable skills are portable from one job to another. Individuals too often acknowledge only the skills gained in paid employment and discount those gained from other aspects of life. For example, an individual who volunteers to chair and organize a Parent Teacher Association event, while working as a data entry clerk, might not recognize skills she is developing in leadership, event planning, and organization. Many individuals focus on the specifics of a job or task instead of considering the skills used to accomplish the job or task. A manager can help to identify skills in several ways: first, by asking an individual to write down current and past life roles; then, by having the individual record the skills used in those roles. For example, an individual might use budgeting, time management, and planning as a part of her role outside the work environment. Those skills could be transferred to an employment situation and harnessed by the employer. A complementary approach is to ask an individual to write a narrative of several achievements or accomplishments, and then identify skills that were a part of the narrative, paying particular attention to patterns of transferable skills. There are also instruments that can assist in clarifying skills, including Leadership Architect (www.lominger.com) and SkillScan (www.skillscan.net ).

### Values

Individuals may find employment that matches their skills and abilities but then experience dissatisfaction. This is often due to a conflict in values between the organization or job and the individual. Values can include areas such as service to others, monetary issues, ethical issues, recognition, and reputation. An organization's values can be expressed through mission statements or strategic plans; they are demonstrated through management behaviors. Values are fundamental to an individual's choice of occupation, job, or employer. Individuals can clarify personal values by exploring those areas they would not compromise and those that give meaning to their life. Managers can assist individuals in clarifying their own values (for example, through using an instrument such as Values

Driven Work, http://www.novaworks.org/valuesdrivenwork) and discussing similarities and discrepancies with those of the organization.

*Interests*

Interests are another important area of self-understanding. Table 7.1 provides a framework for categorizing interests in six broad themes (Grutter 2006; Grutter and Hammer 2005; Hirsh 1995): Realistic (Doers), Investigative (Thinkers), Artistic (Creators), Social (Helpers), Enterprising (Persuaders), and Conventional (Organizers).

*Personality*

An understanding of self includes an awareness of personality and how this significantly affects career choice. Building on Carl Jung's foundational work, Katherine Briggs and Isabel Briggs Myers, created the Myers-Briggs Type Indicator (MBTI), which has undergone many refinements since its original introduction. Personality type provides insights into activities and environments that people will likely find engaging and satisfying (Myers et al. 2003). The MBTI is best administered by a career counselor trained in assessment delivery; it is also accessible directly at www.mbticomplete.com .

*Strengths and Development Needs*

Finally, an understanding of self is essential to recognizing and capitalizing on strengths and identifying critical skill gaps in need of development. Individuals will benefit from seeking opportunities to address gaps as well as enhance strengths. Although formal education may be necessary in some cases, development can also be obtained through on-the-job training, apprenticeships, courses, mentoring, or other types of informal training. Organizations can assist in addressing these needs by offering training and by providing experiences and opportunities within the work setting. For example, a team project can offer an individual the opportunity to develop or enhance skills such as project management, leadership, organizational capability, creativity, or research practice. Encouraging project participation can provide excellent organizational support for individual growth and development.

## Opportunity Identification and Exploration

The second step in the career fitness cycle is gaining a solid understanding of opportunities that may exist within an organization or outside. The focus of this second step is external to the individual. Labor market

**Table 7.1. Framework for describing interests**

| Occupational themes | Common characteristics | Example occupations and activities | Organizational attributes |
|---|---|---|---|
| Realistic: "Doers" | Hands-on, building, repairing, working outdoors, product-oriented, practical, reliable, self-reliant | Mechanic, healthcare technician, computer networking and systems; outdoor activities, "popular mechanics" magazines | "Fix It" Show, not tell or teach Clear, measurable goals and deadlines Chain of command Few meetings/discussions |
| Investigative: "Thinkers" | Analytical, research-oriented, inquiring, rational, independent, insightful about ideas | Pharmacists, clinical lab scientists, environmental studies, mathematics; attending lectures, performing experiments | "Analyze It" Abstract ideas/concepts Complex problem solving Intellectual achievement Leaves details to others |
| Artistic: "Creators" | Self expressive, idea-oriented, creating or enjoying art/drama or music/writing, imaginative, intuitive | Advertising, corporate communications, author, interior designer, performer, chef; reading literature, going to museums, photography | "Create It" Flexibility, originality Creative approaches to problems Aesthetic vision Delegates routine tasks |
| Social: "Helpers" | Helpful, humanistic, service-oriented, tactful, understanding, warm, insightful about people | HR, training, teaching, social worker, counselor, nursing, childcare; enlighten others, organize events, volunteering | "Work Together" Spends time actively listening, trusted Strong team player Pitches in to finish tasks and not burden others |
| Enterprising: "Persuaders" | Persuasive, competitive, results and rewards oriented, ambitious, energetic, confident, leading, status oriented | Marketing, sales management, optician, small business/entrepreneur; chairing committees, debating, campaigning, sports | "Make a Deal" Dynamic, outgoing style Enjoys challenges, leading, visibility Persuasive: a strength and sometimes overdone |
| Conventional: "Organizers" | Systematic, data and detail oriented, monitoring, organizing, orderly, accurate, efficient, persevering | Accounting, financial advisor, medical administration, administrative assistant, software developer, office manager, teller; collecting, home-improvement projects, building models, civic organizations | "Be Sensible" Specific, clear instructions Readily follows procedures and respected leaders Does things correctly and desires proper training Needs time to process and accept change |

information provides insights into the environment outside the organization. This includes sector growth projections, identification of jobs that are in demand, and sector interactions. Examples of such information used in a healthcare organization are given in chapters 4 and 9. An example of sector interactions is that of rising gas prices that affect transportation costs by truck, which may result in decreased demand for transportation services, the number of trucks needed, and the need for associated parts. Thus, multiple industries and markets are affected.

Networking is an excellent way to explore opportunities either inside an organization or outside. While most effective when conducted through personal contact, it has evolved well beyond just job search and also now includes electronic interactions. This latter aspect is frequently covered by the umbrella term *social networking* and supported by Web sites like LinkedIn that foster such connections. Networking is about connecting, sharing common interests and causes, and assisting others with knowledge and additional connections, as well as accessing their networks. Knowledge and information sharing through social and professional networking, whether in person or by using virtual approaches, provide important windows on emerging opportunities.

Exploration of opportunities follows identification. Informational interviews with people in a field of interest can provide excellent anecdotal insights about job specifics or sector trends. Job shadowing can be used by organizations to help individuals considering an internal move gain greater perspective on the requirements of a position and likely fit. It can also be used to provide a perspective on potential areas for individual growth and development. Other external exploration approaches include volunteering, internships, and part-time work. Sustaining career fitness means continuing external exploration on an ongoing basis.

## Direction and Decision

Decisions about career direction need to integrate self-knowledge with knowledge of a continuously changing external environment. An individual with a strong personal portfolio can build on past skills, accomplishments, and experiences along with an understanding of self to make effective decisions regarding future opportunities. Organizational support of such decisions enhances the likelihood of securing alignment of individual perspectives with organizational needs, which in turn enhances productivity. Organizational sponsorship of formal and informal feedback about development, from supervisors, peers and mentors, is an important form of such support. Factors such as emerging technology or shifts in company focus can present unanticipated changes for individuals. A solid grounding in self-understanding provides a compass to navigate such changes. Organizational knowledge of individuals' perspectives and talents enhances the ability to flex assignments as needed.

### Negotiating Favorable Entry

Negotiations prior to an individual accepting a job offer, whether with the current organization or outside, extend well beyond salary and monetary benefits to include, for example, support for lifelong learning and professional development or flexible work hours. An effective negotiation step in the career fitness cycle can cement a strong foundation for the relationship between the individual and the organization. This will increase the likelihood of rapid assimilation into a new position, quickly securing needed productivity. Organizations can assist this process by clarifying performance expectations, necessary skill sets, and the norms of corporate culture.

### Integrating and Excelling in New Situations

Success in a new work environment depends on an individual's ability to adapt readily to a new culture, whether in a new division or a new organization. Organizational support for time spent initially in observing and analyzing the work environment, work flow, pace, nature of relationships, and organizational communications can be an important contribution to successful integration. Communicating the company or division's vision, direction, values, and mission are also important factors that help individuals align expectations, goals, and development plans with organizational priorities. Providing opportunities for growing levels of responsibility, participation on project teams, and continuous learning are also important factors. Watkins states, "Transitions are periods of opportunity" and an individual must "build momentum during your transition" or face "an uphill battle from that point forward" (2003, 1). Watkins outlines strategies for succeeding in a new position that can help guide organizational support in this phase of the career fitness cycle.

### Maintenance or Sustainability

During the maintenance or sustainability stage of the career fitness cycle, some people may become so comfortable in an environment that they become stale, and their contributions decline. The desire to stay may still be strong, but eagerness is diminished. A key challenge is reengagement to regain motivation and energy. Others may continue to be motivated and energized by a combination of the work, the company's mission and direction, rewards offered by the organization, or contributions they make to society. In this case, a key challenge is that of ongoing renewal to sustain this level of focus and commitment. In either case, ongoing assessment and development planning are important contributors to reengagement and renewal. Development can take the form of learning new skills, gaining experience to enrich a current role, or preparing for a new role. This may also be a time to explore external options. Being prepared to stay or go includes, but is not limited to, ensuring that essential skills are up-to-date, actively nurturing a strong network, and having an updated resume and portfolio highlighting recently acquired skills and experience that may target a new career path. Organizations play an important role in engaging complacent employees as well as energizing committed employees by encouraging goal setting, professional development, and regular career conversations to determine how the relationship can continue to be mutually beneficial or if the relationship needs to be fundamentally changed.

### Transition

Inherent in movement through the career fitness cycle are transitions. Transitions by individuals can be categorized as those that are triggered by voluntary or involuntary events. An example of an involuntary event is a layoff or downsizing leading to unanticipated job loss. Survivors of downsizing may also experience the resulting organizational change in the form of an increase or shift in job duties or a promotion or transfer coming at an unexpected or unanticipated time. The uncertainty associated with job insecurity can be particularly debilitating (Burgard, Brand, and House 2009). Voluntary events are those chosen by individuals seeking enhanced organizational alignment, more challenge, or growth in a new career direction. Bridges (1980) describes the response to change events as an internal process of transition, which can be described in three phases: an Ending, the Neutral Zone, and a New Beginning. Organizations can provide support through all stages of this process by helping individuals recognize the opportunities, not only the losses, inherent in change and transition; communicating often and authentically to address fears, questions, and concerns; and providing resources, tools, and services to assist individuals in moving toward new priorities and future success.

## SHARED ROLES

Career fitness is strengthened when responsibility is shared by the employee and the employer. The primary responsibility for career fitness lies with the employee to initiate and manage learning and development. While the organization cannot guarantee an individual's success, the organization can play a significant role in assisting employees to experience increased satisfaction and enhanced effectiveness, and in creating an environment conducive to individual success. Organizations can also assist dissatisfied employees seek other opportunities either within the organization or outside.

**Employee Role**

*Ownership*

An important organizational responsibility is communicating to employees their role in accepting ownership of their career fitness and providing support for this. Employees can acknowledge this need and initiate their career development through discussions about their development with management and mentors, or by participating in career services within an organization. If no formal services are provided, these conversations might occur with Human Resources or a supervisor regarding an interest in growing or developing at work. This may be prompted by dissatisfaction with the current situation or evolving excitement about a new direction. While it is up to the individual to accept ownership, the organization can assist by providing support for managers, supervisors, and mentors to engage in development conversations with individuals. Employees will likely need encouragement to engage in such conversations before they take or accept the initiative.

*Self-Assessment*

Employees can engage in formal or informal self-assessments of talents, strengths, areas for development, and organizational fit. The organization may offer assessments, or some can be accessed through resources such as America's Career Infonet (www.acinet.org), state government employment Web sites, or those referenced earlier in the chapter.

*Feedback*

Candid feedback about skills, interactions, and goals is an important development element. It requires that employees be open to receiving such feedback. Feedback can be requested from managers, mentors, peers, and others inside and outside the organization. Employees will benefit most by listening and asking clarifying questions without being defensive or offering justification. The knowledge resulting from feedback is valuable in validating areas of strength, weakness, opportunities for growth, and decisions about future directions.

*Goal Setting and Action Plans*

Setting goals and developing an action plan are vital to the employee's success in determining career direction and specifying steps either within, or external to, the organization. Components of a development action plan may include education and training, learning from others, and experiential or on-the-job opportunities, within defined time frames. Effective development goals align with current organizational priorities as well as with the reality of the internal and external labor markets. The action plan provides a focus on preparing for the next career steps and may include varied activities, such as gathering information about critical positions and related educational opportunities, applying to schools, gaining financial support, taking on leadership roles, cross-training, choosing or becoming a mentor, or participating in targeted events or teams. An example of a development plan template and a sample are included as appendix C.

### Lifelong Learning

Regardless of the career path chosen or the steps involved, learning will be an integral component. Learning is a lifelong process that occurs both formally and informally. In addition to on-the job learning, it can include interacting with mentors, observing leaders and peers, and learning through colleges, trade schools, and professional associations.

### Resources

A comprehensive development process involves using a variety of resources, including information from online and written sources and direct input from others. For example, conversations with network contacts might provide specific information and guidance that can be augmented with Internet information gathering to validate and generalize. Written information is valuable but may be outdated and therefore unreliable. Online information, while readily available, requires validation. Incorporating people as resources and relying on others' experience and expertise encourages the possibility of deepening the process.

## Manager and Organization Role

The organization plays a critical role in creating the infrastructure to support employee development and career fitness. Elements of this support may include making information widely available about organizational priorities and competencies, offering financial assistance and career coaching, and acknowledging managers for their contributions in developing employees. Managers can translate the organizational priorities into strategies for individual career development and assist the process through ongoing communication and awareness of the employee's goals.

### Developmental Environment

An important role of the manager is to create an environment that encourages employee development and career fitness. Open and ongoing communication with employees is essential in fostering trust and promoting further development and growth. Regular meetings can facilitate candid conversations about the employee's values, satisfaction, motivation, and alignment with the organization's direction. These conversations are most effective when held outside performance appraisals or other performance-related meetings and when focused only on the growth of the individual. These meetings provide a forum for dialog about employee strengths and areas for development.

### Information about the Organization

Another form of valuable feedback from the manager is information about the organization's realities and direction. Current knowledge of the priorities and direction is helpful to the employee in determining a balance between being eager to stay and possibly preparing to go. The manager may choose to engage employees in discussions about the organization's values, mission statement, and goals as well as provide information about management strategies, financial performance, initiatives, and processes. For example, if a company decides to institute new manufacturing strategies to reduce costs, managers need to educate employees on the rationale, processes, contribution, and personal implications. This type of communication encourages commitment to the new process or initiative.

### Coaching and Resources

Employees may not have adequate knowledge to develop a career plan independently. Managers can assist the process through coaching. Managers and supervisors are potentially excellent coaches if they can share practical experiences, make realistic appraisals of organizational opportunities, build on the individual's past performance evaluations, understand and evaluate external factors and trends, bring experience with similar career situations, and be empathetic (Gilley and Eggland 1989). Managers will likely need training in coaching skills to be effective in this role. If the individual's personality type is known, coaching techniques can be modified to most effectively address blind spots and build on strengths (Hirsh and Kise 2000). While it is not the role of the manager to make decisions for employees, managers can identify growth opportunities for employees, primarily within the organization but also externally if appropriate or needed. Once a direction is determined, the manager may inquire about planned action steps and offer feedback based on the manager's experience, networks, and knowledge of company resources. With this knowledge of processes and people, the manager may suggest opportunities such as cross-training, job shadowing, mentoring, or team assignments that would enhance the employee's portfolio of skills and experience as well as individual career fitness. Managers may also recommend employees for projects based on awareness of the employee's development goals and career plan.

*Encouragement and Accountability*

Regular meetings to address the employee's career plan and action steps are motivating and facilitate progress toward development goals. Fournies states, "Without frequent and specific feedback, performance varies and often fails" (2000, 102). Feedback discussion meetings provide periodic deadlines to address accountability, assess progress, and address barriers that might surface. There is mutual benefit to this process of supporting employee development and career fitness. The manager has the opportunity to assist employees in the career development process by offering open communication and feedback. In turn, employees are more committed to their job performance, their teams and projects, and to the organization. Managers who coach their team and employees through the career process also need to remain attuned to their own career development plans. If a manager is stale in her career, she will be less effective in coaching her direct reports about their careers.

## CONNECTING STAGES OF CAREER FITNESS WITH ENGAGEMENT STRATEGIES

### Entry

Before a new employee joins an organization, the engagement process has already been active through hiring interviews, the employment offer, and negotiations. Discussions during the interview and hiring process can provide vital information regarding the values of the new employee, the desired direction for growth and development, and a good sense of fit with the organizational culture. It is beneficial for the organization to stay connected with the new employee prior to the start date. When communication and involvement between employee and organization begin early and are open and honest regarding abilities and interests, "management can increase productivity, improve employee attitude toward work, develop greater worker satisfaction, and greater loyalty" (Gilley and Eggland 1989, 60).

The new employee's first day represents another opportunity to support his career fitness. Orientations that provide information about the company's vision, mission, goals, and values are essential for assisting new employees in understanding the organizational culture both formal and informal. Other strategies for welcoming new employees include introducing them to colleagues, decision makers, resources, and systems within the organization as well as clarifying how their contribution is valuable to the overall organization. Matching the new employee with a tenured employee, whether from the assigned job area or another part of the organization, will assist the individual in navigating the organizational culture and laying the groundwork for a successful career path.

### Integration

Effective employee integration is strengthened by providing training for job-specific tasks as well as by clarifying performance goals and expectations. Training on different technologies or software that may be needed builds a skill set while also addressing organizational priorities. If there is a probationary period, regular meetings during the period will assist in further clarifying the employee's role and building rapport with the individual as well as laying groundwork for a clear career development path. Integration is also an appropriate time for the manager or mentor to provide additional information about resources offered by the organization and engage the employee in targeted projects, teams, and committees that will support development and advance organizational objectives.

### Development

During the development phase, the individual is fully integrated into the organization and aware of his roles and responsibility. The manager has an understanding of the employee's career goals and the skill base he needs to develop. Several activities may be used by the manager or the organization to assist the employee with this aspect of career fitness. Experiential learning in the form of projects or activities provides an excellent approach and might include the following:

- Making presentations to management or vendors, or at professional conferences
- Leading or participating in various team projects and activities
- Mentoring others or being mentored
- Rotating through jobs and departments to gain a greater understanding of the organization's functions
- Participating in job assignments targeted toward developing a specific skill set or knowledge base
- Accepting challenging stretch goals
- Supervising projects or team members
- Teaching others through a formal process or through serving as a subject matter expert
- Assuming team leadership roles

### Transition

During involuntary transitions such as a downsizing or reduction in force, organizations may use outplacement services or internal career services to assist affected employees. These services provide support to individuals in clarifying their aspirations and developing effective action plans for moving forward. For those transitions that are initiated by employees, third-party exit interviews can provide excellent insights into the issues that caused the departure (Elsdon 2003).

## CONCLUSIONS

Careers evolve through stages: the beginning of work life, entry and integration into an organization, continuing development, periodic transitioning, recycling through one or more stages, and sometimes reinvention or making a major change. Managing careers can be compared to physical fitness, a process that is intentional and ongoing. Career fitness is primarily the responsibility of the individual, supported by the organization, and is most effectively achieved through a combination of activities:

- Being keenly aware of internal work motivations and external conditions and trends
- Recognizing and creating events, relationships, and situations—both planned and unplanned—that represent opportunities
- Developing tools and honing skills to capitalize on, and benefit from, these situations

In summary, actively engaging with the career fitness cycle at all career stages is critical. Organizations play a key role in promoting individual career fitness by providing resources, guidance, and services. Managers support career fitness by paying attention to the needs of employees at different career stages and at various stages of organizational tenure. There are many strong and mutual benefits to both employees and organizations for sharing responsibility for employee development and career fitness. Though some managers may be reluctant to support career development believing it provides employees with tools to leave the department or organization, Simonsen (1997) suggests that in a development culture, employees are often willing to postpone opportunities in the present for the sake of the organization's competitive advantage if they trust that their manager recognizes and supports their career interests. Elsdon and Iyer (1999) demonstrate that providing options and choices for individuals reduces attrition. Eager to stay and prepared to go is an approach to proactively managing individual careers that meshes well with the contemporary realities of the world of work. As described in this chapter, applying the critical skills and tools for such an approach in a collaboration of employees practicing career fitness and an organization creating a development culture significantly increases the probability of success for both. In the next chapter, we will explore tailoring approaches to address the needs of different populations.

# CHAPTER 8

# Tailoring Approaches to Address the Needs of Different Populations

*Shannon Jordan, Lisa Franklin and Martha Edwards*

Regardless of our training and theoretical orientations, as counselors, coaches, and managers, we no doubt aspire to be centered on the needs of those individuals with whom we work when focused on their development. Understanding the context within which individuals live and work is the foundation for meaningful and effective development. In a marketplace that often values customization, we are pulled to develop expertise with various population groups, yet in just the two organizations with whom the authors of this chapter work, there are employees representing 102 countries, speaking 66 languages and dialects, working in 1 of over 50 broad occupational areas, and ranging in age from under 20 to 81. The often challenging task of tailoring approaches to address the needs of different populations becomes less about the development of expertise and more about being aware of dynamics, understanding issues, and building knowledge of the infrastructure within which individuals find themselves.

In this chapter, three contributing authors share their experiences working with technical professionals, labor union–represented employees, and age 50-plus individuals. Their approaches to career development services and programs for these three different populations offer suggestions for building our awareness, understanding, and knowledge from both an organizational and an individual perspective. Just as each population is unique, so are the approaches to providing career development support.

## CAREER DEVELOPMENT WITH
## TECHNICAL PROFESSIONALS

Within the high-technology sector, one of the fastest growing segments of the U.S. economy, the telecommunications industry provided over one million wage and salary jobs in 2008 (Plunkett Research 2009). Employment is expected to decline, due to productivity gains, by about 1 percent per year from 2008 to 2018, compared to about 1 percent annual growth for all nonagricultural employment (U.S. Department of Labor 2009b). Rapid technological change and increased global competition have resulted in unprecedented mobility for professionals who can master the latest skill sets. Attracting top talent and minimizing attrition continue to be major concerns for companies in the high-tech industries where movement among organizations is common. Career pathing information in these organizations is sometimes limited as industry leaders scramble to stay ahead of competition and translate technological advances into job functions and workforce needs. The lack of a clear road map detailing positions and career paths can lead to frustration among the rank and file of these companies as employees question their value, contributions, and development, sometimes with little feedback or direction from management. With this in mind, we will explore career development with technical professionals building on experience with a multinational telecommunications company in 2008 and 2009.

### Description of the Population

About 50 percent of the client population worked within the engineering functions: test, software, hardware, systems, and applications engineers, and a handful of others in highly specialized engineering disciplines specific to the industry. The other half of the client population comprised business services and operations professionals working in marketing, business development, project management, program management, finance, or legal functions. Many of these professionals had engineering backgrounds themselves or had spent most of their careers working in the high-tech industry. Nearly 80 percent of the clients held at least a bachelor's degree; several had doctorates in the engineering disciplines. The majority of the clients were Caucasian, followed by Asian (mainly of Indian or Chinese descent). Women were slightly in the majority of the client population. The clients' ages ranged from 25 to 45, with the majority having fewer than five years of service with the company. This was a highly educated, technically savvy, motivated group of individuals.

### Career Growth Opportunities and Challenges

The economic environment changed dramatically over the course of the project. Clients were not only trying to navigate their career paths in a complicated, matrixed, fast-growing high-technology organization but also during what turned out to be one of the most tumultuous years for the U.S. economy. The threat of unemployment and perilous economic conditions added to the challenges faced by employees. Perhaps not surprisingly, it also enhanced their commitment to improving their current work environments based on fear of job loss.

The challenges most of the employees encountered were similar to those faced by others in fast-moving, high-technology organizations. Typical concerns were the decision as to whether or not to leave a technical function to take a managerial role; the challenges of how to communicate with teammates and a manager who may be in a different location; and the issue of how to communicate one's accomplishments and contributions in a matrixed environment when the project lead and manager may be two different people. Opportunities to impart the concepts of driving a career and assessing individual interests, values, motivated skills, and work style abounded. While this was a highly educated, technically savvy group, most had either never been exposed to the career development process, especially if from a different culture, or had not taken the time to reflect on, and consider, their own needs.

### Approaches

The career development program was provided as a benefit for employees at all levels. The initial strategy was to launch an à la carte selection of services positioned for the proactive, high-performing employee. These services included individualized, confidential career coaching appointments (up to four one-hour sessions), career-related assessments, and workshops covering such topics as career management, work style and motivators, developing in role, and building relationships. The services were designed to provide individuals with opportunities to self-assess on a number of career development constructs as a foundation for an online development planning process already available through the company's learning and development department.

The following story illustrates the clarity that self-assessment can bring to the development process. The client was a 38-year-old male engineer in a highly specialized field, at the company two years, and part of a fast-moving, newly formed division. His reasons for engaging in individual career coaching included the goal of career progression (wage/title) and the desire for increased satisfaction in his current job. The results of an interest inventory indicated preferences in the artistic area, namely writing and communications. When queried about his interests, he disclosed that he'd always been a writer but had pursued a more technical field, perceiving this to offer more employment opportunities. In his spare time, he wrote a community blog and was working on his first novel. During the course of career counseling sessions, he asked a most poignant question: "Does anyone ever leave this place to pursue a dream?" The dream he described entailed becoming a published writer, yet this dream was tempered by a high need for financial security and a low tolerance for risk. He acknowledged that he had never considered integrating writing into his work. He was a get-it-done, execution-oriented, company-first kind of professional. He and his career coach discussed opportunities for introducing writing into his job in a way that both added value to his department and met his needs as an individual. He indicated that he had recently been selected to represent his team and attend an intensive training around a new technology. The idea that emerged out of the coaching sessions was to create a manual to share the new training knowledge with his teammates—a technical writing effort of sorts. The timing was ideal.

In the weeks following his sessions, the engineer went through a semi-annual performance review process. In preparation for the review process, his manager asked him to select two competencies that he thought were critical to developing in his role and then a third competency that appealed to his growth as an individual. His manager was to do the same, and then the two would discuss their results until there was agreement on a development plan for the upcoming year. Armed with a more solidified understanding of his personal interests, values, personality style, and strengths, the engineer reported that the development discussion went very smoothly. He proposed the technical writing goal as the third competency. His manager loved the idea and suggested this employee incorporate the writing function into his job description, enabling him to handle any future technical writing needs for the department! It had never dawned on this engineer to integrate his love of writing into the job.

This client's experience was not an isolated case. Many clients reported anecdotally that clarifying interests, skills, strengths, values, and personality type supported development planning. Once clients were able to clarify what they wanted, they found it easier to communicate how to align their development with the organization's objectives. The process equipped individuals with the ability to drive their own career development; this was not a new concept, but it was one that seemed fresh to this particular group of technical employees. The self-assessment piece became the cornerstone of the client work and the fabric of both individual coaching and group workshop options. Many professionals indicated they had never taken the time to think about their personal goals, let alone think about how to marry those goals with the company's objectives and business needs.

A second story involved a female engineer of Asian descent who had sought career coaching to prioritize goals. As a high performer, she admitted that by default she routinely adjusted her vision, priorities, and goals to meet the needs of the company but had never really taken the opportunity to consider her personal goals. In her discussions with a career coach, she realized that attending to her personal goals (meeting other women engineers weekly for lunch, taking nature walks, and becoming more assertive in her personal communications) positively affected her engagement, productivity, and outlook at work. She was able to broaden her network, feel more energized during the day, and confidently initiate a previously dreaded conversation with her manager regarding a promotion. Career conversations built upon a framework integrating professional and personal aspirations and concerns benefitted both the employee and the organization.

## Key Learnings

Two key learnings stand out from these and other experiences working with technical professionals; one relates to content and the other to structure. Rather than wanting to talk just about career progression or next steps, most clients appreciated the opportunity to explore in more depth the meaning of work in their lives. They were interested in how to enhance their relationships with their managers and their teams, in how to stay motivated and engaged. The coaching was more holistic than had been expected. One PhD-level engineer brought in a journal and a wish list of things he wanted to accomplish in his lifetime, and asked for assistance in creating a mission statement so he could best prioritize this wish list. In a similar vein, as part of the foundation workshop, participants created a career lifeline indicating times when they were highly engaged in their work, when it flowed comfortably. This provided insights into themes around interests, strengths, and values. The engineering clients were particularly engaged in this exercise, often creating two- and three-dimensional graphical depictions of their individual paths.

In terms of the structure of the services, technical clientele responded well to the use of assessment tools. It is likely that the validity and reliability of the instruments, grounded in research, provided a familiar framework and structure to complement the sometimes fluid nature of counseling conversations. Workshops and opportunities for group engagement were also well received. A year into career services operations, groups of employees who had built relationships with each other in the workshops started, of their own volition, to form affinity groups. Employees with common career development concerns (working mothers, new managers) would agree to exchange contact information and occasionally meet in common areas around the organization. At the time of writing this book, the career services team was also exploring the use of social media tools such as moderated blogs, wikis, and other knowledge networks to provide ongoing support. These technically savvy, largely introverted employees, many of whom were engineers, welcomed such customized connections.

## CAREER DEVELOPMENT IN A LABOR UNION–REPRESENTED ENVIRONMENT

### Description of the Population

More than 15 million workers in the U.S. belonged to a union in 2009 (U.S. Department of Labor 2010a). They were teachers, nurses, truck drivers, carpenters, cooks, postal carriers, and employees in numerous other occupations across a variety of industries. Each worked under a collective bargaining agreement negotiated between the respective employer and union. Each agreement, or labor contract, defined the terms of employment for wages, hours, benefits, and so on. Explicitly or implicitly, items in the agreement also influence individual career decisions. A union member, just as others managing their careers, wants to learn new skills, advance within an organization, and maintain financial stability and job security. Like others in a nonrepresented environment, he wants to fulfill his potential and aspirations. The difference is in the influence of the labor contract on career options. By having a firm grasp of the contract and the environment in which it is implemented, the career counselor or mentor can help the union member with his desired development or transition.

### The Career Counselor/Mentor's Role

Among the many tools used when serving union members, probably the most essential is the labor contract. The company's Human Resource department or a union representative should be able to provide a copy. The counselor or mentor will want access to a copy for each union represented at the organization. In the contract the counselor/mentor will find the job classifications under the union's jurisdiction; corresponding wage scales, and types of employees (for example regular, temporary, on-call) covered by the agreement; how and when job vacancies are posted and how a request for transfer is handled; an explanation of how seniority affects job changes, as well as explanations of many other issues pertaining to employment rights. Armed with this knowledge, she can better see how an employee can move laterally or vertically within the organization and the possible consequences attached to any job or career transition. She can better help the employee navigate his way through the organization.

Understanding the terms of the contract is just the beginning. It is also important to be alert to the needs of various constituencies. Labor and management will each have their separate, though not necessarily competing, interests, motivations, and goals, and these will affect employees. Behind the scenes, there might be contract negotiations or organizing underway, changes in leadership, or tensions between unions, any of which could have ripple effects throughout the organization. In many ways, a counselor/mentor assisting union members needs to be a tightrope walker, neither leaning too far toward labor nor toward management, but maintaining a steady, neutral balance between the two. In the end, of course, it is the employee the counselor/mentor serves, but in the interest of her client, the counselor/mentor must pay attention not only to the labor contract but to the political climate in which that contract exists.

By gaining the trust of union representatives, as well as management, the counselor/mentor can form invaluable partnerships that in the end benefit the employee. Listening to the concerns expressed by labor and management is key. Building trust may, however, take time. The counselor/mentor may need to assure labor that she is a neutral party, not a representative of management, and that she has only the best interests of her clients, the union members, in mind. In some organizations, labor may view the appearance of a career counselor on the scene as a sign that layoffs are looming. The counselor/mentor will need to clarify the nature of her role.

It is crucial too, for the counselor/mentor to respect the role of the shop steward. Counselors/mentors are by nature helpers and so might naturally feel the impulse to advocate when an employee complains of problems on the job. This responsibility falls to the shop steward. According to Murray, within the workplace a shop steward is "the eyes and ears of the union" and is "authorized to receive, investigate, and attempt to settle complaints before they become formal grievances" (1998, 164). Stewards, who also have other union responsibilities, are employees of the company, not of the union, and usually work in a full- or part-time position while carrying out their union duties.

## Case Studies

Just as each labor contract will be unique, so of course will each employee. The case studies that follow illustrate how career counseling in a union environment can unfold. In each case, the employee wants to remain with the current employer and to stay in a union position (names and identifying details have been changed to maintain confidentiality). In actuality, this won't always be true. Finding out the client's preference, if one exists, in the initial conversation can save time in the counseling process. The procedure for moving from a union into a nonunion position will likely have its own set of rules; the counselor may need to confer with the Human Resources department about what those are. A collective bargaining agreement is unique to the union and the employer who crafted it; therefore, the case studies below are not intended to represent a particular union or employer.

### Case Study 1

Janice is a 47-year-old secretary. For five years, she has been happy with her job. However, due to changes in technology, she is facing the prospect that it will be phased out in the not too distant future. Anxious and wanting to respond to her situation proactively, she seeks the career counselor's assistance. The career counselor and Janice agree to begin with an interest inventory. After reviewing the results with her career counselor and narrowing her choices to a few occupations, Janice does extensive research. She volunteers at a clinic, conducts informational interviews, and shadows another employee on the job. As it turns out, the career Janice is most interested in falls under the jurisdiction of another union. Before laying out an educational plan, Janice and the counselor investigate answers to the following:

- Bidding rights: Do members of Janice's union (Union A) have bidding rights to positions in Union B, the union which represents her chosen occupation? In other words, assuming at the time of application Janice is equally qualified for the position as are members of Union B, will she be given equal consideration for the job? Or does the fact that she's coming from a different union result in her being ranked differently in the recruiting process possibly even as an external candidate?
- Seniority: Will Janice's years of seniority with the company be considered in the hiring process? Or will she have to start at the bottom of the ladder?
- Wages: Will she be starting at the bottom of a pay scale in Union B? She knows that if she stays in Union A, her hourly wage cannot drop below its current level—even if she moves to a different, lower-paying position.

As it turns out, a job candidate from Union A will be considered as an internal candidate when applying for a position with Union B, but priority will be given to members of Union B, a much larger union with potentially more applicants. Janice's seniority with the company will not be factored into the hiring process. If she chooses to accept a position under Union B's jurisdiction, she will retain her seniority in regard to her benefits, but she will start at the bottom of that job classification's pay scale. After discussing her options at length with her career counselor over several months, Janice decides that having a career she will find meaningful outweighs any concerns she has about these issues. She enrolls in school and begins training for a new career.

### Case Study 2

Denise has held the same receptionist job for seven years. Although she enjoys the work, she is unhappy in her department. She feels alienated from her co-workers and has received two consecutive poor performance reviews from her supervisor—unjustly so, she feels. Denise is not receptive to exploring how her own behavior might be contributing to the situation. She desperately wants to change jobs and has decided her only option is to apply for a position outside her union. She has already consulted with her shop steward when she seeks the assistance of the career counselor. Before taking any action, Denise needs to consider these issues:

- Performance: If Denise applies for a job under another union's jurisdiction, or a nonunion position, will her performance reviews be taken into account in the selection process?
- Transfer process: If Denise were instead to transfer to another position within her union, would her past performance be considered? What is considered for an intraunion transfer?

Denise's performance reviews will be taken into account if she applies for either a position within another union or a nonunion position, and that will likely eliminate her from consideration. Both Denise's shop steward and her career counselor advise her to transfer to a position within her union, where only her seniority and ability to meet the minimum qualifications will be factored in. This way, she can remove herself from a stressful situation and then build up a record of positive performance reviews over time. The counselor also refers Denise to the company's Employee Assistance Program (EAP) for help dealing with her stress. Denise eventually transfers to the same job in another department, although this means switching to a less desirable evening shift.

### Case Study 3

Mark is a few years from retirement. For the past 12 years, he has worked as a stock clerk at a warehouse. He wants to remain with this employer until he retires, but he is bored with his job and would like to branch out into something new. So that he can retain seniority, he wants to stay within his union. His current job is just a few miles from his home, and he does not want a longer commute. When he first consults a career counselor, his expectations are high, but his options are few. With the help of his career counselor, he learns he needs the answers to these questions:

- Jurisdiction: What positions does his union have jurisdiction over and where? His employer might have other campuses close to his home, but that doesn't mean his union will have jurisdiction at those campuses.
- Job classifications: If his union does have jurisdiction over other positions within an easy commute, how do those positions compare to the job he currently holds? Will they provide the challenge he is seeking? Will there be opportunity for advancement? How do the wages compare?

As it turns out, Mark's union does not have jurisdiction over positions outside the warehouse. After exploring several options that will require a longer commute, Mark decides to look for ways to increase his satisfaction on his current job. His counselor recommends he complete a transferable skills analysis to help remind him of his talents and to gain a better sense of what skills he most enjoys using. Then, with the consent of his manager, Mark begins taking on projects within his department that enable him to use those skills. He also seeks out a role as a mentor to an employee at a lower grade level, which gives Mark the opportunity to pass on his knowledge and to do one of the things he loves most—train others.

### Summary

Although career counseling and mentoring in this environment can seem daunting, it isn't necessary for the counselor to be an expert on unions to counsel union members. As long as she familiarizes herself with the labor contract, respects the culture, and remains neutral, she will succeed in helping her clients make informed decisions about their careers as they navigate their way toward new opportunity and advancement.

## CAREER DEVELOPMENT WITH AGE 50-PLUS EMPLOYEES

### Demographic Shifts

The annual growth rate of the age 55 plus population in the U.S. is projected to increase by more than 27 percent over the 2000–2050 time period compared to the previous 50 years (M. Toossi 2002, 2006). Globally, due to a decrease in infant mortality rates, improved city infrastructures, reduced birthrates, and advances in healthcare and better nutrition, average world life-expectancy has reached 68 (World Health Organization 2009). And we haven't yet seen the effect of new biotechnologies on aging. Our great-grandchildren may not look a day older than 110!

With extended life spans, we have the unfolding of multiple career paths. There is no longer one career, one company, one gold watch. This 20th-century pattern is being increasingly replaced by an unpredictable and flexible personal work history. Modern work lives are filled with breaks in careers, restructured departments, new trainings and certificates, rotating managers, and constantly improving technologies.

> You may start a PhD program at age 50.
>
> Begin a successful business at age 55.
>
> Build your greatest building after age 60.
>
> Michelangelo did.
>
> Go into space at age 76.
>
> John Glenn did.
>
> Meet the love of your life at 77.
>
> Run your first marathon at age 90.

Age is no longer the predictor of our driving needs, primary involvements, or central values. Within today's business organizations, employees are experimenting with job changes, even career changes, at unexpected ages, and they will turn to career specialists within the organization for guidance during these many transitions. Age 50-plus workers are skilled, experienced, knowledgeable, seasoned, and ambitious—and seeking fulfilling and challenging work. Workforce developers—career counselors, managers, mentors, and human resource professionals—can help them continue to build value for the organization, reach their full potential, and grow their careers through their fifties, sixties, and beyond.

In discussions with career counselors who have worked with older workers, themes emerged that speak to critical challenges and opportunities facing organizations dealing with a large 50-plus population in their workforce:

- Generational conflicts
- Ageism
- Modest computer skills
- Desire for less physically demanding work
- Difficult decision: career change after age 50
- Beyond retirement: what's next?

## Generational Conflicts

Age diversity in the workforce is increasing as several generations work side by side, often within the same department and sometimes on the same teams. Each generation has its own lens for viewing the work world, with differing work values and work styles, depending on a shared history (Zemke, Raines, and Filipczak 2000, 4).

Here is an example: a 58-year-old woman is being written up for poor performance by her new, 32-year-old manager. The employee has never been written up before and has always received good recommendations during her 20-plus years of work at this organization. All of a sudden, her thoughts of retirement at age 62 are subject to doubt. There have been layoffs at this organization, and she feels headed for redeployment or a performance plan, neither of which seems a tolerable option. After speaking with her career counselor, the employee determines she has too much anger and hurt around the issue to judge her options clearly. She decides to talk further with her EAP counselor and several close friends during the next few weeks to let off some steam before contacting the human resources consultant for a head-to-head session with her manager. Within the following weeks, the situation with her manager does not resolve, but the employee feels less desperate and is thinking about a prudent way to approach the problem. Does she want to leave the organization for an early retirement and live on significantly less money? Does she want to go out into the workforce again—after having been with this company for 23 years—and see what she could find during a recession? Will the stress of continuing to report to this manager cause illness? There are no easy decisions. Eventually, she decides to accept the current management situation, but to try to work more closely with another group on a new project. She begins a performance plan with her manager but feels more hopeful for a change in the near future. As it turns out, her department is headed for a reorganization later in the year. She feels this will be the chance to change her reporting relationship. She feels that at the heart of this problem there has been a generational power struggle between herself and her far younger manager about whose work style should prevail.

Whether a worker is being managed by a significantly younger manager, managing a younger team, or has become the only older worker on a younger team, generational differences can create tensions. Workforce developers hear from older employees about their performance insecurities, their anger at having their authority questioned, and their hurt feelings over being unacknowledged or disrespected. It's a natural point of confrontation in business when ambitious 20-year-olds feel the need to prove their value and age 50-plus workers seek work-life balance without the stresses experienced in their twenties and the pressures of their thirties. Career counselors/mentors can facilitate emotional movement by simply listening to the stories without judgment. They can provide information on how to handle work situations when intergenerational differences become an issue within hiring processes, interviewing, promotions, managing, performance reviews, and close, age-diverse teamwork.

### Ageism

Ageism is discrimination due to age. If it exists in the workplace, does this preclude older workers from promotions or from being hired for new positions? Not necessarily, if they are properly prepared to deal with ageism within their organization. Age discrimination occurs when assumptions are made about a worker simply because of his age. Age diversity means employing people of all ages based on a clearly defined set of skills, talents, and attributes.

A workshop for older workers, 35 to 55 years old, was conducted at John F. Kennedy University in Northern California in 2006. During the workshop, small groups were formed and asked to list common strengths of age 40-plus workers. They were also asked not to include the phrase "life experience" on their lists. Surprisingly, the lists from each group were short and lackluster. There was little mention of political, social, managerial, and leadership factors, such as broad industry knowledge, institutional knowledge, negotiation skills, presentation skills, delegation, training abilities, motivational leadership, efficiency measurements, complex problem solving, budget planning, hiring and staffing, professional networks, process management, and conflict management.

The teams then repeated the exercise, brainstorming the perceived strengths of younger workers. In this case, the lists were long and came readily: technologically sophisticated, quick learners, able to work long hours, acute memory capability, agile, greater physical strength, enthusiastic, and creative, among others. This workshop group consisted of older adults, who seemed able to list their own fears and shortcomings quite easily but could not speak to their strengths effectively. If older workers are more focused on their potential weaknesses than aware of the abundant variety of complex skills they have gained through many years of work experience, they may not know how to sell themselves in an interview or may even avoid new job opportunities altogether due to a fear of competing with younger workers. Career and workforce developers/mentors can coach older workers about how to make the most of their interviewing and networking opportunities by focusing on these areas:

- How to deal with disguised or undisguised age-oriented questions
- How to overcome negative stereotypes during an interview
- How to best handle an interview with a younger manager
- How to develop and tell success stories that showcase complex skill groups
- How to demonstrate an increasing amount of responsibility and challenge in a chronological resume
- How to showcase growth in technology skills and a commitment to lifelong learning

Some specific suggestions about how to deal with ageism when it is encountered in the workplace are provided by Harkness (1999). Age discrimination does exist, but career specialists can do much to bolster confidence and to better prepare employees to overcome the most common prejudices of ageism in the workforce.

### Modest Computer Skills

Older workers who have used computers infrequently during their work life may have developed only modest computer skills. For example, a nurse in the workforce from 1970 to 2000 would record the majority of her work in hard copy form, not using electronic files. She might know how to write and send an email, but may not know how to make a table, write a report, create a PowerPoint presentation, or conduct an investigation on the Internet. In today's work world, such computer skills are essential.

As technology becomes more present in all industries, advanced computer skills are increasingly seen as mandatory for employers. Career and workforce developers/mentors may have to deal with this issue in their own communication with older employees as well as in supporting clients' job search activities. For example, with a recent client, several problems in email communication had to be overcome before career counseling could begin. The counselor taught the client basic email and Internet computer skills before working with the client on job searches. Assessing computer skill levels is not easy because a lack of these skills can be hidden from managers and co-workers . . . and from counselors. Older workers may not want to reveal inadequacies, so they may hide their computer knowledge gap, inadvertently creating a roadblock to investigating new job opportunities. Workforce developers/mentors can maintain a list of computer classes available locally and be familiar with the level of instruction.

### Desire for Less Physically Demanding Work

Even though older adults are living longer than previous generations, they are not necessarily living more healthfully. Many trades can cause stress on a worker's body by his later years. In the healthcare sector, for example, work can be physically demanding, depending on the amount of time spent standing, the weight of equipment used, and the amount of direct contact with patients. It is not uncommon for surgery technicians who are on their feet all day; imaging technicians moving heavy equipment; physical therapists manipulating limbs; and dialysis technicians, medical assistants, and sonographers working with patients and equipment to complain about the stress caused to their bodies during work.

If a 50-plus worker is in discomfort or physical pain during the working day, she may start exploring new options even though other aspects of her present job are still fulfilling. There are several options, but no easy paths. Here are some examples:

- She could work with the pain and discomfort during her last few years before retirement.
- She could work part-time and postpone retirement.
- She could take a management position even though she might not enjoy or feel prepared to be in a management role.

The available options suggest a number of questions: How much schooling would be required for a new position? Can the employee handle changing from being an expert at her present work to being a beginner in a new field? If she is already at the top of her pay scale, does she take a decrease in salary to make a change, and will the exchange be worth the effort?

Career and workforce developers/mentors can provide support and a place for clients to talk freely about their health concerns without fear of retribution. They can encourage development of realistic perspectives, taking financial and medical issues into consideration. Knowing the medical leave and disability policies of the organization is critical so that all options can be included in the analysis. Creative brainstorming and flexible company policies will aid the older worker in finding a path that allows her to be at her best for the organization, for herself, and for her family.

### Difficult Decision: Career Change after Age 50

After age 50, a worker may for the first time be able to visualize the end of his working life. This shift in perspective can bring unexpected insights about a current career path and lead to experimentation within that career path. Some 50-plus clients feel they need to give more to their organization before retirement. Some feel they have not yet reached their peak, especially if they have not been challenged much in the last 5–10 years. If an employee has felt undervalued and underutilized, he may crave a project where he can face new challenges and gain recognition. Another employee might look forward with a financial advisor and realize he may need to be working and saving for another 10–20 years. Layoff fears can be another motivator in a 50-plus worker's desire for job change. Driven in part by technological advances, departments are reorganizing frequently, and employees are being dislocated. Facing the loss of health benefits at age 50 or older may spark thoughts and anxiety about career alternatives. A worker might hold her breath and hope change doesn't happen . . . at least not in her department . . . at least not this year. To change or not to change? This becomes a difficult question for the older worker!

For example, one of the chapter's authors began a significant career transition at age 45 from the multimedia industry into the field of career development. It took her five years to complete a graduate program because she was still working fulltime and wanted to pay for her education as she progressed. However, the effort was fully worthwhile, and the result has been a rewarding and fulfilling new career path forward.

Career and workforce developers/mentors, by being sensitive to the challenges of job change for older workers, can brainstorm with their clients potentially attractive options for a worker seeking job change within his organization. A career change might require new schooling; however, special projects, mentoring, new training, or lateral moves could be more practical alternatives, and just as satisfying. The employee has much to think about when considering job change: finances, health concerns, stress tolerance, risk tolerance, relationships with spouse and children, and time management. If a change is made at age 50 or older, it should be made with due consideration, reality checks, careful planning, and guidance from career and workforce developers.

### Beyond Retirement: What's Next?

If a 40-plus worker decides to stay in an unchallenging or unfulfilling job for a period of time, her fifties could then be a good time to explore alternatives. Work, either paid or in a volunteer capacity, after age 60 can become part of the most satisfying stage in a person's life. Career and workforce developers/mentors can help employees find volunteer activities within professional organizations or in local community enterprises that will stretch their skills and make the most of their talents. Many businesses have ties to community nonprofit organizations and local educational institutions. These entities can be accessed to find fulfilling and challenging engagements for older workers. Career and workforce developers/mentors can help an employee identify such opportunities. Career and workforce developers/mentors can also help an employee learn how to approach her manager about exploring internal and external options.

### So How Old Is Old?

We build perceptions of how work and retirement operate when we are young. Our world is changing, though, and we are shifting our psychological perspectives on aging to adapt. Middle age, senior, and old age are being redefined. With so many Baby Boomers willing and able to work, will businesses encourage older workers to develop their careers throughout their fifties and sixties? Or will an outdated view of aging and institutionalized ageism prevent older workers from having desirable choices?

Career and workforce developers/mentors have a wonderful opportunity to help shape the future for older workers, for organizations, and for the benefit of both. For example, if part-time work were a more common option, how many Baby Boomer workers would stay in the workforce? With the first group of 77 million Boomers in the U.S. moving into their sixties, now is the time to work together to develop options for older workers, for their benefit and for the benefit of organizations and our communities.

### CHAPTER SUMMARY

Whether the client is a technical professional seeking increased job satisfaction, a union member considering surrendering security for a career she'll be passionate about, or an age 50-plus worker trying to navigate a power struggle with a much younger boss, the challenge for the career specialist/mentor is the same: how to tailor her approach to meet the individual's unique needs. Having an understanding of the context within which a client makes his career decisions can enhance the work that the career specialist/mentor and client do together, making it more meaningful and rewarding, resulting in a happier and more productive worker and workforce for the organization. In the next chapter we will explore two examples of how organizations have approached providing workforce and career development services with this goal in mind.

# CHAPTER 9

# Example Case Studies: Healthcare and High-Technology

*Zeth Ajemian, Mark Malcolm and Ron Elsdon*

To illustrate applications of the principles we have been exploring, we will now look at two case studies. The first, from the healthcare sector, illustrates the implementation of a broad-based workforce and career development initiative within an organization. The second, from the high-technology sector, illustrates the implementation of a career development pilot project sponsored from within a particular group as an initial step.

## Kaiser Permanente

*Zeth Ajemian and Mark Malcolm*

### BACKGROUND AND FOUNDATION

Kaiser Permanente (KP) is the largest nonprofit health plan in the U.S., serving more than 8 million members in nine states and the District of Columbia as mentioned in chapter 4. The organization employs more than 150,000 people in wide-ranging disciplines, with a common commitment to providing high-quality, affordable healthcare. KP endeavors to foster a trusting and inclusive work environment to engage each person's skills, experience, and abilities in continually improving service and performance for members. In 1997 KP and the Coalition of Kaiser Permanente Unions (the Coalition) created the Labor Management Partnership (LMP) to strengthen the relationship between unions and the organization, emphasizing cooperation and collaboration as central tenets. This relationship is embodied in national agreements that are established and renegotiated every five years. It is in this context that workforce and career development take place for KP's labor union–represented population, which is the focus of this case study.

### The Tipping Point: LMP 2005 National Agreement

The strong emphasis on workforce development was probably one of the least expected directions that the 2005 national agreement (Kaiser Permanente 2005) would take. To prepare for bargaining a new agreement, the Coalition surveyed its some 90,000 members on their specific interests. The many local unions that comprise the Coalition cover wide-ranging job functions from administrative through technical. While workforce development had been identified in the 2000 national agreement, no one had anticipated how important it had become to the membership of the Coalition. Interest in access to education and career development scored highly with the members and from that became an important goal for labor in the new agreement.

In preparation for the 2005 negotiations, management identified their own set of issues for shaping the KP workforce. Workforce planning was becoming a critical necessity. Movement toward the implementation of an electronic medical record system promised to affect thousands of jobs and reshape how clinical work itself was delivered. Critical shortfalls in key staffing categories and the lack of clearly defined pipelines to support the changing needs of a large, complex healthcare organization were a continuing concern.

### Identifying Common Interests from Different Perspectives

As bargaining began, common interests were identified as the basis for negotiation. At the most basic level, labor was concerned about career development as it supported both lifelong learning and as a strategy for serving membership's interests. For management, workforce development was seen as a method of addressing dislocation of the workforce as a result of changing practice patterns and technology. In terms of the changing skills required to staff a modern healthcare provider, KP was faced with the classic conundrum of make or buy. Both parties could agree that KP would benefit greatly if workforce planning and development could help to make the workforce of tomorrow from the existing talent. If this could be accomplished, both parties would clearly win.

### WORKFORCE PLANNING AND DEVELOPMENT— KAISER PERMANENTE STYLE

Workforce planning and development as it was shaped and bargained in 2005 followed the general topography of the organization. It is a national program, but it is regionally implemented. There may be agreement about the general categories of programs and initiatives, yet they are shaped in large part by the regional workforce planning and development committees established by the agreement. These committees are co-led by management and labor, and include a variety of stakeholders within each region.

### The Taft-Hartley Trusts

The 2005 agreement brought into play two Taft-Hartley trusts (Taft-Hartley Act 1947) to offer career development and upgrade training programs and services for their respective memberships. The first funded was the Service Employees International Union United Healthcare Workers— West (SEIU UHW) & Joint Employer Education Fund (Education Fund), which includes employers other than KP and serves the SEIU employees of KP's four western regions. A second trust, named after the colorful labor leader Ben Hudnall, was established to serve the remaining bargaining units in all KP regions. The Education Fund, a multiple employer–single union trust, and the Ben Hudnall Memorial Trust (BHMT), a single employer–multiple union trust, may differ somewhat in structure, but they are each governed by trustees from both management and labor. Thus, both labor and management have a partnership role in determining programs and benefits that will be funded through the trusts.

### Building the Infrastructure

With an emphasis on sustaining and strengthening the workforce for the benefit of both employees and KP, infrastructure was needed to support workforce planning and development, career development processes, and education and training as delivered through the two trusts. An organizational infrastructure for workforce planning and development was created that consisted of a national guidance team and regional strategy and implementation teams. Developing a national program to be implemented regionally required technology tools to help it become a reality. The national agreement called for information to be available for workforce planning purposes, along with Web-based career development tools, publication of career paths, career counseling services, and support for education and training. All of these challenges have been met and in some cases are undergoing second-generation developments. For example, the workforce planning and development teams spearheaded the creation of tools to facilitate workforce planning projections, created a workforce planning dashboard, and built online career path information. An online system was developed for employees to make appointments with career counselors, sign up for workshops, find information on critical positions in each KP region, search career paths in every KP region, and see what particular educational benefits were available. Additional information about this system is provided in chapter 4. The educational benefits include tuition reimbursement and stipends that cover employee compensation for time spent in educational activities. Third-party providers, with specialized expertise in career development, were engaged to deliver career counseling services that included project management, career counselors located in each region, content provision of services, and metrics development and tracking. To see how this unfolded in practice, we will now look at the launching of an initiative in one of the regions in KP—Southern California.

## EXAMPLE OF THE INITIATIVE LAUNCH IN ONE REGION

Establishing a new service delivery initiative for employees can be a logistical challenge for any large organization. However, developing a regional workforce development initiative targeting training, career counseling, and a variety of other in-person career services to over 43,000 employees represented by 11 unions at 15 hospitals, over 100 medical office buildings and clinics, and in both in-patient and out-patient settings, and in a geographical area spanning six counties was a particularly daunting task. This was the challenge KP Workforce Development (WFD) representatives faced when they began a workforce development/planning initiative for union employees in KP's Southern California region. This section will discuss both the challenges and lessons learned about developing and implementing a workforce planning and career development initiative from the KP Southern California regional perspective, the largest region in the organization. The following topics will be covered:

- Importance of sponsorship
- Working within a complex organizational structure
- Workforce data
- Working with individual facilities
- Importance of early success
- Identifying priority positions and related action steps
- Implementing career counseling
- Program metrics: measuring success
- Summary of learning

For years KP representatives had discussed the need to create a workforce planning and development initiative to help identify and forecast organizational staffing needs as well as provide career upgrade services for the unionized workforce. For the employees, a workforce development initiative would build upon the KP tradition of investing in its workforce, supporting employee career growth, and contributing to making KP the best place to work. Labor representatives advocated for KP employees to have the tools, flexibility, and access to develop new skills or upgrade their current skills for career advancement and wage progression. For KP as an organization, many felt that key workforce and business challenges necessitated planning for, and investment in, the workforce. There were a number of reasons for this belief:

- Shortages of people to staff critical positions such as in nursing and allied health occupations (e.g., radiology technologists, respiratory therapists, and clinical lab scientists) were occurring.
- Implementation of new technologies, such as digitized medical record systems, required large-scale redeployment of staff into new roles within the organization (based on KP's commitment to employment and income security for union employees).
- Opening new hospitals required staff planning in advance as well as investment in training to secure skilled staff providing the best possible service for KP members.
- Evolving demographics, due to increased immigration to the Southern California region and the aging of the population, meant the organization needed to prepare its employees to provide expanded services to a diverse population with evolving needs.

All of these pressures culminated in the inclusion of a workforce development initiative as part of the LMP 2005 national agreement. Regional thinking and leadership on these issues were instrumental in framing and implementing the initiative in Southern California.

### Importance of Sponsorship

In Southern California, getting buy-in and executive sponsorship early on were key to success in establishing the workforce and career initiatives. Lack of sponsorship had caused previous attempts to fail. Even though the negotiated, national LMP agreement of 2005 laid out a high-level framework for KP regions to follow, without local management support, the initiative would fail. Key leaders in Southern California including the Regional LMP Council co-chairs (the regional labor coalition coordinator and the chief operating officer) and a senior vice president recognized the value of workforce and career initiatives and made a commitment to support them. These initiative champions helped educate key leadership within Patient Care Services (nursing), Human Resources, and ambulatory practice about the urgency of addressing workforce issues at KP in a comprehensive and coordinated manner. Additionally, the recently negotiated 2005 national LMP agreement was a contract between KP and the Coalition, and there was accountability for following through on implementation. Finally, the allocation of funding to the two Taft-Hartley workforce development trust funds provided legitimacy and tangible support.

### Working within a Complex Organizational Structure

KP's organizational structure is relatively complex, and consequently presented barriers to initiative implementation. KP is comprised of three distinct business entities: the Kaiser Foundation Health Plan, the Kaiser Foundation Hospitals, and the Permanente Medical Group. Operational and fiscal arrangements can differ significantly, since the Medical Group is a for-profit entity and the Foundation and Health Plan are nonprofit. The Medical Group, with its doctors, support staff, and outpatient service clinics and medical office buildings, can have workforce needs and staffing structures that differ from that of the in-patient hospitals. It was essential that the new WFD initiative accurately identify the needs of each business entity within the organization in order to succeed at addressing the multitude of workforce issues throughout the organization.

There is a similar complexity on the labor side at KP.

- Employees are represented by multiple international and local union entities. There are seven international unions that comprise the Southern California Coalition of Unions, collectively representing over 43,000 employees: the Service Employees International Union United Healthcare Workers—West (SEIU UHW), United Nurses Association of California, Office and Professional Employees International Union (OPEIU), Teamsters, United Steel Workers, Kaiser Permanente Nurse Anesthetists, and United Food and Commercial Workers (UFCW). This number of unions increases to 11 if multiple UFCW local unions are counted.

- There are significant union occupational and geographic jurisdictional complexities. Each union represents certain types of job classifications at KP, in different geographies. For example, SEIU UHW represents most technical positions in the Los Angeles area medical centers, while OPEIU Local 30 covers the same classifications at the San Diego medical center.

- Union membership in the LMP introduces additional complexity and opportunity. As part of the Coalition, these union employees are also part of the LMP and therefore eligible for benefits from workforce development LMP trust funds. Exempt management positions and some unionized workers (pharmacists, for example, are in a union which is not part of the Coalition) are not eligible for the WFD services funded by the two trust funds.

- Relationships among unions and the trust funds also must be considered. SEIU, the largest single union, chose to disseminate workforce development funding through a separate and preexisting (in the Northern California region) trust, called the SEIU UHW & Joint Employer Education Fund. All of the other participating Coalition unions are served by a separate trust (Ben Hudnall Memorial Trust) set up as a result of the 2005 Agreement.

Despite these complexities, many workforce-related negotiations with the unions were executed via the Coalition of which each union was a part. However, in most cases for implementation of training programs or redeployment processes, each union had to be consulted separately, thus adding to the complexity of designing and implementing career services for their respective member employees.

For the implementation of KP HealthConnect (the digitized medical records system for KP), a separate, national agreement was negotiated with the Coalition, and then regional agreements were drawn up with each union. Workforce development services could only move forward when agreements like these were in place, a process that can take extended time to execute. Consequently, working with the Coalition as a cohesive unit, whenever possible, to strategize about workforce issues was crucial to advancing the initiative.

Because the workforce development program was an LMP initiative, each level and component of the initiative required labor and management representatives' guidance and input into decision making. Although the LMP had existed in the organization since 1997, there was still significant work needed to overcome more traditional adversarial approaches between labor and management. In Southern California, as with other regions, the WFD initiative was led by labor and management co-leads, who chaired a Regional Labor and Management Workforce Development Committee (the Committee). Each Coalition union was represented on the Committee as well as on each WFD subcommittee. Representation on the committees integrated each of the labor unions directly into decision making and policy development.

To add to the complexity, there were challenges in the relationships among the different levels of the organization: national (program offices), regional, and the medical centers. While, this is a common occurrence among different levels of a hierarchical organization, there was a constant need to foster approaches that eliminated isolated, disconnected business practices in favor of collaboration, coordinated planning, and use of best practices. For example, there was a need to address situations where medical center program decisions about the development of various training and career programs were being made in isolation. This could occur if one medical center developed a curriculum for a particular occupational training activity without working with other medical centers, leading to logistical inefficiencies and avoidable costs.

Consequently, for all of these reasons, attempting to design a proactive, forward-thinking and well-organized workforce development and career initiative was challenging on many levels. The organization was complex and multileveled on both the management and labor sides, so collaboration was a challenge. For WFD planners early on, simply identifying existing career training programs was not possible because there was no centralized program database. These various organizational complexities required an initiative development effort that was inclusive in its planning, using the LMP to encourage collaboration between labor and management representatives at multiple levels of the organization. This included consensus decision making and development of programs to address a variety of high-priority issues facing both the organization and its participating unions.

### Workforce Data

A specific example of the challenge associated with building a workforce development initiative within a complex organization was the effort to locate core workforce data. In order to understand the workforce challenges facing the organization and to prioritize work and allocate resources efficiently, basic employee information was essential. Examples of this data included various job classifications and headcount; numbers by union and medical center; vacancy and turnover rates; and demographic information such as retirement rates. Unfortunately, while some of these data points were collected and stored in various forms, they existed in multiple databases, within separate systems, in different departments with little or no sharing across platforms. For example, the recruitment data system tracked turnover, hiring, and career transfer data, while the Human Resources departmental data system collected demographic data and payroll information. It was important that workforce planners be able to view data representing the entire employee life cycle from the point people were recruited and hired until the time they retired, left, or were terminated. This required merging multiple data sources into one common, searchable, and easily accessible database. The development of this online, Cognos-based, database instrument with over 80 data points on the KP workforce required the involvement of 10 organizational units and funding from multiple sources, in an effort that took almost two years to accomplish. Getting these various parties to the table required extensive relationship building and encouragement. This tool then allowed for comprehensive analysis to identify priority areas for workforce investment.

### Working with Individual Facilities

Successful regional WFD initiative development required that medical center staff engage in the process of helping shape implementation to directly address their needs. The national agreement recommended creation of medical center WFD committees to address local training and other career-related issues. Initial hesitation in forming such local committees was overcome when it was clear to the medical centers that such a committee structure was more effective in providing access to trust funds and superior to ad-hoc, event-driven approaches. It also became clear that medical centers needed flexibility to develop processes in a way that met their specific needs. An imposed, central strategy would not only be resisted, it would be ignored. Allowing local flexibility also created a degree of local accountability through prioritization of efforts and resources by local leadership.

### Importance of Early Success

Despite the larger program objective of providing career upgrade services to employees to address a variety of critical position shortages and other challenges, many saw workforce development, early on, as simply addressing one specific business need: reduction of staff due to the implementation of the organization's new, five-billion-dollar digital medical records technology, KP HealthConnect. This major technology implementation project launch happened to coincide with the start of the workforce development initiative in early 2005. The objective of the technology effort was to implement a digital medical records system and rapidly achieve economies through staff reduction. It primarily affected chart room file clerks, whose job was to retrieve patient paper medical charts when requested by a doctor. The digital system eliminated the need for paper charts and accommodated the scanning of existing paper files. Today, the digital system provides doctors with instantaneous electronic access to patient information.

KP went into national bargaining with the Coalition to negotiate a redeployment agreement in connection with KP HealthConnect prior to, and separate from, the LMP national agreement. This agreement, in tandem with the 1999 LMP Employment Security Agreement (E.S.A.) dictated that employees affected by the implementation of a new technology would be able to (a) protect their wages and benefits for up to one year if needed, (b) receive career counseling and training if needed, and (c) be redeployed into new jobs upon receiving appropriate training, given appropriate seniority to bid on these jobs and demonstrating the ability to meet the new job requirements. It was decided that the newly formed workforce development initiative would coordinate this redeployment effort because it involved career counseling, training, and placement in new jobs. As such, WFD created a process by which local labor and management teams at each affected medical center department would work together to prepare employees for the transition. Based on their seniority in the department, employees would either stay in the department performing a similar or modified (scanning versus retrieving charts) function, get a new job outside of the department, or elect to sever from the organization and receive an agreed-upon number of weeks of health coverage or payout.

Because the trusts were not yet funding career upgrade training programs at this early point in the process, WFD concentrated mostly on the redeployment efforts. In under two years, over 600 employees were successfully transitioned into new roles as a result of the project. The disadvantage of being associated with coordinating redeployments was that WFD's larger program objective of providing career upgrade training to fill a wide array of critical workforce needs of the organization was temporarily less evident. However, the successful redeployment of hundreds of workers, who otherwise would have been laid off, into new jobs within the organization addressed a concrete and immediate need from both labor and management perspectives. There was tremendous pressure to execute on these redeployments in order to save costs, considering the multi-billion-dollar expenditure associated with the implementation of the new system. At the same time, from labor's perspective, it was important that these employees were given an opportunity to be redeployed into different jobs rather than simply terminated from the organization. Workforce development's early success in meeting these objectives created significant value for the initiative by gaining credibility with stakeholders.

### Identifying Priority Positions and Related Action Steps

Given the multitude of workforce challenges facing the organization, how did the WFD regional committee identify the priority issues and allocate limited program funds in an efficient and effective manner? Many talked about the need to fill critical or hard-to-fill positions. However, there was rarely consensus about which jobs were most critical to the organization. Different people had different perspectives. It was common to hear about the nursing shortage, not only at KP, but throughout California as well as in the rest of the country, based on high rates of projected nurse retirements and the increased demand expected through Baby Boomer retirements. Did that mean that nurses should be ranked as the highest priority position by the WFD regional committee? Some believed so. However, at KP, the data showed that many positions had high vacancy rates, other positions had high turnover rates, or they had many employees within five years of retirement. Various medical centers and departments identified other needs. As a result, it soon became clear that a systematic and comprehensive process was needed to prioritize occupations.

The WFD regional committee developed a strategy to identify priority positions rather than critical, hard-to-fill, or in-demand positions. Priority positions were those occupations that were determined to be facing the highest degree of current or upcoming challenges. A three-step, comprehensive process was developed to identify the problem areas and appropriate solutions. The first step was to access data from the newly created workforce development dashboard. Out of the 80 workforce metrics on the dashboard, the workforce development committee targeted 8 as most relevant to the challenges faced by various occupations:

1. Vacancy rate
2. Average age of an open job requisition (how many days it has been open)

3. Average time to fill a requisition (number of days from requisition being opened to offer acceptance)

4. Number of external hires (vs. hires of internal candidates)

5. Percentage of external hires to all new hires

6. Percent within five years of retirement (relative to the specific occupation's average retirement age)

7. Voluntary turnover of those with fewer than two years of service

8. Total turnover

All positions covered by the Coalition that required at least an associate's degree or certificate or a license were analyzed against these eight metrics. Lower-skilled positions were also prioritized based on their need with respect to redeployment due to new technologies, but these were not included in this particular data analysis. Occupations ranking in the top 10 of any metric were then subject to review by the WFD regional committee.

The second step involved management and labor subject matter experts being assigned to focus on the corresponding positions in what became known as Do-It subgroups. By analyzing the data, providing subject matter expertise (perspectives from specialists, department managers, recruiters, HR representatives, labor representatives, and educators, among others), and interviewing employees, root causes were identified for the areas of concern (e.g., high vacancy rates, turnover).

The third step was to examine external labor market and industry information about the positions to determine whether KP's experience was similar to, or different from, regional trends. Workforce planning leads felt that it was important to incorporate an understanding of industry-wide trends that might affect the workforce at KP (e.g., new government regulations, fluctuating labor market conditions, changes in education requirements). Government data sources such as the Bureau of Labor Statistics and the State Employment Development Department, as well as private health care industry reports, were surveyed for this analysis.

Once the KP data and external data were considered and various subject matter experts were able to provide their qualitative input, solutions were developed to address the issues identified for each occupation. These solutions primarily focused on, but were not limited to, the development of training programs to address various occupational needs. Solutions could also involve approaches such as examining experience requirements, hiring, and staffing strategies, as well as gathering additional diagnostic data through exit interviews to assess the causes of turnover. Once the solutions were agreed upon by the labor and management subgroups, they were reviewed with the WFD regional committee for final approval and implementation. When implemented, this process was well received by labor and management leadership. It provided a means to evaluate the workforce needs of the organization that was systematic, comprehensive, grounded in data and subject matter expertise, and measured against external occupational and industry trends.

## Implementing Career Counseling

An important component of the initiative was the provision of career counseling services. These services provide employees with support in clarifying their aspirations and linking their aspirations to opportunities in the organization. The career counseling services enabled people to build confidence in their ability to progress in KP. They also provided people with practical information about how to access internal resources such as stipends, as well as external educational resources. For example, in the Ben Hudnall Memorial Trust, an organization with specialized expertise in career counseling and development (Elsdon, Inc.) was contracted to deliver career counseling services in Southern California and other KP regions. It was therefore possible to readily share learning about effective career counseling approaches in KP among the different regions, and to share content, such as workshop materials. The third-party provider was able to assure participants receiving career counseling that their conversations would be held in confidence, an important component of building trust about such sensitive areas. In addition, the third-party provider created and monitored extensive metrics to track the implementation of career counseling services. This helped in guiding the evolution of these services and in communicating progress.

## Program Metrics: Measuring Success

Measuring outcomes and successes is a challenge. Other LMP programs such as Attendance (an initiative to improve employee attendance) and Workplace Safety (to reduce workplace injuries) were measured strictly quantitatively and involved Performance Sharing Programs, which resulted in employees receiving an annual bonus for meeting organizational metrics targets. Improved employee performance, as measured by increased attendance and decreased workplace injuries, directly related to the outcomes sought from these programs. Workforce development was fundamentally different, involving more intangible outcomes. Unlike these other programs, employee participation in training and career upgrade programs could not be mandated unless dictated by government regulation or compliance requirements. Participation in the workforce development training programs was largely voluntary and dependent upon individual motivation.

However, by mid-2009 over 6,000 union employees had accessed one or more WFD services, an impressive total considering that one of the trust funds had only been operational in the region for about two years and the other for about two and a half years. So use rates were strong. But what were the specific initiative outcomes? How did this activity benefit the participating individuals? The organization? KP's patient members? And, how was the organization to measure each of these areas? A metrics framework was created to address these questions. It is summarized in Figure 9.1.

This framework connects resource investment in workforce initiatives to outcomes from the perspective of individual employees and the organization, as well as the influence on patient care. Some of the metrics elements were readily available and were therefore identified as being in the short-term category. Others will be accessible in the longer term as systems to provide access are established. This framework builds on that described in chapter 5, represented in Figure 9.1 by the arrow in the lower part of the diagram, which begins with reaction and extends to value created. The overall framework of Figure 9.1, which is a work in progress, allows labor and management representatives to assess the effectiveness of development resources such as training, stipend, and career counseling programs. WFD representatives are able to provide concrete measurements of numbers of participants in program initiatives and numbers completing training, receiving a job related to training, receiving a certificate as a result of training, and securing wage progression as a result of training.

Additionally, at the time of this writing, the influence of investment in training and other resources on organizational cost metrics such as cost of turnover, overtime, and use of registry (contract) workers was being explored. Metrics associated with career counseling are used to guide the evolution of career counseling service delivery. These metrics include activity levels, knowledge gained, behavior changes, and actions taken. As described in chapter 5, this information is generated by the career counselors and from surveys of career counseling clients. Future plans for overall metrics include exploration of the influence of workforce and career development activities on organizational outcomes and patient perspectives.

## SUMMARY OF LEARNING

Following is a summary of key points from this case study.

- Building stakeholder support: building support of key stakeholders at multiple levels is essential to successfully developing and implementing workforce and career development initiatives broadly across an organization.
- Building on existing collaborative structures: it is important to use existing collaborative structures, in this case the Labor Management Partnership, to support the launch of workforce and career development initiatives.
- Navigating organizational complexity and culture: vital to the success of workforce and career development initiatives is building an understanding of, and navigating, the complexity and culture of an organization. This means

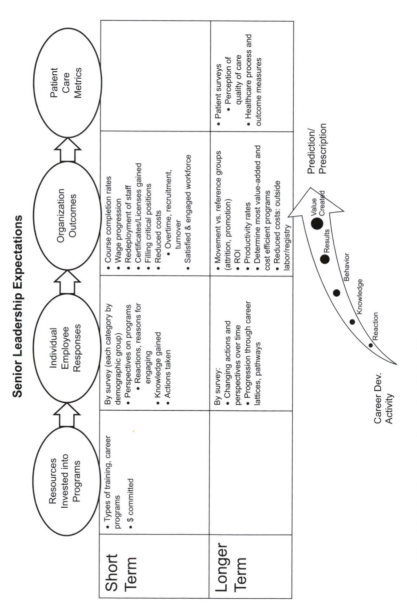

Figure 9.1.  Metrics framework used at Kaiser Permanente

gathering multiple perspectives about needs and issues, and providing consistent communication to relevant groups and individuals about progress.

- Understanding the value of short-term successes in order to implement long-term change: addressing short-term needs of the organization initially is an important step in gaining credibility with stakeholders to support larger, more visionary goals of the initiative. In this case, redeploying hundreds of chart room workers early on was integral to demonstrating that career development could produce concrete benefits from both a labor and management perspective.
- Aggregating workforce data: creating systems that provide comprehensive data about the workforce, centralized in a single data repository for easy access, is essential in supporting and prioritizing initiatives.
- Developing strategies for identifying priority initiatives: establishing clear, systematic processes for prioritizing focus areas is necessary to progress efficiently with limited resources.
- Establishing useful methods for measuring initiative successes: despite the challenging task of measuring success of development processes, it is important to establish a metrics framework that clearly communicates initiative outcomes at the individual and organizational level.

Having examined implementation of a broad, system-wide workforce and career development initiative, we will now explore the pilot introduction of a career development component in a high-technology organization.

## High-Technology Organization

*Ron Elsdon*

Is it possible to start a career development initiative in an organization without support at the institutional level but rather with sponsorship at a local HR level? This case study illustrates the opportunities and challenges in such a situation. This organization is in the high-technology sector, well established, having been in existence for more than 20 years. It has more than 12,000 employees worldwide with the majority in a single U.S. location in multiple facilities. Rapid organizational growth placed a premium on hiring people with specialized technical expertise; indeed, a quantitative technology orientation was central to the organization's culture. The company's founders and senior management maintained a commitment to the local community. Policies were oriented to creating a supportive work environment resulting in the organization being on Fortune's list of the best places to work. However, this was also a hard-driving culture, with an implicit expectation that people work long hours. Business units operated in silos and tended to hoard talent, which limited ease of internal mobility. No formal workforce planning or development functions existed, and the perceived need for such activities was just emerging. Not surprisingly, given this situation, support for career services emerged at the local HR level rather than at the institutional level.

The sponsors of the career services initiative were part of an HR staffing group that recognized the need to create a development environment that encouraged people to stay and develop within the organization, which had a relatively low attrition rate for its sector. The project sponsors also saw an opportunity to reduce barriers to mobility within the organization. At project conception, they were encouraged by the success of career development initiatives in other high-technology settings, for example, the case described by Elsdon and Iyer (1999). Since the new initiative was driven by local sponsorship, it was challenging to collaborate with some other groups, such as learning and development, which were already extensively resourced. The introduction of career services in this situation is most appropriately considered as a pilot, given the limited resources available. In spite of this limitation, there was much progress in building a career services foundation to support individuals while adding value to the organization.

We will examine the various stages of the project, beginning with building the infrastructure, and then explore the learning resulting from the project. For the project's primary sponsor, the main driving force for career services was furthering individual development, with success judged primarily by anecdotal feedback. Organization-level metrics were acknowledged as important for long-term project sustainability. An important initial question was the extent to which services would be delivered internally or by a third party. Balancing considerations were these: on the one hand, the benefits of relationships and knowledge of the organization from internal resources; and on the other hand, expertise in career services delivery, content, project management, and progress tracking, coupled with the ability to maintain client confidentiality, from a third party. The approach selected was a partnership of internal and third-party resources, building on the strengths of each and recognizing that for the high-technology organization's project manager, there was a preference to rapidly shift to internal delivery.

## BUILDING THE INFRASTRUCTURE

Infrastructure building included the following components:

- Project team
  - The third-party project team consisted of one full-time project manager, integrating project management responsibilities and career services delivery, and one part-time career coach dedicated to service delivery. Each person brought considerable depth of experience in the career counseling and coaching field as well as alignment with the high-technology organization's culture. The terminology career coach, rather than counselor, best fit this organization's culture. The organization provided a

dedicated project manager, focused on creating interfaces within the organization, internal communications, and some group service delivery, in addition to committed administrative support personnel.

- Project tracking and metrics capability
  - The third-party provider created customized, online databases to track time allocation; individual client interactions; demographics and outcomes; aggregated assessment results; and feedback both from group delivery sessions and from individual client sessions. Information specific to individual clients was maintained in confidence by the third-party provider; aggregated metrics were provided to, or accessible by, the high-technology organization.
- Career services delivery content
  - The third-party provider created an initial online repository for content, such as workshop materials, that evolved over time with the creation and inclusion of new items. In addition, a portal for accessing online assessments was provided.
- Communication processes
  - In concert with the project team, the high-technology organization's project manager spearheaded the development of communication materials, internal branding for the initiative, and an outreach schedule for engaging with the organization.

## PROJECT EVOLUTION

Once the team and infrastructure were in place, the focus shifted to prioritizing outreach into the organization. An important initial consideration was that of pacing outreach to match the scale of available delivery resources, given the scale of the employee population. With this in mind, a measured outreach process began with those groups that, based on prior contacts, were enthusiastic about using the services given their needs and perspectives. Initial outreach consisted of conversations with business unit HR leaders about components of career services delivery and their value to the organization. This laid the groundwork for presentations to a broader employee audience within these business units, which covered access to, and the value of, the services. In parallel, outreach presentations were also given to special interest affinity groups in the organization that crossed business unit boundaries. During this initial phase, a primary emphasis was also on establishing a core protocol for working with individuals and validating demand for the services. An ongoing challenge was the need to stay focused on career-related issues even though there were requests to provide general skill building training, for example, in general leadership development. While this was well within the capability of the team, it was outside the scope of the project, residing in the domain of the learning and development group. As the first project phase progressed, it became clear that demand for career services was substantial and growing. At that point, it became necessary to examine how the approach to service delivery should evolve to accommodate demand.

In entering a second project phase, several months after project introduction, delivery emphasis shifted as the team determined that a blend of seminars for up to 20 people each (e.g., engaging in the career process, exploring assessment results) coupled with preceding or following individual sessions could permit greater scale of delivery to a broader population for the same level of resource commitment. The number of individual sessions for each person was reduced since some of the content could be covered in a group setting. The career services team acknowledged that engagement preferences varied by individual, with some people preferring a group format and the resulting interaction, and with others more comfortable in the privacy of individual sessions. Consequently, a variety of individual and group engagement combinations were created and offered as choices. The approach to outreach also shifted with the delivery of larger-scale (typically 40–80 people) introductory sessions that provided some experiential content related to career development and an introduction to the services. Also during this second project phase, contract extensions were given to the third-party provider for service delivery; however, these were of sufficiently short duration to preclude hiring additional project staff. Ultimately, with additional personnel changes and a growing emphasis on the group approach, the project moved entirely to internal delivery, the project foundation having now been well established.

## TRACKING PROGRESS

Process and outcome metrics provide a basis for strengthening delivery and communicating progress, as mentioned in chapter 5 (see Figure 5.1). Outcome metrics include the first three levels of Kirkpatrick's framework (1998): addressing individual reactions to the services, knowledge gained, and behavior changes. They can extend to organizational results (as outlined in Kirkpatrick level 4), financial return, and the ability to predict how resource commitments create value. This means moving eventually from descriptive metrics to predictive models that can allow prescriptive approaches (Elsdon 2003, 99). In the early project phases, the focus was on the first three levels of the Kirkpatrick framework, in addition to process tracking. These metrics were available in real time and accessible by the high-technology organization in aggregate form. The metrics components were as follows:

- Career coach time and activity
- Measures of individual career coaching
  - Population demographics and attributes
  - Career coaching progress and outcomes
- Workshop feedback

## Career Coach Time and Activity

Career coach time and activity provide insights into the changing dynamics of the project, including time spent with individuals, in groups, in learning, and on administrative activities. The initial time spent learning about the organization rapidly transitioned to a primary focus on individual career coaching and then to a growing emphasis on workshop and seminar delivery. During the foundation building phase of approximately 17 months, more than 450 individual career coaching sessions were provided for more than 230 clients. More than 540 people participated in over 35 workshops.

## Measures of Individual Career Coaching

Measures of individual career coaching provide insights into the demographics of the served population receiving individual career coaching and into their attributes. This information was gathered from two sources: first from the career coaches as new clients engaged, then directly from clients through an online survey feedback process administered semiannually. Let's first examine some of the information gathered by career coaches. Demographics indicate the extent to which services reach needed groups; attributes provide insights into characteristics of the served population and how to adjust services accordingly. The demographic elements tracked were as follows: gender, ethnicity, age, years of service (with the organization and in the position), functional area and facility, job title, education level, and nature of employment (full- or part-time). It was particularly important for the organization that services were used by the technical population, and they were indeed major participants. The numbers of men and women using the services were about equal. There was significant ethnic and age diversity in the client group. About two-thirds of the individual clients had up to five years of service, reflecting the value of career services in strengthening relationships with a population early into the organization, which is particularly vulnerable to attrition.

Aggregated results of individual assessments provide insights into the characteristics of the served population. The population was oriented strongly toward an objective, rational approach to decision making based on results from the Myers-Briggs Type Indicator (Myers 1998), rather than a subjective, values-based approach. This is not surprising given the technical and quantitative orientation of the organization. It speaks to the need to provide a well-reasoned, rational basis for engaging with career services and a logical, structured approach to creating a path forward for individuals. There was also a significant orientation toward taking in information holistically rather than incrementally, pointing to the importance of placing these services in the context of individuals' career trajectories. The predominant interest areas for the served clients, as determined by the Strong Interest Inventory (Borgen and Grutter 2005), were those reflecting research/

investigation and creativity. This is consistent with the need for technical creativity in the organization. It also underlines the importance of using creative outreach approaches to appeal to people who may want to engage in career services. Regarding preferred approaches to conflict, avoiding dominated as the preferred approach to conflict management, as measured by the Thomas-Kilmann Conflict Mode Instrument (Thomas 2002). This was followed by accommodating. Avoiding as a means to resolve conflict has the benefit of minimizing time spent on relatively unimportant issues. However, it has the significant drawback of limiting interchange from different perspectives that result in creative solutions to issues. It can also cause small problems to fester and grow. Addressing other approaches to conflict management, such as collaboration, was identified as a potentially valuable skill development area for the organization.

Insights into how clients learned about career services and the steps they took as a result of career coaching come from the career coach perspectives and the results of client surveys. Both showed word of mouth as the predominant way clients learned about the services, with events (such as the large group sessions) also significant. Not surprisingly, growth in participation comes when those early into the process tell others about their positive experiences. People indicated that the top priority reason for engaging was to address progression and mobility, followed by increased satisfaction in their current roles. Indeed, the career services team was closely connected to resources that could assist with internal mobility. For individuals, engaging with career services was about progressing on a career trajectory, not just progressing in a position. Reflecting some of the challenging aspects of the culture, respondents indicated dissatisfaction with their current positions was also a significant factor drawing people into the process.

As a result of engaging in career coaching, people investigated internal job opportunities, built their career support networks, and sought relationships with mentors. Here, the role of the career coaches was central to identifying and encouraging these connecting steps. People indicated that they gained greater understanding of what their career drivers were, how to connect with others, and what resources were available within the organization. They developed greater confidence in their ability to find and pursue new career paths and career opportunities within the organization. These are important factors that can contribute to reduced attrition. People also actively explored ways to increase their satisfaction in their current roles as well as exploring new opportunities inside and outside their current areas.

A series of 9 questions gathered feedback about the value individuals received from the career coaching process. These responses were uniformly high (averaging over six on a seven-point scale), reinforced by strongly supportive anecdotal comments. Feedback also included a series of 15 questions exploring peoples' perspectives about the organization, building on, and extending, a framework mentioned by Elsdon (2003, 92). These responses provided insights into areas of opportunity, such as peoples' perception that they were working well below their potential, opening the possibility for significant productivity improvement. A question probing how long people anticipated remaining with the organization generated a response pattern described in quantitative modeling (Elsdon 2003, 136–44), which shows people falling into one of two primary groups based on anticipated tenure with the organization. The organization's leadership is in a position to strongly influence the transition of people from one group to another, and so affect attrition. Analyzing the relationship among responses to different questions showed that the time people anticipated remaining with the organization, and their approach to working at full potential, were directly related to their pride in working at the organization. Peoples' perceived proximity to working at their full potential, and therefore their productivity, were also directly related to their strength of affiliation with their work group in the organization.

### Workshop Feedback

Complementing feedback from individual sessions was the feedback from workshops. A series of 10 questions completed by participants probed for their perspectives about the workshop experience and its value for them. As with the individual sessions, responses were uniformly high, again averaging more than six on a seven-point scale. The workshop feedback process also highlighted opportunities to refine delivery approaches.

## SUMMARY OF LEARNING

What can we learn from this case study that might inform work elsewhere? Let's explore a number of aspects. It is helpful to examine lessons learned from three perspectives:

- Structuring a project
- Content and delivery
- Processes and outcomes

### Structuring a Project

This project benefitted greatly from the enthusiasm and zeal of its primary internal sponsor, who was able to garner sufficient support for initial resource allocation. This support was critical to early adoption of the services in selected parts of the organization. It was highly effective in quickly mobilizing a pilot project. However, the lack of broader institutional support presented a significant challenge, resulting in short-term contract extensions that limited the ability to recruit and the opportunity to build a larger project vision, including breadth of contribution and value creation. This was compounded by the absence of workforce planning and development functions, so career services were focused largely at the individual level. Workforce planning and development functions provide an important window into future organizational needs and a framework for individual development, while also reducing barriers to mobility. With this in mind, the following are key learning points about structuring a project:

- Pilot delivery of career services can be effectively sponsored at a local level in an organization to enhance individual development and strengthen local workforce capability. Organizational transformation, however, requires a larger-scale initiative supported at the senior institutional level, coupled with parallel workforce planning and workforce development processes.
- Contractual commitments for service delivery should be of sufficient duration to provide adequate continuity for staff engagement, project planning, and execution.

### Content and Delivery

It was possible to rapidly initiate this project because of the strong relationships of internal project champions within the organization, the third party's significant prior experience in designing and implementing career services delivery, and the expertise of the delivery team. Key points of learning related to content and delivery were the importance of the following:

- Internal project champions providing links to, and relationships with, key sponsors in the organization, who can provide insights into departmental needs and access to the employee population
- Leveraging the capability of experienced external resources that bring strong content knowledge of the career field applied in individual and group settings, and experience with program metrics, as a basis for outreach and communication with the organization
- Providing a confidential setting for career-related conversations so that people are confident that their exploration of personal development and progression will provide a platform for future growth with no negative repercussions
- Flexing the nature of delivery processes as needed, for example, shifting the balance between individual and group delivery
- Providing substantial autonomy for the project managers and team so that outreach and delivery can be rapidly tailored to the needs of specific client groups
- Maintaining a clear focus on the project scope of career related issues

## Processes and Outcomes

Establishing relevant metrics at project inception and enabling timely access provide a sound basis for monitoring progress, continuing to strengthen delivery processes, communicating progress, and developing understanding about the potential for future contributions. Key learning related to processes and outcomes is as follows:

- Implement comprehensive tracking and metrics to ensure a sustainable project
  - Establish key metrics at project inception
  - Ensure that metrics are readily accessible on an ongoing basis
  - Incorporate both anecdotal feedback, which a carries a strong emotional component, and quantitative feedback that can be translated into value contribution and predictive and prescriptive recommendations
- Build sufficient project scale so that the delivery is team and content based rather than personality based
- Seek opportunities to partner with other groups in the organization that bring complementary skills (e.g., learning and development) or include members who can benefit from the services (e.g., special interest affinity groups)

We can now return to the question posed at the beginning of this case study: is it possible to start a career development initiative in an organization without support at the institutional level but rather with sponsorship at a local HR level? We have seen in this case that it is possible to build a strong foundation for a pilot project that benefits individuals and adds value to the organization. Extension beyond a pilot to an initiative that creates organization-level transformation requires institutional support at the most senior levels. It requires the coupling of individual career development with organization-level workforce planning and development. Organizations that view their workforce as a strategic asset will adopt such a comprehensive approach and reap long-term benefits. Others, such as in this case study, will begin their exploration on a smaller scale, anticipating a broader transformation at some future time. There are still other organizations that will ignore these important opportunities. Those organizations put their long-term survival in jeopardy.

It is our hope that both case studies will contribute to an understanding of how workforce and career development initiatives can be implemented, and can benefit individuals and organizations. The final chapter provides perspectives on weaving together the threads that we have been exploring in the book.

# CHAPTER 10

# Weaving the Threads Together

## Ron Elsdon

The threads in this book are woven from many voices. Each person speaks from the heart and from life experience. Their reflections on workforce strength and career development come from a range of experiences that include observations over time, perspectives of working with various demographic and employment groups, reflections on the effects of learning, results of being present for people along their career paths, and observations of the social and political fabric of organizations. These reflections speak to development of individuals and, as a result, development of organizations. From this process of observing and assessing, of sitting beside, themes that emerge about building workforce strength fit into the following three broad areas:

- Context—why build workforce strength
- Content—what to include
- Implementation—how to move forward

Let's look at each in turn.

### CONTEXT: WHY BUILD WORKFORCE STRENGTH

Workforce strength directly affects people's daily work lives, the organizations with which they affiliate, and the communities in which they live. This is shown schematically in Figure 10.1.

Our authors describe how workforce strength helps bring meaning and fulfillment into individual working lives, how it enables organizations to

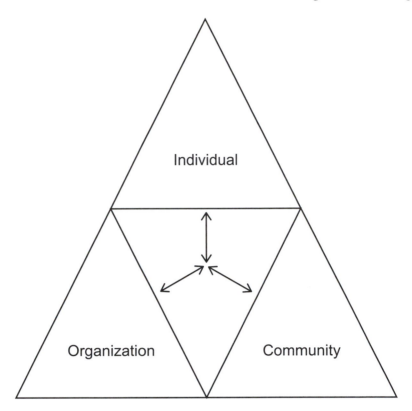

Figure 10.1.  Schematic interconnection of individuals, organizations and communities

operate more effectively, and how it is intimately connected to communities. The many stakeholders, both within and outside organizations, benefit from workforce strength. These include internal stewards entrusted with securing the future prosperity of organizations; suppliers and customers exchanging services or products with organizations; and community entities such as educational institutions, or local and federal taxing bodies, linked with organizations through giving or receiving.

These interconnections take place in an ever-changing external environment. How relevant is workforce strength as this external environment shifts? Let's consider three examples defined by different economic circumstances (which can also mirror national economies at various stages of social and political maturity):

- Recession
- Relative stability
- Rapid growth

### Recession

In a recession, shrinkage or slow growth of Gross Domestic Product (GDP) leads to rising unemployment, constrained job openings, and organizational focus on cost containment. This described the U.S., and some other developed economies, in 2008 and 2009. In these circumstances organizations benefit from building workforce strength since doing so addresses the following critical needs:

- Enhanced operating and delivery efficiency
- Effective use of workforce capabilities
- Strengthened affiliation through individual development
- Redeployment of internal resources as needed
- Flexing in response to reduced demand for products or services
- Preparing for an upcoming recovery

### Relative Stability

During a period of relative stability, the emphasis becomes one of maintaining a vigorous organization able to deliver value and continue to evolve in new directions. Building workforce strength in these times addresses the following critical needs:

- Enhancing and developing core organizational capabilities
- Maintaining flexibility to make evolutionary adjustments as needed
- Sustaining the enthusiasm and vitality of those in the organization so they are able to identify and seize new opportunities:
  - Identify new business areas
  - Incorporate new processes and technologies
- Strengthening affiliation through provision of clear career paths
- Securing ongoing operating efficiencies to address competitive challenges

### Rapid Growth

During a period of rapid growth, the ability to move, to adjust and rapidly build new capabilities becomes paramount. Organizations benefit from building workforce strength as it addresses the following critical needs:

- Flexing to respond to rapidly evolving business requirements
- Rapidly growing core capabilities
- Rapidly identifying and integrating emerging workforce needs
- Strengthening affiliation by encouraging people to secure emerging opportunities that arise from organizational growth
- Creating a strong foundation for the future evolution of the organization

In summary, while the emphasis shifts according to the economic situation, the value contribution of building workforce strength, both immediate and longer term, is significant whether the economy is contracting, stable, or growing.

## CONTENT: WHAT TO INCLUDE

Building workforce strength, particularly capability and flexibility, means supporting individual and organizational development. Our authors have explored aspects of content knowledge supporting such development from a practitioner perspective. This can be viewed in the following broad categories:

- System-level workforce planning and development
- Individual career development
- External relationships and knowledge

### System-Level Workforce Planning and Development

We have seen that workforce planning examines current workforce capabilities, future workforce needs, and potential gaps. Workforce development addresses how to close those gaps. Integrating both workforce planning and development with career development provides a powerful foundation for building workforce strength. System-level workforce planning, while requiring cross-functional relationships, also requires technology-based approaches to aggregate information across geographic and operating boundaries. In approaching workforce planning, there are natural tensions to resolve that vary according to the needs of an organization:

- The need for consistency in building workforce strength across the organization while accommodating local factors
- The need for a comprehensive, consistent workforce information structure across an organization, while being flexible to accommodate changes over time
- The need for breadth of access to information by many potential stakeholders balanced with the need to protect proprietary information
- The need for precision and for speed

By focusing on defining critical workforce planning information that is required to make effective decisions, it is possible resolve such tensions. While securing complete workforce planning information might, on the surface, seem like an ideal basis for decision making, it is likely unattainable since the information base is constantly shifting and can quickly become overwhelming in scale and complexity. As a result, judicious selection of key information becomes paramount. Here, relationships with key stakeholders are central to defining content needed for effective decisions. Such information clarity can then inform workforce and career development initiatives.

### Individual Career Development

The individual's emerging knowledge, enthusiasm, and commitment are at the core of workforce strength. Maintaining the centrality of the individual means supporting people at each step of development, from building self-belief, to understanding the skills associated with career fitness, to engaging in effective decision making about a path forward, to building confidence to take action, and to acquiring the skills needed to secure emerging opportunities. This means encouraging individual behaviors of initiative and perseverance in a context of career interdependence. It also means recognizing the growing importance of different forms of relationship that individuals have with their work. Organizations compete with potentially attractive nontraditional work options such as portfolio careers.

We have seen how strengthening affiliation with individuals is important as a means to increase individual fulfillment and organizational productivity while reducing attrition. Affiliation is supported by an organization that sponsors individual development. Consequently, those organizations that value individual career development will enhance their competitive position. Direct personal contact is a key component in this development support because it is valued highly by those generations currently in, and just entering, the workforce. Reflecting growing workforce diversity, career development initiatives need to be tailored to specific groups in an organization, for example represented and nonrepresented employees, those with particular, specialized backgrounds, and those at different stages in their career life cycles. From an organizational perspective, career development initiatives provide a bridge from the needs of the individual to the needs of the organization. This bridge is built on relationships, augmented by technology.

### External Relationships and Knowledge

We have seen how external workforce information needs to flow both to and from organizations. Such interlinking requires organizations to continuously communicate evolving needs to educational institutions. External information sought for workforce planning includes a variety of items:

- Changing economic conditions that affect demand for products or services
- Availability of people with particular skill sets in a given location

- Actions of competitors that might influence workforce conditions (e.g., drawing from, or adding to, the employment pool, influencing compensation levels)

Building workforce strength at a system level includes incorporating approaches that provide access to such information and developing needed external relationships.

## IMPLEMENTATION: HOW TO MOVE FORWARD

Our exploration of moving forward and implementing approaches to building workforce strength underscores the need to address the following:

- Tailoring approaches to the values and culture of an organization
- Building relationships, sponsorship, and partnerships
- Acquiring the broad array of skills needed
- Creating effective communication and outreach
- Measuring progress and adjusting as needed
- Addressing organizational change aspects

### Tailoring Approaches to the Values and Culture of an Organization

The extent to which an organization values people and their development is fundamental to the success of workforce initiatives. This is shown by a willingness to commit funds to individual development, including HR in major strategic decisions, and supporting the development of direct reports as an important management and leadership competency that is tracked by the organization. Successful implementation builds on these attributes; their absence may preclude building workforce strength at the institutional level.

Whether an organization operates with substantial local autonomy relative to central direction is another important cultural attribute. Where central direction dominates, workforce initiatives are implemented most effectively when first sponsored at senior levels. On the other hand, where local autonomy dominates, local pilot projects can generate support and the impetus for eventual system-wide implementation. Assessing whether the organization responds better to a top-down or a bottom-up approach, or some combination, is an important early consideration.

It is also important to gauge the nature and extent of information needed for decisions about workforce initiatives. Some organizations implicitly accept the value of such initiatives. In this case, defining metrics that will sustain the project over time, if sponsors change for example, becomes an important focus. Close linkage to business metrics such as attrition or movement rates already in use can be particularly effective. Other organizations, particularly those with long investment horizons, may require intense detail and analysis before implementing a workforce initiative. Creating a framework that provides a rationale for the initiative, and milestones along the implementation path, can address this need.

### Building Relationships, Sponsorship, and Partnerships

Relationship building is central to the initiation, implementation, and delivery of processes addressing workforce strength. These relationships are internal and external. Internally, securing sponsorship is a crucial first step. With centrally guided organizations, sponsorship will be required at senior levels. Local sponsorship is needed for organizations with distributed authority. Time invested in securing support from sponsors at the beginning will be rewarded later when reaching into the organization for information or to promote delivery capability. In the delivery phase, building mutually trusting relationships with clients is an essential part of processes such as career counseling. Positive experiences lead to word-of-mouth support so the activity gathers momentum. In the workforce planning and development areas, interfaces are needed with groups such as operating management, unions, HR, and organizational development and learning. Externally, relationships include partnering with entities that bring specialized resources, for example, educational providers, career counseling providers, and providers of technology such as human resource information systems. The relationships begin in a project proposal stage, often building on prior project successes. An organization's workforce planning and development implementation infrastructure needs to include resources for managing these relationships.

### Acquiring the Broad Array of Skills Needed

The opportunity to create proprietary advantage by building workforce strength stems in part from the broad array of skills involved. This breadth makes it possible to tailor approaches to the specific needs of an organization, an essential aspect of successful implementation. It also adds to the challenge of implementation. We have seen how the skills, attributes, and knowledge needed include the following:

- Content knowledge of the career and workforce fields
- Career and workforce development delivery expertise
- Project management skills
- Analysis and metrics development capability
- Database construction and application know-how

- Written and verbal communication skills
- Relationship-building attributes
- Group delivery capability
- Curriculum development expertise
- Knowledge of effective approaches for adult learning
- Organizational savvy
- Strategic understanding of workforce and organizational issues
- Effective teaming

These areas include working well with people in an individual or group setting, applying content knowledge in core development areas, managing resources well, understanding and working effectively within the social and political fabric of an organization, analyzing data to track progress, and deploying technology to gather and communicate information. This means bringing together a diverse team of people, with wide-ranging perspectives and viewpoints. It is in this setting that creativity can flourish, leading to a path of special value to an organization. Indeed, a well-functioning team can act as a role model for building broad-based workforce strength. Teams charged with building workforce strength grow in effectiveness over time as shared skills develop, which is exactly the path sought for the overall organization.

### Creating Effective Communication and Outreach

Since workforce and career development are unfamiliar to many people, active promotion is important at implementation and to sustain interest. For those services designed for individuals, such as career development, there are a variety of effective outreach approaches that include brown bag sessions, e-newsletters, introductory briefings, and co-location close to high-traffic areas. Important precursors to communication initiatives are listening to the needs of the organization and building clarity about the purpose of the services and the primary messages. As more people participate, word of mouth becomes increasingly significant. This can be augmented effectively with vignettes that communicate the value of services.

For those activities such as workforce planning and development, which operate at the system level, continued interaction with business and organizational planning processes, and operational, learning, and organizational development departments, can help ensure ongoing relevance and translation to action. This interaction needs to include listening to understand critical issues, and communication of outcome and process metrics. Ongoing interaction with external entities such as educational institutions helps ensure that the organization's needs are communicated and that the organization stays current with the evolving educational environment.

### Measuring Progress and Adjusting as Needed

Measures of progress address processes and outcomes that result from committing resources to building workforce strength. This descriptive information is a foundation for guiding and adjusting future initiatives. Decisions about future direction are then informed by predictions that flow from the measurements of prior activity. The tools of mathematical modeling can assist here. Measurement includes both qualitative and quantitative aspects. For example, scaled survey responses are typical quantitative measures. Such quantitative measures are particularly helpful in identifying overall themes, in making comparisons across subgroups, and in projecting the influence of future resource commitments. They also link directly to financial and economic aspects of organizational progress. Qualitative measures, on the other hand, are anecdotal in nature, providing excellent insights into individual perspectives. Creating and using measurement frameworks, such as those described in the book, provide linkages among metrics and communicate relevance to the overall direction of the organization.

### Addressing Organizational Change Aspects

Building workforce strength can be described in the following broad steps:

- Establishing a foundation
- Developing, guiding, and implementing changes
- Achieving and monitoring needed outcomes
- Realizing future potential

These steps require organizational change, which can be a challenging proposition. For that reason it is helpful to draw on accumulated knowledge from the field of organizational change. This begins by acknowledging two fundamental approaches to organizational change (Cohen 2005, 7):

- Analysis-Think-Change
  - Give people analysis; as a result, data and analysis influence thinking, and these new thoughts change behavior or reinforce changed behavior
- See-Feel-Change
  - Help people see; as a result of seeing, something hits the emotions, and emotionally charged ideas change behavior or reinforce changed behavior

In Analysis-Think-Change, which is frequently the main focus in the organizational world, the premise is that facts are sufficient to sway opinion and behavior. An example of See-Feel-Change, on the other hand, is Rosa Parks' refusal to give up her seat on a bus in Montgomery, Alabama, in 1955. This visible act of courage and defiance became a symbol for the Civil Rights movement. Cohen finds that the See-Feel-Change approach is most effective, which means helping people see a truth that influences their feelings. It is similar to the appreciative approach introduced in chapter 6. Frequently the See-Feel-Change component is missing in an organizational setting, so it is not surprising that change efforts flounder. In Elsdon, Inc. reviews of the results of exit interviews with organizations, we have found that a combination of both approaches is most powerful in generating movement to action. So a central aspect of taking steps to build workforce strength is to include both the emotional and the analytical components in communicating the path forward. What might this mean in terms of stages to guide change? Figure 10.2 summarizes the framework outlined by Cohen (2005, 3).

There are three primary stages:

- Creating a climate for change
- Engaging and enabling the whole organization
- Implementing and sustaining

Each stage has two or three components. In the first stage at the base of the triangle, the focus is on creating a rationale for change that includes

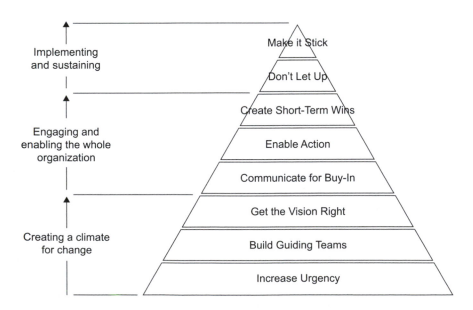

Figure 10.2.   Key steps needed to guide organizational change

a sense of urgency, a structure, and a collective vision. While these steps are presented as occurring sequentially, in practice there is much overlap and iteration. The second stage is one of engaging and enabling the whole organization. Here, the emphasis is on moving to action, with a strong focus on communicating (listening and expressing), supporting action steps, and establishing those short-term wins that energize. This is followed by the third stage of implementing and sustaining, where a primary emphasis is on reinforcing the change process so that the organization does not regress to its prior state.

Before beginning a change initiative, an important question is whether the right pieces of the jigsaw are assembled. Watkins (2003, 98) sheds some light on this question, proposing that the following five items need to be in place before moving forward:

- Awareness
  - A critical mass of people acknowledge the need.
- Diagnosis
  - It is clear what needs to be changed and why.
- Vision
  - There is a compelling vision and solid strategy.
- Plan
  - The expertise exists to create a detailed plan of action.
- Support
  - There is a sufficiently powerful supportive coalition.

Given a critical mass of people who acknowledge the need for change, knowledge of what needs to be changed and why, a compelling vision and solid strategy, the expertise to create a detailed action plan, and a sufficiently powerful supportive coalition, then it makes sense to proceed. If any of these key elements is missing, then an initial focus on collective learning may be more appropriate. Addressing the challenges of organizational change in building workforce strength means considering both logic and emotion in communications, assessing readiness, creating the needed climate, engaging the organization, and sustaining the approach. Taking these steps will do much to secure the needed path forward.

So we come full circle, recognizing the importance of integrating relationship with analysis, of process with outcomes, of individual needs with organizational and community needs. In this integration of people and systems, of emotion and logic, we see a pattern begin to unfold that strengthens individuals, organizations, and communities. That pattern is the beauty and the essence of building workforce strength.

# Appendix A

# Examples of Accrediting Bodies in the United States

Following is a list of regional educational institution accreditors:

- Middle States Association of Colleges and Schools (MSA)
- New England Association of Schools and Colleges (NEASC)
- North Central Association Commission on Accreditation and School Improvement (NCA CASI)
- Northwest Commission on Colleges and Universities (NWCCU)
- Southern Association of Colleges and Schools (SACS)
- Western Association of Schools and Colleges (WASC)

There are several national accreditors that establish and issue accreditation within specific bodies of knowledge, including health education (ABHES); continuing education (ACCET); distance learning (DETC); and theological education (ATS). There are also bodies that provide accreditation for specific professions or educational programs that have a strong emphasis on scientific or technological rigor, or on practice standards, including those on this partial list:

- Accreditation Board for Engineering and Technology (ABET)
- Accrediting Commission of Career Schools and Colleges of Technology (ACCSCT)
- Accreditation Council on Pharmacy Education (ACPE)
- Accrediting Council on Education in Journalism and Mass Communication (ACEJMC)

- American Association on Marriage and Family Therapy (AAMFT)
- American Association of Nurse Anesthetists (AANA)
- American Culinary Federation (ACF)
- Association of Collegiate Business Schools and Programs (ACBSP)
- Commission on Accreditation of Allied Health Education Programs (CAAHEP)
- Council on Aviation Accreditation (CAA)
- National Accreditation Agency for Clinical Laboratory Sciences (NAACLS)
- National Association of Industrial Technology (NAIT)
- National Association of Schools of Art and Design (NASAD)
- National Council for Accreditation of Teacher Education (NCATE)

Some of these bodies grant accreditation to entire institutions, whereas others accredit only specific programs. Some fields may have multiple accreditation bodies, each of whose accreditation regulations and standards may vary considerably.

# Appendix B

# Prior Learning Assessment

Examples of institutions providing prior learning assessment approaches (cited Web sites accessed November 12, 2009):

- College Level Examination Program (CLEP): http://www.collegeboard.com/student/testing/clep/about.html
- Defense Activity for Non-Traditional Education Support (DANTES) Subject Standardized Tests (DSST): http://www.getcollegecredit.com/
- Excelsior College Examinations: https://www.excelsior.edu/Excelsior_College/Excelsior_College_Examinations
- Empire State College: http://www.esc.edu/esconline/online2.nsf/html2/olcreditforpriorlearning.html
- Advanced Placement Tests: http://www.collegeboard.com/student/testing/ap/about.html

# Appendix C

# Development Plan Template and Sample Development Plan

| DEVELOPMENT PLAN TEMPLATE | |
|---|---|
| Employee Name: | Job Title/Classification: |
| Manager Name: | Division/Unit: |
| Date: | Department: |
| Strengths: | Development Needs: |

| LEARNING ACTIVITIES | | | |
|---|---|---|---|
| *Training / Seminars* | *Timing* | *Coaching / Mentoring* | *Timing* |
| | | | |
| *Special Assignments* | *Timing* | *Other* | *Timing* |
| | | | |

| SAMPLE DEVELOPMENT PLAN | |
|---|---|
| Employee: XXX | Job Title/Classification: Team Leader |
| Manager Name: XXX | Division/Unit: XXX |
| Date: XXX | Department: XXX |
| Strengths:<br>• Results oriented; achieves targets and goals<br>• Communicates effectively with team members to motivate and encourage<br>• Customer focused, both internal and external | Development Needs:<br>• Expand knowledge of company's international activities<br>• Enhance understanding of cultural differences in the workplace<br>• Learn to manage conflicts among employees more effectively |

| LEARNING ACTIVITIES | | | |
|---|---|---|---|
| *Training / Seminars* | *Timing* | *Coaching / Mentoring* | *Timing* |
| • Attend course or seminar focusing on supervisory skills, with emphasis on cultural competence and conflict management | To begin by 6/xx | • Based on 360 degree feedback, seek a manager / program lead to be a mentor, meeting 1–2 times per month for six months | To begin by 3/xx |
| • Participate and/or present at international conference | By end of year | • Volunteer as a mentor in organization's formal mentoring program for new hires | Express interest now |
| *Special Assignments* | *Timing* | *Other* | *Timing* |
| • Become team member on an international project | By 7/xx | • Participate in 360 degree feedback process<br>• Delegate *** tasks to team members in order to develop others while also making time for self-development | 2/xx to 3/xx<br><br>Start now |

# References

Ajzen, Icek, and Martin Fishbein. 1980. *Understanding attitudes and predicting social behavior.* Englewood Cliffs, NJ: Prentice Hall.

American Airlines. October 17, 2008. AMR Corporation reports a third quarter profit of $45 million. Available at: http://www.aa.com/intl/jp/aboutUs_en/pr_result3q2008.jsp (accessed 3/22/10).

Andreas, Steve, and Charles Faulkner, eds. 1994. *Neuro-linguistic programming: The new technology of achievement.* New York: Quill/William Morrow.

Barnett, William P., and Anne S. Miner. 1992. Standing on the shoulders of others: Career interdependence in job mobility. *Administrative Science Quarterly.* 37, no. 2, 262–81.

Becker, Brian E., Mark A. Huselid, and Richard W. Beatty. 2009. *The differentiated workforce: Transforming talent into strategic insight.* Boston: Harvard Business School Press.

Becker, Brian E., Mark A. Huselid, and Dave Ulrich. 2001. *The HR scorecard: Linking people, strategy, and performance.* Boston: Harvard Business School Press.

Bedbury, Scott. 2002. *A new brand world: 8 principles for achieving brand leadership in the 21st century.* New York: Penguin Books.

Bee, Helen L. 1987. *The journey of adulthood.* New York: Macmillan Publishing Company.

Beisser, Arnold. 1970. The paradoxical theory of change. Available at: http://pioneersofchange.net/library/articles/Paradoxical%20Theory%20of%20Change.pdf (accessed 8/28/2009). Originally published in Joen Fagan and Irma L. Shepherd, eds., *Gestalt therapy now: Theory, techniques, applications.* New York: Harper Colophon Books, 1970.

Berkowitch, Anne, Anne Pauker Kreitzberg, and Charles B. Kreitzberg. 2009. Leveraging social networks in a downturn: Better, cheaper, faster ways to drive business results. American Management Association webinar, Jan. 14, 2009.

Berry, Leonard L. 1995. *On great service: A framework for action.* New York: Free Press.

BlessingWhite. 2007. State of the career report 2007. Princeton, NJ. Available at: http://blessingwhite.com/content/reports/2007%20State%20of%20 the%20Career%20Report%20Final%20Rev.pdf (accessed 9/25/2009).

BlessingWhite. 2008. The state of employee engagement 2008: North American overview. Princeton, NJ. Available at: http://www.blessingwhite.com/% 5Ccontent%5Creports%5C2008EmployeeEngagementNAOverview.pdf (accessed 9/4/2009).

Block, Peter. 1993. *Stewardship: Choosing service over self-interest.* San Francisco: Berrett-Koehler.

Bloch, Deborah. 2005. Complexity, chaos, and nonlinear dynamics: A new perspective on career development. *Career Development Quarterly.* 53, no. 3, 194–207.

Borgen, Fred, and Judith Grutter. 2005. *Where do I go next?* Mountain View, CA: CPP.

Bridges, William. 1980, *Transitions: Strategies for coping with the difficult, painful, and confusing times in your life.* Cambridge, MA: Da Capo Press.

Bright, Jim E. H., and Robert G. L. Pryor. 2008. Shiftwork: A chaos theory of careers agenda for change in career counseling. *Australian Journal of Career Development.* 17, no. 3, 63–72.

Buckingham, Marcus, and Donald O. Clifton. 2001. *Now discover your strengths.* New York: Free Press.

Burgard, Sarah A., Jennie E. Brand, and James S. House. 2009. Perceived job insecurity and worker health in the United States. *Social Science and Medicine.* 69, 777–85.

Cherniss, Cary, and Daniel Goleman. 2001. *The emotionally intelligent workplace: How to select, measure, and improve emotional intelligence in individuals, groups and organizations.* San Francisco, CA: Jossey-Bass & Wiley.

Cohen, Dan S. 2005. *The heart of change field guide.* Boston: Harvard Business School Press.

College Board. 2009. Economic challenges lead to lower non-tuition revenues and higher prices at colleges and universities. Available at: http://www.college board.com/press/releases/208962.html (accessed 3/9/2010).

Cooperrider, David L., and Diana Whitney. 2005. *Appreciative inquiry: A positive revolution in change.* San Francisco, CA: Berrett-Koehler Publishers.

Council for Higher Education Accreditation. 2009. Degree mills and accreditation mills. Available at: http://www.chea.org (accessed 10/2/2009).

Cox, Allan, with Julie Liesse. 1996. *Redefining corporate soul: Linking purpose and people.* Chicago: Irwin Professional Publishing.

DePree, Max. 1992. *Leadership jazz.* New York: Dell.

Digest of Education Statistics. 2008. National Center for Education Statistics. U.S. Department of Education, Institute of Education Sciences. Available at: http://nces.ed.gov/programs/digest/d08/tables_3.asp#Ch3aSub7 (accessed 3/8/2010).

Dikel, Margaret F. 2009. Networking and your job search. Available at: http:// www.rileyguide.com/network.html (accessed 3/8/2010).

Duffy, Ryan D., and Bryan J. Dik. 2009. Beyond the self: External influences in the career development process. *Career Development Quarterly.* 58, no. 1, 29–43.

Elliott, Charles. 1999. *Locating the energy for change: An introduction to appreciative inquiry*. Winnipeg: International Institute for Sustainable Development.

Elsdon, Ron. 2004. Affiliation, development and value creation. Available at: http://www.elsdon.com/learning_resources1.htm (accessed 11/20/2009).

Elsdon, Ron. 2003. *Affiliation in the workplace: Value creation in the new organization*. Westport, CT: Praeger.

Elsdon, Ron, and Seema Iyer. 1999. Creating value and enhancing retention through employee development: The Sun Microsystems experience. *Human Resource Planning*. 22, no. 2, 39–47.

Erickson, Rita. 1989–2009. Personal files.

Erickson, Rita. 2000. Unpublished research.

Erickson, Rita. 2004. Unpublished research.

Fairlie, Robert W. 2009. *Kauffman Index of entrepreneurial activity 1996–2008*. Kansas City, KS: Ewing Marion Kauffman Foundation.

Fournies, Ferdinand F. 2000. *Coaching for improved work performance*. New York: McGraw Hill.

Friedman, Thomas. 2008. *The world is flat 3.0*. New York: Picador USA.

*Gallup Management Journal*. 2002. Building a highly engaged workforce: How great managers inspire virtuoso performance. Available at: http://gmj.gallup.com/content/238/Building-Highly-Engaged-Workforce.aspx (accessed 8/19/2009).

Gardner, Howard. 2006. *Changing minds: The art and science of changing our own and other people's minds*. Boston: Harvard Business School Press.

Gelatt, H. B., and Carol Gelatt. 2003. *Creative decision making: Using positive uncertainty*. Boston: Course Technology/Thomson Learning.

Gilley, Jerry W., and Steven A. Eggland. 1989. *Principles of human resource development*. Reading, MA: Addison-Wesley.

Gladwell, Malcom. 2008. *Outliers: The story of success*. New York: Little, Brown.

Gordon, David, and Graham Dawes. 2005. *Expanding your world: Modeling the structure of experience*. Self-published. Available at: http://expandyourworld.net (accessed 9/17/2009).

Greenhouse, Steven. 2005. How Costco became the anti-Wal-Mart. *New York Times*, July 17, 2005.

Grutter, Judith. 2006. *Career exploration: Using the Strong and MBTI tools to help you chart your course*. Mountain View, CA: CPP.

Grutter, Judith, and Allen L. Hammer. 2005. *Strong interest inventory: User's guide*. Mountain View, CA: CPP.

Guinn, Vicki. 2009. Personal communication.

Hammond, Sue A. 1996. *The thin book of appreciative inquiry*. Plano, TX: Kodiak Consulting.

Harkness, Helen. 1999. *Don't stop the career clock: Rejecting the myths of aging for a new way to work in the 21st century*. Palo Alto, CA: Davies-Black.

Harter, James K., Frank L. Schmidt, Emily A. Killham, and James W. Asplund. 2006. *Q12® meta-analysis*. Omaha, NE: Gallup Organization.

Haughton, Laurence. 2004. *It's not what you say... It's what you do*. New York: Currency Doubleday.

Head, Thomas C., Peter F. Sorensen, Jr., Bernard H. Baum, Joanne C. Preston, and David L. Cooperrider. 1998. *Organizational behavior and change: Managing human resources for organizational effectiveness*. Champaign, IL: Stipes.

Hill, Linda A. 1996. Building effective one-on-one work relationships. Boston: Harvard Business School Publishing, 9–497–028. Available at: http://hbr.org/product/building-effective-one-on-one-work-relationships/an/497028-PDF-ENG?Ntt=linda+hill+building+effective+one-on-one (accessed 3/9/2010).

Hirooka, Masaaki. 2006. *Innovation dynamism and economic growth: A non-linear perspective.* Cheltenham, UK: Edgar Elgar.

Hirsh, Sandra A. Krebs. 1995. *Strong interest inventory resource: Strategies for group and individual interpretations in business and organizational settings.* Mountain View, CA: CPP.

Hirsh, Sandra A. Krebs, and Jane A. G. Kise. 2000. *Introduction to type and coaching: A dynamic guide for individual development.* Mountain View, CA: CPP.

Holmes, Stanley, and Wendy Zellner. 2004. The Costco way. *Business Week.* Available at: http://www.businessweek.com/magazine/content/04_15/b3878084_mz021.htm (accessed 12/5/2008).

IBM. 2008. Unlocking the DNA of the adaptable workforce: The IBM global human capital study 2008. Available at: http://www-935.ibm.com/services/us/gbs/bus/html/2008ghcs.html (accessed 12/7/2008).

Intrator, Sam, and Megan Scribner, eds. 2007. *Leading from within: Poetry that sustains the courage to lead.* San Francisco: Jossey-Bass.

Jaffe, Dennis T., Cynthia D. Scott, and Glenn R. Tobe. 1994. *Rekindling commitment: How to revitalize yourself, your work, and your organization.* San Francisco: Jossey-Bass.

Kafka, Franz. Available at: http://www.themodernword.com/kafka/kafka_quotes.html (accessed 12/5/2009).

Kaiser Family Foundation. 2009. Trends in healthcare costs and spending. Available at: http://www.kff.org/insurance/upload/7692_02.pdf (accessed 3/9/2010)

Kaiser Permanente. 2005. Kaiser Permanente, 29 local unions agree to new five-year agreement. News release. Available at: http://ckp.kp.org/newsroom/national/archive/nat_050929_lmprelease.html (accessed 9/11/ 2009).

Kaplan, Robert S., and David P. Norton. 1996. *The balanced scorecard.* Boston: Harvard Business School Press.

Kaye, Beverly, and Sharon Jordan-Evans. 2008. *Love 'em or lose 'em: Getting good people to stay.* 4th ed. San Francisco: Berrett-Koehler.

Kegan, Robert, and Lisa Laskow Lahey. 2001. The real reason people won't change. *Harvard Business Review.* Nov. 2001, 84–92.

Kelly, Kevin. 2006. The speed of information. *The Technium.* Available at: www.kk.org/thetechnium/archives/2006/02/the_speed_of_in.php (accessed 8/17/09).

Kirkpatrick, Donald. 1998. Great ideas revisited. In *Another look at evaluating training programs,* comp. D. Kirkpatrick, 3–8. Alexandria, VA: American Society for Training and Development.

Kotter, John P., and Leonard A. Schlesinger. 2008. Choosing strategies for change. *Harvard Business Review,* Best of HBR, July–Aug. 2008. Available at: http://hbr.org/product/choosing-strategies-for-change-hbr-classic/an/R0807M-PDF-ENG (accessed 3/9/2010).

Krumboltz, John D., and Al S. Levin. 2004. *Luck is no accident: Making the most of happenstance in your life and career.* Atascadero, CA: Impact.

Laborsta. International Labor Organization. http://laborsta.ilo.org (accessed 11/17/2008).

Leibowitz, Zandy B., Caela Farren, and Beverly L. Kaye. 1986. *Designing career development systems.* San Francisco: Jossey-Bass.

Levy, Frank, and Richard J. Murnane. 2005. How computerized work and globalization shape human skill demands. Available at: www7.national academies.org/CFE/Educ_21st_Century_Skills_Levy_Paper.pdf (accessed 1/23/2009).

Lichty, Amy E. 2000. Unpublished annual report of the Professional Development Center.

Mallon, David. 2009. Social software in enterprise learning: Getting started. Washington, D.C.: Human Capital Institute webinar, Sept. 8, 2009.

McCall, Morgan W., Michael M. Lombardo, and Ann M. Morrison. 1988. *Lessons from experience: How successful executives develop on the job.* New York: Lexington Books.

Meister, Jeanne C., and Susan Tonkin. 2009. From zero to 360 degrees: How four generations view performance reviews. Washington, D.C.: Human Capital Institute webinar, July 16, 2009.

Mitchell, Kathleen E., Al S. Levin, and John D. Krumboltz. Planned happenstance: Constructing unexpected career opportunities. *Journal of Counseling and Development.* Spring 1999, 77, 115–24.

Moore, Geoffrey A. 1995. *Inside the tornado.* New York: HarperCollins.

Murray, R. Emmett. 1998. *The lexicon of labor,* New York: New Press.

Murrell, Audrey J. 2009. Mentoring up, down and sideways accelerates performance. Washington, D.C.: Human Capital Institute webinar, Aug. 13, 2009.

Myers, Isabel Briggs. 1998. *Introduction to type.* Mountain View, CA: CPP.

Myers, Isabel Briggs, Mary H. McCaulley, Naomi L. Quenk, and Allen L Hammer. 2003. *MBTI manual.* 3rd ed. Mountain View, CA: CPP.

National Association of Colleges and Employers. 2009. Experiential education survey. *NACE Research.* Available at: http://www.naceweb.org (accessed 8/31/2009).

National Center for Education Statistics. 2002. Special analysis 2002. Available at: http://nces.ed.gov/programs/coe/2002/analyses/nontraditional/index.asp (accessed 8/24/09).

National Center for Education Statistics. 2009. Web tables: Undergraduate financial aid estimates by type of institution in 2007–2008. Available at: http://nces.ed.gov/pubs2009/2009201.pdf (accessed 3/06/10)

Nevis, Edwin C. 1987. *Organizational consulting: A gestalt approach.* Cambridge, MA: Gestalt Institute of Cleveland Press.

Nevis, Edwin C., John Lancourt, and Helen G. Vassallo. 1996. *Intentional revolutions: A seven-point strategy for transforming organizations.* San Francisco: Jossey-Bass.

Nocera, Joe. The Sinatra of Southwest feels the love. *New York Times,* May 24, 2008. Available at: http://www.nytimes.com/2008/05/24/business/24nocera.html?scp=1&sq=nocera%20may%2024%202008&st=cse (accessed 3/9/2010)

Nonaka, Ikujiro, and Hirotaka Takeuchi. 1995. *The knowledge-creating company.* Oxford: Oxford University Press.

Phillips, Jack J. 1997. *Return on investment.* Houston: Gulf.

Phillips, Jack J., and Patti P. Phillips. 2009. Measuring what matters: How CEOs view learning success. *Training and Development.* Aug. 2009, 44–49.

Pizzigati, Sam. 2008. Long live the statistical middle class. Washington, D.C.: Institute for Policy Studies. Presentation, June 5, 2008.

Plunkett Research, Ltd. Plunkett's telecommunications industry. Available at: http://www.plunkettresearch.com/Industries/Telecommunications/tabid/77/Default.aspx (accessed 08/12/2009).

Rogers, Everett M. 1962. *Diffusion of innovations.* New York: Free Press.

Roosevelt, Theodore. 1910. The man in the arena. Speech at the Sorbonne, Paris, France, April 23, 1910. Available at: http://www.theodore-roosevelt.com/ (accessed 3/9/2010).

Rosenbluth, Hal T., and Diane McFerrin Peters. 2002. *The customer comes second: Put your people first and watch 'em kick butt.* New York: Harper Collins.

Rucci, Anthony A., Steven P. Kirn, and Richard T. Quinn. 1998. The employee-customer-profit chain at Sears. *Harvard Business Review.* Jan.–Feb. 1998: 83–97.

Ruse, Don, and Stacy Chapman. 2009. Using workforce planning to get and stay in front of the global recovery. Washington, D.C.: Human Capital Institute webinar, July 30, 2009.

Saez, Emmanuel. 2009. Striking it richer: The evolution of top incomes in the United States (Update with 2007 estimates). Available at: www.econ.berkeley.edu/~saez/saez-UStopincomes-2007.pdf (accessed 9/21/2009).

Saner, Marc. 2004. Ethics codes revisited: A new focus on outcomes. *Policy Brief No. 20, June 2004.* Institute on Governance, Ottawa. Available at: http://www.iog.ca/publications/policybrief20.pdf (accessed December 4, 2008).

Schein, Edgar H. 1978. *Career dynamics: Matching individual and organizational needs.* Reading, MA: Addison-Wesley.

Schein, Edgar H. 2006. *Career anchors participant workbook.* San Francisco: John Wiley & Sons.

Schutt, Donald A. 2007. *A strength-based approach to career development using appreciative inquiry.* Broken Arrow, OK: National Career Development Association.

Schwartz, Peter. 1996. *The art of the long view: Planning for the future in an uncertain world.* New York: Doubleday.

Seagraves, Theresa. 2003–2006. Private communication, unpublished data.

Seligman, Martin E. P. 2006. *Learned optimism: How to change your mind and your life.* New York: Simon & Schuster.

Sharf, Richard S. 2005. *Applying career development theory to counseling.* Belmont, CA: Brooks/Cole CENGAGE Learning.

Sheldon, Kennon M., and Laura King. 2001. Why positive psychology is necessary. *American Psychologist.* 56, no. 3, 216–17. Available at: http://education.ucsb.edu/janeconoley/ed197/documents/sheldon_whypositivepsychologyisnecessary.pdf (accessed August 19, 2009).

Simonsen, Peggy. 1997. *Promoting a development culture in your organization: Using career development as a change agent.* Palo Alto, CA: Davies-Black Publishing/Consulting Psychologists Press.

Southwest Airlines. October 16, 2008. Southwest Airlines reports third quarter financial results. Available at: http://www.southwest.com/about_swa/press/prindex.html (accessed 3/3/2010).

Spencer, Lyle M., Jr., and Signe M. Spencer. 1993. *Competence at work: Models for superior performance.* New York: John Wiley & Sons.

Stone, Hal, and Sidra Stone. 1993. *Embracing your inner critic: Turning self-criticism into a creative asset.* Albion, CA: Delos.

Sue, Derald Wing, and David Sue. 2007. *Counseling the culturally diverse: Theory and practice.* New York: John Wiley & Sons.

Taft-Hartley Act. 1947. Available at: http://vi.uh.edu/pages/buzzmat/tafthartley.html (accessed 9/11/2009).

Thomas, Kenneth W. 2002. *Introduction to conflict management.* Mountain View, CA: CPP.

Toossi, Mitra. 2002. A century of change: The U.S. labor force, 1950–2050. *Monthly Labor Review.* May, 15–28.

Toossi, Mitra. 2006. A new look at long-term labor force projections to 2050. *Monthly Labor Review.* Nov., 19–39.

*Training.* 2008. 2008 industry report: Gauges and drivers. Nov.–Dec., 16–34. Available at: http://www.trainingmag.com/msg/content_display/training/e3id4195d3ce547a2accfccdd7ce0292456 (accessed 12/7/2008).

U.S. Census Bureau. 2009. Income, poverty, and health insurance coverage in the United States: 2008. Available at: http://www.census.gov/prod/2009pubs/p60-236.pdf (accessed 3/3/2010).

U.S. Department of Education. 2009. Diploma mills and accreditation. Available at: http://www.ed.gov/students/prep/college/diplomamills/accreditation.html#recognized (accessed 8/13/09).

U.S. Department of Labor, Bureau of Labor Statistics. Career guide to industries, 2010–11 Edition: Healthcare. Available at: http://www.bls.gov/oco/cg/cgs035.htm (accessed 3/7/2010).

U.S. Department of Labor, Bureau of Labor Statistics. 2009a. Economic news release: Table 2. Families by presence and relationship of employed members and family type, 2007–08 annual averages. Released May 27, 2009; annual average data from 2007 and 2008. Available at: http://www.bls.gov/news.release/famee.t02.htm (accessed 3/2/2010).

U.S. Department of Labor, Bureau of Labor Statistics. 2009b. Employment projections: Employment and output by industry. Available at: http://www.stats.bls.gov/emp/ep_table_207.htm (accessed 3/8/2010).

U.S. Department of Labor, Bureau of Labor Statistics. 2010a. Economic news release: Union members summary. Available at: http://www.bls.gov/news.release/union2.nr0.htm (accessed 3/2/2010).

U.S. Department of Labor, Bureau of Labor Statistics. 2010b. Job openings and labor turnover survey: January 2010 Available at: http://www.bls.gov/schedule/archives/jolts_nr.htm#current (accessed 3/9/2010).

Vanitzian, Alysia, and Michele Croci. 2009. New Frontiers in Talent Management at Farmers/Zurich. Presentation, Aug. 2009, American Society for Training and Development meeting, Los Angeles.

*Washington Post.* 2009. U.S. workers' wages stagnate as firms rush to slash costs. May 3, 2009.

Watkins, Michael. 2003. *The first 90 days.* Boston: Harvard Business School Press.

Whitfield, Edwin A., Rich W. Feller, and Chris Wood. 2009. *A counselor's guide to career assessment instruments.* 5th ed. Broken Arrow, OK: National Career Development Association.

Wilke, Joe, and Nick Sorvillo, 2004. Targeting early adopters: A means for new product survival. Available at: http://kr.en.nielsen.com/pubs/2004_q1_ap_adopters.shtml (accessed March 9, 2010).

World Health Organization. 2009. World health statistics. Available at: http://
    www.who.int/whosis/whostat/en (accessed 8/24/2009).
Zemke, Ron, Claire Raines, and Bob Filipczak. 2000. *Generations at work: Managing
    the clash of veterans, boomers, Xers and Nexters in your workplace.* New York:
    American Management Association.

# Index

# About the Contributors

ZETH AJEMIAN, MA, is the director of workforce planning and development for Kaiser Permanente's Southern California region. In this capacity, Zeth leads a labor and management program initiative that provides strategic staff planning and career upgrade services for over 43,000 Kaiser Permanente unionized workers in the region. Before coming to Kaiser Permanente, Zeth was the associate director for workforce development and research at the Los Angeles County Federation of Labor, where he developed training and career ladder programs for member AFL-CIO unions. Zeth's background is in industry sector and labor market analysis with the intent of identifying and supporting growth industries that provide opportunities for high-wage jobs with career ladder potential. Zeth received his bachelor's in political science from Pitzer College and his master's in urban planning with an emphasis on economic development from the UCLA School of Public Policy.

NANCY ATWOOD, MA, has over 20 years of diversified experience as a career and college counselor in business and education settings, helping individuals navigate transitions and identify ways to maximize their opportunities and potential. She is currently a career counselor with Elsdon, Inc. providing career services to Kaiser Permanente employees in the Pacific Northwest. Nancy received a BA in social science and sociology from Colorado State University; she completed graduate work in industrial management at Clarkson University and received an MA in college student personnel from the University of Portland. She is a member of the National Association of Career Development and the Oregon Association of Career and Technical Education.

MICHELE DEROSA, MA, is a career development (CD) professional with extensive experience working with individuals and groups in diverse settings: organizations, colleges, consulting groups, and private practice. Currently, she works for Elsdon, Inc. as part of Kaiser Permanente's workforce development initiative providing career services to union-represented employees. Writing for this book fulfills one of Michele's own professional development goals to use a different voice to influence and empower others to recognize and pursue their potential. Michele worked in recruitment and CD for NASA's Jet Propulsion Laboratory and at DBM, where she designed an internal CD program for a major airline, CD webinars for a high-tech firm, and leadership workshops for United States Olympic Committee coaches. She teaches part-time at California State University–Northridge and at Antioch University in Los Angeles. Michele received her BA in English and theater from the University of California–Santa Barbara and her MA in educational psychology and counseling from California Polytechnic State University–San Luis Obispo. Michele can be reached at mdrosa@earthlink.net.

ANNA DOMEK, MS, is a career counselor and experiential learning coordinator at Sacramento State University and adjunct professor at American River College, where she teaches work experience. Anna received her BA in psychology and history from the University of California–Davis and her MS in counseling with an emphasis in career counseling from Sacramento State University. Anna has experience in counseling, advising, and working with a variety of clients and students from diverse backgrounds in community colleges, four-year universities, and private and nonprofit organizations. Anna is a member of the American Counseling Association and the National Career Development Association. Anna can be reached at adomek@elsdon.com.

CYNTHIA (CYNDI) BRINKMAN DOYLE, MEd, is a licensed professional counselor in the state of Texas, a national certified counselor, and a master career counselor. She graduated from the University of North Texas with a BA degree in counseling and human resources and a master's of education degree in counseling. Her counseling experience has encompassed over 15 years of career counseling and career development for a variety of populations and industries as well as individual therapy. She is currently in private practice in Denton, Texas. Cyndi can be reached at cyndi.doyle@yahoo.com.

MARTHA EDWARDS, MA, is a career counselor with Elsdon Inc., currently working at Kaiser Permanente's administrative headquarters in Oakland, California. With the Elsdon group, she serves union members within Kaiser Permanente who are seeking career growth opportunities. She also works at Kaiser Permanente as a workforce consultant, and recently finished managing the development of a career-planning Web site for healthcare workers featuring over 50 different career paths. Martha earned her master's degree in career development at John F. Kennedy University's School of Management in Orinda, California. During her graduate program, she counseled students and alumni at the University of California–Berkeley, Haas School of Business, and Saint Mary's College in Moraga, California. Prior to her career counseling work, Martha was multimedia director for Age Wave, a niche advertising agency in San Francisco, which specializes in marketing and research projects for the 50-plus population. Martha can be reached at martha_a_edwards@ yahoo.com.

RON ELSDON, PhD, is founder and president of Elsdon, Inc. Ron specializes in the workforce and career development fields, providing organizational consulting, individual career counseling and coaching, public speaking, publishing, and lecturing. Ron has more than 25 years of leadership experience at diverse organizations in a broad range of sectors, and has been an adjunct faculty member at several universities. He has authored numerous publications and has spoken regularly at national and regional events in the career and workforce development fields. With his co-author, Ron was awarded the Walker Prize by the Human Resource Planning Society. He holds a PhD in chemical engineering from Cambridge University, a master's degree in career development from John F. Kennedy University, and a first class honors degree in chemical engineering from Leeds University. Ron can be reached at renewal@elsdon.com.

RITA ERICKSON, MS, is an organizational development consultant and career coach with more than 15 years of experience working in high-technology, professional services, and healthcare environments focused on aligning individual passion and talent with evolving organizational strategy. A former economist, human resources manager, executive recruiter, industry analyst, and project manager, she currently leads Elsdon Inc.'s organizational career development initiative within Kaiser Permanente. She thrives in organizations experiencing transformational change, where she coaches clients to discover and leverage their strengths, build future capability, and create sustainable competitive advantage. Rita holds an MS degree in organizational behavior with honors from Benedictine University, a graduate certificate in career development from John F. Kennedy University, and a BA in economics with highest distinction from

the University of Illinois at Chicago. Rita can be reached at rita.erickson@
att.net.

LISA FRANKLIN, MS, is a career counselor with Elsdon, Inc. providing
career services to more than 2,000 union members at Kaiser Permanente in
Northern California. Throughout her 20 years in the counseling field, she
has enjoyed tailoring services to meet the unique needs of the populations
she has served, including injured workers, immigrants, low-income adults,
and dislocated workers. She holds a master's degree in counseling from
California State University–Hayward and a bachelor's degree in English
and a certificate in human resource management from San Francisco State
University. Lisa can be reached at lisafranklincareercounselor@live.com.

SHANNON JORDAN, MA, holds designations as a national certified
counselor, national certified career counselor, and master career counselor.
At the time of this writing, Shannon was a project manager and career
counselor with Elsdon, Inc. providing career counseling in the high-tech
sector, having previously provided career counseling in the healthcare
sector. Shannon also founded an award-winning career development
center for the extended studies division of a large state university, which
she directed for 10 years before moving into organizational career development consulting work. During her university work, Shannon served
as the academic director of a certificate program to train counselors and
human resources professionals in the art of career counseling and also
taught courses at the graduate level. Shannon holds a bachelor's degree in
business and a master's degree in career counseling, and has completed
additional graduate training in human resources, organizational development, executive coaching, distance coaching, instructional design, and the
expressive arts.

AMY LICHTY, MS, is a career professional with over 15 years experience
implementing career systems for companies focusing on talent management. She is a career consultant with Elsdon, Inc. providing career coaching for represented employees at Kaiser Permanente in Colorado. Amy is
a master career counselor and principal of Dreamweavers Institute. Her
passion is bringing about purposeful renewal for people and organizations. She earned her post–master's degree in career guidance from California State University–Long Beach, her MS in developmental therapy
from the University of LaVerne, and her BA in human development from
Pacific Oaks College. Amy can be reached at amy.lichty@dreamweavers
institute.com.

MARK MALCOLM, MA, earned his bachelor's degree in political science from the University of Chicago and his master's degree in industrial

relations from the University of Minnesota. He has three decades of human resources experience, including technical and executive recruitment in healthcare, IT, and engineering. He has served in a variety of senior HR executive roles. Currently, Mark directs a variety of workforce development initiatives as part of Kaiser Permanente's National Workforce Planning and Development team. Mark can be reached at mark.j.malcolm@kp.org.

DARLENE MARTIN, MS, is a career consultant with Elsdon, Inc. providing career services for represented employees at Kaiser Permanente in Georgia. Darlene is a national certified career counselor and a certified career development facilitator instructor and master trainer. She earned an MS degree in counseling and psychology from Chaminade University of Honolulu and a BA in social science from the University of Hawaii–West Oahu. Darlene can be reached at ldm1264@yahoo.com.

MICHELE MCCARTHY, MEd, has more than 25 years' experience in employee development and career transition coaching in both federal government and private sector organizations. She graduated summa cum laude from Duquesne University, Pittsburgh, with a master's degree in counseling psychology and is a nationally certified counselor. Currently, Michele is a career counselor with Elsdon, Inc. providing services to Kaiser Permanente's workforce planning and development task force in the Mid-Atlantic region. There, she assists nurses, medical assistants, radiologists, and other union staff to leverage educational opportunities and enhance career mobility. In her spare time, Michele is an artist and enjoys teaching families to use creativity to soften the effects of technology on today's youth. Michele can be reached at success605@aol.com.

BOB REDLO, MA, is the director of national workforce planning and development for Kaiser Permanente. In addition, Bob is co-director of the Ben Hudnall Memorial Trust, a Taft-Hartley trust that provides funding for education and training to union members at Kaiser Permanente. Bob and his team, with labor's partnership, have initiated the groundwork for a national workforce development program at Kaiser Permanente. Prior to Bob's current position, he was the senior HR consultant at Kaiser Permanente's San Francisco medical facility. Bob has also served as an HR consultant at a number of other Northern California medical facilities. Bob serves on a number of community organizations and committees for the California Community Colleges, California Hospital Association, and other national and local workforce planning organizations. Before joining Kaiser Permanente, Bob was chair of the Center for Labor Research and Education at the University of California–Berkeley. Bob holds a BA in political science from State University College at Oswego, New York, and an MA from the Rockefeller College of Public Affairs and Policy at the University at Albany (State University of New York); he has also completed doctoral course work at the University at Albany–SUNY.

RICHARD VICENZI, MS, has more than 20 years' experience in organizational change issues, executive coaching, career management, workplace diversity, and staffing and recruitment. His current work includes career counseling with Elsdon, Inc. His past corporate clients have included Fortune 100 companies, privately held businesses, and nonprofit organizations. He has also been an effective career coach across a wide range of disciplines for people in roles ranging from individual contributor to senior executive. Richard received a BA in economics from the University of California–Riverside, and an MBA. from the University of California–Los Angeles. In addition, he received an MS in advanced management from the Drucker School of Management at Claremont Graduate University, where he also completed doctoral coursework in organizational design and strategic management.